Shadows In My House
Of Sunshine

Published in the United States by
Beckham Publications Group, Inc.
P.O. Box 4066, Silver Spring, MD 20914

Library of Congress Control Number: 2007923098

ISBN: 0-931761-28-X

10987654321

Shadows In My House
Of Sunshine

A Journey of Discovery

Emilie Betts

To Nancy
warm wishes
Emilie Betts

June 21, 2007

THE **Beckham**
PUBLICATIONS GROUP, INC.
Silver Spring

To Bob
Who made it possible

"How difficult it is to take the affairs of a lifetime and arrange them at the river's edge."

ANON

Contents

Preface

"By wisdom a house is built, and by understanding it is established;"

— Proverbs 24:3

WHEREVER I have gone I have found building my own nest to be one of life's most exhilarating experiences. Looking back on the many places that I have called home, I see old houses, new houses, double houses, single houses, farmhouses, houses at the seashore, houses in the country, apartments, rented rooms, even tents—all connected in some way to the one before. Every door I have walked through has opened other doors in my mind, pushing me into new territories, teaching me principles on which I could build my life. Interwoven in all these many places that I lived, twenty-nine in all, was the underlying value of truth and love and the binding of family ties. It was not only where I lived, but how I lived that was most important.

We all need a place of our own where we can "be"—a place to express ourselves—a private place where we don't have to answer to society's whims. This place is the well from which we drink the waters of survival. It is the nurturing place for mind, body, and soul.

This place is called home.

Acknowledgments

I am deeply grateful to my family and friends who reached out to me during the writing of this book. Their love and support kept the process moving along between bouts of doubt and writer's block. I also would like to thank the editors who shared their thoughts and guided me in shaping many thousands of words into readable form—Matie Molinaro and Ina Chadwick. But special thanks go to Karen Tesoriero, whose untiring efforts from the beginning saw this baby grow to maturity.

Thank you all for being a part of these stories and an inspiring part of my life.

Prologue

OUR comfortable white bungalow was shaded by century old trees and graced with a lush lawn that felt like chinchilla to our bare feet. A river not far away was always gurgling and singing. On lazy summer afternoons, when I grew weary of swinging on the old tire, I would stretch out on the velvety grass and listen to the bees buzzing in the flowerbeds and the singsong of Rosie and Yanna working in the kitchen. This was my first home—my house of sunshine—where I first experienced the wonder of my existence.

This was in 1922. My brother Buddy and I were toddlers, blissfully drifting from one day to the next, caught up with important things like giving tea parties in our play house or staging a battle with our toy soldiers under the century old oak trees. When the weather was warm and full of the clicking and buzzing of insects, we played in the field of bluebells by the pond, where we fed the swans and took horsy rides on our patient St. Bernard dog. In winter, we spent our time with Rosie and Yanna in our warm kitchen that was filled with delectable smells like bacon or chocolate cookies. They loved us to death, clucking over us, just like the plump mother hens in our hen house. When we were tired and cranky, they took us on their laps and rocked us, while singing German songs, and when we were good, they made us Pennsylvania Dutch molasses crumb pie.

Our world and the world of Mother and Daddy seldom met except in the evening, when our nursery rhyme quilts were pulled up and we were tucked into our beds in our sleeping porch. Then, as I listened to the lapping of the river nearby, sometimes Mother would read us a story from

"The Bookhouse," before she said goodnight. This was a treat for us, since she and Daddy were not at home most of the time.

Their life was the glittering world of entertainment, where their concert bookings were always full. They were included in chic musical circles in New York and attended many openings on Broadway and The Metropolitan Opera. There were lavish parties in our home, when the antiques and candelabras in the living and dining rooms were polished to perfection, and the house was filled long into the night with the laughter of people whose names I had trouble pronouncing—Madam Schumann-Heink, Fritz Kreisler, Amilita Gallicurrchi, all prominent stars of the day. I remember how Rosie dressed us in our Sunday clothes to meet these famous people and then, after curtsying and bowing, being whisked off to our playroom. Mother and Daddy loved to show us off. So did my teenaged sister and brother, Dorothy and Charles. It wasn't often in the 1920's that mid-life parents were blessed with two little ones, eighteen months apart.

When I was five years old, we had a very fancy wedding for my big sister Dorothy. I was going to be flower girl and Buddy the ring bearer. At last, we were able to be in that magical world—the one with Mother and Daddy and the grownups. I loved every bit of it—loved the chance to prance down the aisle in my pink organdy dress—loved sitting cross-legged behind a palm at the reception, goggle-eyed at the beautiful women in their short silk dresses. My mouth hung open watching them flaunt their shiny black cigarette holders and I knew I would be just like them someday.

Then, not long after the wedding, Mother put us to bed one night with a frown on her face. She couldn't read to us, she said. There were people downstairs waiting for her and she had to hurry. Mother was upset. But I was curious to find out why?

Buddy and I counted to fifty and then crept to the top of the stairs. We heard a babble of voices but over them was Mother's high-pitched voice. My heart turned over. Then I heard Daddy. "Now Lil, calm down. We're trying to figure things out so let's all get our heads together." He didn't sound like Daddy at all. After a while, Buddy and I silently crawled back to our sleeping porch, our heads swimming with the strange talk. We had no idea that day—October 24, 1929—would be the beginning of a completely new life for all of us.

CHAPTER 1

Leaving River Road

IT was cold on the flagstone steps—so cold that my bottom was becoming numb and I could feel Buddy shivering as he cuddled up close to me. Sitting with our chins in our hands, we had been watching the moving men parade by all morning, carrying boxes and furniture. After a while, to break the monotony, we made up a guessing game about what was under the blankets.

"Oh, there goes the sofa," or "That's Daddy's chifferobe," and "Look, I see Nana's painting." Some people bought Nana's paintings and hung them on their walls but to me, she was my dark and scary cloud, always flitting around the house in her dirty black dress. And the night when the men in the white coats came to take her away, I was scared and glad at the same time. I never saw her again but I'll never forget the sound of her wailing like an injured animal as they put her in the big black car.

Buddy and I had fun with our moving game until I saw the pale blue legs of my bed go by and I wanted to run up to the mover and shout, "Put it back! It belongs in the house."

But I didn't. I just sat there and watched and wondered why we were leaving our house. When Mother came out of the house to check on the movers, I pulled at her skirt to talk to her.

"Not now, Emilie Louise, can't you see I'm busy?"

"But why are we moving?" I asked. "I love my house. I love my big dog and the swans in the pond. And why did Rosie and Yanna leave us? Who's going to put us to bed and make us oatmeal in the morning? Don't they love us anymore?"

But Mother had gone back into the house so I stopped whining and started thinking about the day our dear nursemaids left us. "Goodbye, my little darlings," Rosie had said, her flushed cheeks shimmering with tears. "We'll come to see you when you are settled." I clung to her roundness, breathing in her familiar soapy smell. I remembered how the black feathers on Yanna's Sunday hat bobbed up and down as she covered me with goodbye kisses.

"Ya, ya, mine little child. We will come see you soon," she said. Her mouth turned down, as though she was going to cry. Pressing her soft face against mine, she whispered in my ear. "Mind your Momma and take care of Buddy." And then I watched two people that I loved drive away in Mr. Van Doren's shiny gray Cadillac taking my safe little world with them. I loved Mr. Van Doren, Daddy's old friend, too, but why did he take Rosie and Yanna away. He was the one who found them for us. He had always been like a guardian angel for us. Mother's voice jerked me back to the present.

"Just take care that Buddy doesn't climb into the truck or get in the way."

She turned back to directing the men. "That's an antique clock so be careful. Make sure you wrap it securely and put it on the top of things and not the bottom." She was cross and tired and had a worried look on her face that chased away all the smiles.

Finally, the driver hopped down from the back of the truck, closed the doors with a loud bang and shouted, "OK, boys, let'r roll."

Slowly, the truck pulled away from us—away from our house and our meadow—and when it disappeared from sight, my stomach heaved and I started wailing.

"Oh, come on, Emilie Louise," Mother said in a brisk no-nonsense tone. "We have to make sure they didn't forget anything." And she took us by the hand and led us back into the house.

Nobody said a word. Our footsteps made hollow sounds on the bare floors and the echoes followed us from empty room to empty room. I brushed away tears with the back of my hand and looked around. It was all strange and familiar at the same time—the windows without our damask draperies—the bare floors showing marks where the rugs had been—the dining room holding memories of Sunday dinners after church, when Rosie and Yanna would lay the table with our best china and cook something special for dinner. I could almost see the sunlight flooding the room, bouncing off the crystal and silverware in shimmering waves that lit up dust specks in the air.

As Mother held Buddy and me by the hand, we walked from room to room, our footsteps echoing our sadness. I didn't want to leave my house of sunshine. Oh, how I would miss Rosie and Yanna and my beloved St. Bernard and the white swans in the pond. All I could take with me was my blue bed.

Our house had started feeling different long before moving day. Many nights, after we were put to bed, we had eaves-dropped on Mother and Daddy arguing downstairs and it upset us. Mother did most of the talking. "You make me sick," she would say with disgust. "Here we are without a dime because of your bad business judgment. What was the matter with your head, anyway? How could you have put all our money into just one stock?"

I could just picture Mother shaking her finger at Daddy. She didn't get angry often but when she did, she looked just like the wicked stepmother in Cinderella and not like my mother at all. There had been a long silence. Finally, I heard Daddy say in a sad voice, "This is happening to everyone, Lil. It's just not us. Nobody could have foreseen the bottom falling out of the market. I thought I had made a good investment. Besides, our broker urged me on—you know he did. He told us it was a sure way to get a fat nest egg."

"Well, if he was so smart," my mother had shot back, "why didn't he advise you to put some money in another place beside the market—real estate or a trust for the children's college education. Why didn't he do that?"

Then Daddy got mad and had shouted "I give up trying to talk to you. You just don't understand the whole picture!"

"Really," Mother had replied in her haughty tone. "You think I don't understand? I wouldn't have lost all of our money. Perhaps you've inherited some of your mother's confusions in your business dealings."

At that point, we had heard a kitchen chair scrape on the floor and a fist bang on the table. "You leave my mother out of this," Daddy had yelled. And then the back door had slammed shut and all was quiet. Daddy had left. Was he leaving for good? Would he come back?

By then we were confused and unhappy and had crept back to bed.

One day, right before we moved, I said to Buddy, "Now I think I know why Mother isn't wearing her sparkly rings. It's because Daddy doesn't have a job anymore and there isn't any money left and I'll bet she sold them to pay bills."

Buddy was busy eating a cookie and just nodded.

"And," I went on, "I'll also bet that's why Daddy isn't like our Daddy at all. I've seen him come home late at night, wobbling up the stairs.

There was still no response from Buddy.

"Maybe what we should do is break open our piggy banks and give them the money."

"Okay," Buddy finally said. But we never did it because our lives had really changed. There were no more parties with exciting singers from the New York Opera—no more pretty dresses or big roast dinners or our wonderful Saturday afternoon movie times in Daddy's theater. Because of the Crash, the lights were turned off and the doors were locked. It had all happened so fast. But the biggest change of all was that we were going to leave our house by the river and move seven miles down the road to a town in Pennsylvania called Easton. It was scary and exciting all at once.

When we were following the moving truck on the way to the new house, Mother told us we were going to live in a neighborhood. "A neighborhood? What's that?" I asked.

"It's a place where there are streets and houses on each side of you," Mother explained. "It's on Pierce Street in College Hill and the people who live there are called "neighbors."

"Oh," I said full of wonder. Maybe in our new neighborhood Buddy could play ball with other boys and I would have girlfriends to play house with. Now I perked up.

Our new house was a red brick bungalow—not at all like my white house of sunshine. But it did have a shady front porch where Buddy and I were told to sit during the move. Mother lost no time and, with her arms moving like a traffic cop, she directed the moving men.

"The big sofa and chairs go in the den with our Stromberg Carlson radio—mind you don't nick the wall—the velvet love seat and Victorian chairs go in the front room with the rest of the antiques, and the oval dining table and high backed chairs go in the next room," she said.

When the gilt-framed mirror was hung over the elaborately carved sideboard in the dining room, I did a little dance in front of it and was absorbed in making funny faces until Mother shooed me out of the way. The draperies were finally hung and our new house began to look like home. I wandered around with Buddy two steps behind me. We were like curious squirrels—opening closets and peeking inside then running up and down the steps, giggling and making a racket until Mother yelled at us that we'd better stop or she'd come down with another one of her headaches.

That night, when I saw my blue bed all made up and ready for sleep, the feeling of being lost softened and when I climbed into the freshly laundered sheets, everything seemed safe for now.

Despite the huge change from our festive life on the River Road, we settled into a comfortable routine on Pierce St. Each night, after the dinner dishes were washed and put away, everyone found their favorite spot in the little den and listened to Lowell Thomas with the latest news from all over the world. His familiar goodnight "So long until tomorrow" still rings in my head. We couldn't wait for the "programs," with stars like Jack Benny and Mary Livingston or Amos and Andy. Our stomachs ached many times from laughing so hard, and for a little while we forgot our troubles.

But Daddy had no steady work and unfortunately spent too much time at the local tavern. He would try to tell us he was having good luck in finding jobs but he never came home with a job or a check in his pocket. Whenever he didn't turn up for dinner, the house took on darkness—a feeling that something bad was about to happen. It usually did. Too many nights Daddy would come stumbling home, around midnight, soused and irascible and I would lie awake listening to the haranguing from my mother. But sunshine the next morning and the promise of new adventures always swept away the gloom of the night..

I would urge Buddy to finish his breakfast. "C'mon, Buddy, hurry up. Let's climb the cherry tree before the robins eat them all. And then we can play on the tennis court. Mother gave me some string so we can fix the net and I found a couple of old balls that still have some bounce." And off we'd go.

It wasn't until after dinner, when we would play kick the can or one giant step, or watch with wonder and delight at the fireflies blinking from inside the mayonnaise jars, that the old fears of Daddy not coming home would start creeping in. But the prospect of school starting in a few days filled me with happy anticipation and chased away my sadness. We would be going to March school and Mother was very happy about this, since this school was the best in the city. And we could walk there. I was so excited I drove Mother crazy.

"Will you stop that constant twitching," she would say, sounding very cross indeed. "What is the matter with you, Emilie Louise,that you can't sit still for a minute? I do declare you are coming down with St. Vitis dance. I will have to call Dr. Fretz."

She shook her head and I sulked. Now I worried that there was something wrong with me and I would examine my face in the mirror daily to see what St. Vitis was doing to me.

The first day of school finally came and the twitching turned into wings. My feet barely touched the ground as Buddy and I skipped and ran the whole six blocks, feeling very grownup with our new book bags and a nickel in our pockets for milk money.

But when I walked into the classroom, the kid's chattering stopped and all eyes turned to me—the new kid on the block. My euphoria evaporated as I stood there looking at everyone as they looked at me. I knew I was different. I didn't look like the other girls. They all had on freshly ironed flowered dresses and I was wearing a bilious green crocheted dress cut down from one of my sister's. It was worse than awful. I felt my face flame. But I put my head high and strode past each set of curious eyes all the way to the back of the room where nobody could see my tears.

The image of that first day still haunts me, but the minute the soft-spoken teacher Miss Crobaugh, passed out our first books, I was transformed. From that time on, my hungry mind gobbled up the magic of words and numbers and as the days went by, I forgot all about my funny clothes.

Our principal, Miss Allen, lived by the slogan emblazoned on a sign above her office door "Learn to do by doing" and she made sure we followed her belief. Sometimes she would teach a class instead of sitting in her office and when she taught ours, I held my breath hoping she wouldn't call on me. I always got tongue-tied and said the wrong thing, fearful she would use her rod on my knuckles. She didn't hesitate to use it on a head that was nodding off or on fingers passing a forbidden note. But it was through Miss Wenzel and Mrs. Corper, my music and art teachers that I found out how classical music could lift my heart and putting paint to paper made me very happy.

My favorite teacher, Miss Mitman, held her cooking class in a sunny room, lined with shiny sinks and stoves. She was a jolly, gray-haired spinster, whose rimless glasses had a habit of tumbling off her nose. "Okay, my little chefs," she would say, after telling us one of her awful knock-knock jokes. "Here's what you do with a basketful of apples."

And then she showed us how to use an apple peeler and how to mix the ingredients for the piecrust. We were clumsy at first, spilling flour on the floor and knocking things over. But she praised us. She said we were the best class ever and I proudly marched home at lunchtime with my carefully wrapped apple tart. When I handed it to my Mother her face broke into a big smile and her eyes shone with pride. That day, our meager lunch turned into a celebration.

One day, our art teacher announced there was to be a soap carving contest. I ran all the way home eager to start looking in our encyclopedia for ideas. I finally found a picture of a ferocious looking grizzly bear standing on his two back legs. That's it, I said to myself. That's what I'll carve.

I could hardly sleep the night before the contest and I was first in my seat in the art room the next morning. When the small carving knives and big bars of Ivory soap were passed out, I sat there holding the soap and knife, frozen, not knowing how to start but slowly, I started chipping away and with each stroke of the knife, I began to see my bear hiding inside. I worked away, losing all sense of time until I handed my bear to the teacher. When I heard "and the first prize goes to Emilie Louise for her carving of the bear," I paraded around holding up my bear for everyone to see.

Learning new things from Monday to Friday kept my mind opened up. I loved March School. It gave me a place where I could be happy and not afraid as I was in the Pierce Street house.

But weekends were another story. Then we had to visit my ailing Grandmother—my mother's mother. Buddy and I hated these visits— hated her dark and smelly kitchen with flypaper hanging everywhere. It gave us the creeps. I remember walking up to her rickety iron bedstead and feeling embarrassed talking to this ancient lady with a sunken mouth and a wrinkled gray face.

"Hello, Grandma," I mumbled.

"Mama," I heard my mother say, "It's Buddy and Emilie Louise."

She turned her head toward us and held out her skeletal arm. She whispered something unintelligible in a raspy voice that sounded as if it could have come from a hovering ghost. Buddy and I stood there, not knowing what else to say. Finally Mother broke the silence and we escaped into the sunshine and the broken-down arbor swing. There we waited, swinging back and forth, dodging yellow jackets and eating half-rotten concord grapes until Mother came for us. We didn't care that the yard was a shambles—it was so much better than sitting around in Grandma's fly-infested kitchen.

Ironically, the only fun we ever had at Grandma's was after her funeral. Buddy and I were being ignored so we went exploring to see the rest of the house. We went into the dim, dusty parlor, which was full of ancient furniture. It was eerily silent and I was convinced there were ghosts in every corner. I tugged at Buddy's sleeve. "C'mon, let's get out of here. It's too spooky for me."

A few more turns and we were in the dining room. I looked around. There on the sideboard was a glass carafe filled with a golden liquid. "Hey, what's this?" I took off the stopper and carefully poured some into one of the little glasses. It was delicious. It warmed my throat all the way down - better than tea with honey.

"Buddy, come over here and have some of this," I whispered. "You won't believe how yummy it is." By the time we finished off the bottle we were floating. When Mother came looking for us, we were playing "Gotcha," falling all over each other and laughing like little hyenas. She saw us, saw the empty bottle and immediately knew what we had done. We had gleefully sipped down a whole carafe of Grandma's dandelion wine.

"Oh, just wait 'til I get you two home. How dare you come in here and take something that isn't yours! I'm ashamed of you," she snapped..

And before any of the relatives could see her tipsy little kids, she pulled us down the dusty hallway and out the front door where she dumped us in the back seat of my sister Dot's car. Buddy and I were still in a woozy world and collapsed in a fit of giggles, while we waited for Dot and Mother to take us home.

Mother had a unique way of pretending that our lives had not taken a turn for the worse. She had a prescription for our ailing spirits that always involved planning small surprises for each holiday—ones that would keep us occupied and enthusiastic, despite the lack of money and Daddy's bouts of drunkenness. Mother had provided red construction paper and white paper dollies for us to make our Valentines long before February and when cupid had come and gone, she was already thinking of something green for us to wear on St. Patrick's Day.

"Remember," she would say, "You have some Irish blood in you." And she would straighten up and tilt her head—I knew she was remembering her proud heritage. These little things she did offset the dreariness of those hard times when her little black purse was very thin and anonymous food baskets were left on the back porch. When the baskets would appear, my mother shed grateful tears while my father put his head in his hands, ashamed to see his family on the dole. Once I heard her say "God bless Palmer Van Doren. If it wasn't for him, we'd all go to bed hungry."

It was our first Christmas in the Pierce Street house and excitement built steadily as we counted the days to December twenty-fifth. The boxes of tree lights, ribbons, the crèche and the delicate ornaments were brought up from the cellar. We set to work; Mother pressing the Christmas ribbons, Daddy patiently winding each light to the branches of the tree and Buddy and I carefully hanging the ornaments. Sister Dot would often pop in with some cookies or a casserole. Sometimes dear Uncle Dick, her husband, came along with her, carrying a big Vogue pattern book. His father owned Laubach's Department store, the best store in Easton and when a new book arrived in the fabric department, he always brought me the old one. He called me "kid" and grinned widely when he saw how it delighted me. I could hardly wait to look through it.

"Gee, thanks Uncle Dick," was all I could say before I dashed off to my room to cut out the pictures of the ladies and play paper dolls.

At Christmas we also got our hopes up about seeing my older brother, Charles. He wasn't home much, away for months at a time playing drums with a traveling dance band. We crossed our fingers hoping he would surprise us and come home for the holiday.

A few days before our first Christmas in the Pierce Street house, I woke up one night to the sound of loud noises. Buddy was awake, too. We got out of bed pressing fingers to our lips—for silence and crept down the stairs toward the noise of hammering. We saw a light in the living room. Slowly we opened the door. And there he was—our brother Charles, hard at work building a Christmas village. He had traveled all night on a bus from Cincinnati so he wouldn't disappoint us.

"Charles!" we yelped! We both ran pell mell into him, hugging him with all the strength in our small arms. "Oh, you didn't forget. You came home. Oh! Oh! Oh!"

During the previous months, while I had been singing on stage at school assemblies, Buddy had made friends with an older boy in the neighborhood who had a bicycle. Buddy used to hang around him hoping to get a ride. Then one day the boy started to fix up his old bike. He sanded and repainted it until it shone like new and then parked it in front of his house with a "For Sale" sign on it. Buddy raced home and pleaded with Mother to buy it for him.

"I just don't have the extra money," she said sorrowfully.

It wasn't long before the bike and the "For Sale" sign had gone. Buddy was heartbroken.

On Christmas morning, Buddy stared, with his mouth wide open, at this very same bike, standing by the Christmas tree. Somehow, Mother's penny pinching had paid off and made a small boy's dream come true. He was out the door in a flash, and on his bike, flying down the street. Finally, after the first thrill of owning a bike had leveled off, Buddy gave me some rides on the back. I clutched him around his waist, my heart pounding, as he pumped the pedals, narrowly missing trees and fences as we wobbled around the block.

Although Mother had done her best to make Christmas happy for us, Charles was the one who made the difference. When he appeared, the whole house glowed from his sunny disposition. He was able to turn the meager holiday into a fun time for all of us and somehow the Christmas village he built eased my disappointment in not getting what I had asked Santa to bring me. There were no lavish presents and just a few holiday goodies under the tree—no roast beef or chocolate cake for dinner—just things we needed, like socks and mittens. I was too young to realize it took money to buy the dolls and dresses I yearned for. Before I went to sleep that Christmas night, the sad place in my heart wondered if I would ever again wear a pretty party dress and dance around the way I used to.

When we lived in my house of sunshine by the river, Sunday was a very special day. We got to wear our best clothes and go to town with Mother and Daddy to the church with the tall white steeple. Mother always looked beautiful in her flowered hat that dipped and waved as she walked us over to the church school. Here we would spend the worship hour with Sister Edith while Mother sang in the church choir and Daddy played the organ. Sister Edith's smile, the Bible stories she read to us in her soft voice—the ones about Jesus and his disciples—the unforgettable scent of crayons mixed with the clean starched smell of her freshly laundered gray habit is a very warm memory.

Sister Edith opened my mind to the power that guides us and watches over us and it was through her that my religious beliefs took root. Those Sunday mornings, when we marched around the room singing "Onward Christian Soldiers," I sang so loudly that the congregation in the sanctuary must have thought a wayward cherub had flown in.

But now, at Pierce Street, we didn't have nice clothes and Mother wouldn't take us to church. I knew it embarrassed her to be seen shabbily dressed in a house of worship. Daddy's one suit was worn and shiny and Mother's coat was years old and threadbare. I looked at her when she would put it on to go the store. Her face was sour and showed how much she hated that coat. I wondered if she felt the way I did when I had to wear that hideous green dress to school.

Mother's faith was strong and not being able to worship in church every Sunday must have filled her with remorse. But "rise above it" was her slogan and as long as it didn't cost any money, she found a way to meet the challenges.

Snow squalls and chilly temperatures ushered in our first Easter on Pierce Street. But there were warm spells that coaxed the crocuses out of the ground, and this told us spring was not far away. Easter would be coming. For weeks, Mother had carefully hoarded a small store of chocolate bunnies and jellybeans—as much as her black purse would allow—so Buddy and I would have something in our baskets. Easter eve, we went to bed with visions of egg hunting in the morning and wondering what the Bunny would leave us. We had no inkling of the surprise Mother had planned.

On Easter morning, it was still black outside when I was awakened by someone gently shaking me, urging me out of the warm deep of sleep. Slowly swimming toward consciousness, I dimly made out Daddy's face bending over me.

"Time to get up," he said softly. "It's snowing hard and we have a long way to go. Mother has breakfast waiting in the kitchen so put on your warmest clothes and come on down."

I looked at the clock. Three o'clock? I was completely mystified. I dressed quickly and joined everyone in the kitchen where they were having hot chocolate and oatmeal.

"Fuel for the long walk," my mother explained as she dished out my cereal.

"Put on your warmest jacket and take two pairs of gloves." Whirligigs inside of me started to dance.

We locked the house and began walking. Streetlights cast eerie thin haloes as the snow, driven by the gusty March winds, swirled wildly around us. Mother and Daddy took the lead while Buddy and I struggled to keep up behind them. We trudged along, heads bent to the wind, down the long hill to the macadam road. To take my mind off the bitter cold, I started making up stories. I imagined I heard singing. Then a magnificent gold-encrusted coach drawn by four prancing white horses stopped and took me aboard. We flew through the sky to a large stone castle with red and blue flags flapping gaily from the many turrets. Inside, we joined a party in full swing with catchy music and dancing and delicious food to eat. And there he was—the Easter bunny—handing out yellow baskets filled with chocolate eggs.

But walking so long in the icy cold wind finally shattered my golden coach fantasy, leaving me as befuddled as I had been. Where were we going? I could not figure out what we were doing on a deserted road in the dark of night when we should have been home in bed.

We pushed on. My feet had lost all feeling and my nose just didn't seem to be a part of my face anymore. Now we were huffing and puffing, this time up a hill. I was very tired and thoughts of my warm bed kept teasing me. Suddenly the hill flattened out and there in front of us was Cottingham Stadium and our high school's playing field. The sky was starting to streak with the first signs of Easter dawn as we followed the assembling crowd to our seats.

"What are we doing here?" Buddy wailed. He was not impressed being in the stadium at the crack of dawn.

"Just be patient. You'll find out," Mother answered.

We brushed the fresh snow off one of the stadium benches and gratefully sat down on the hard wooden seats. After walking for hours, these seats felt like down cushion. I looked down on the field and could dimly make out the outlines of a cross and a large rock. People dressed in long robes were taking their places. As the day brightened, everything came into focus and there in front of me was a beautiful tableau about to tell the story of the first Easter—the story of the resurrection of Jesus.

A minister stepped forward and began to read from the Bible as the choir sang softly in the background to accompany him. He told the story of Mary Magdalene going to the tomb after Christ had been crucified and finding it empty. Now the choir gave full voice to Handel's "Messiah" celebrating Christ's glorious resurrection. Next to me my teary-eyed mother, shivering in Mrs. Laubach's cast off spring coat, was singing joyously along with the choir. I felt a little tug on my heart as I gazed at her thin face lit by an inner radiance. I shall always remember how pleased she looked when she said, "This is the story of Easter, children. Happy Easter to you."

Mother always gave what she could and managed to keep our hopes alive. Without a penny extra after eking out enough to pay for food and our other expenses, she had planned this Easter morning surprise with nothing but love in her heart. I knew this was her way of thanking God for watching over us. So I sang the closing hymn with all my heart, just as I had sung in Bible school with Sister Edith in our beautiful white church.

But the singing in my heart stopped when Buddy and I heard we were moving again. This time Mother did not mince words or tell us to buck up. With a catch in her voice, she said "Our house has been sold and the new owners want us out as soon as possible. For the time being, we have rooms with Miss Bliss so you two better think about what you want to take with you. We have to put everything else in storage." She looked very tired.

After the news, Buddy and I sat out on the back steps to talk about it.

"Who is Miss Bliss? I never heard of her and I don't want to move," he said, his brown eyes filling with sadness. "I don't want to leave my friends and the clubhouse we built. Why do we keep moving all the time? Other kids' families stay in one house. We don't. Why?"

I sighed and said, "I guess it's because Daddy doesn't have a job and can't pay the bills. Mother said it would be for just a little while. I have to believe her."

Buddy put his head on my shoulder and we sat together on the steps for a long time.

The truck pulled away taking our belongings to the storage warehouse just as my sister Dot arrived to drive us the few blocks to Miss Bliss. I sat in the back seat of her car biting my nails and trying hard not to cry. When we arrived at the boarding house, we unloaded our suitcases and dropped them on the sidewalk in front of a run-down building with smudgy windows and peeling trim. Grass was growing in the broken cement walkway. I shuddered. This is it? This is what Dot had found us after our rental house on Pierce Street was sold? Couldn't she have done better than this, I thought?

We trooped into a dismal interior that smelled of old cabbage dinners and even older dust. It was obvious from the murky light that Miss Bliss, the landlady, had nothing higher than twenty-five watt bulbs in the lamps. Everything had a surreal underwater tint.

And then Miss Bliss appeared out of the shadows. One look at her wizened face made me think of a dried apple doll. She sniffed audibly when she saw Buddy and me.

"Huh, kids." I heard her mutter.

There were two rooms for the four of us—a shared bath with other boarders, and a two- burner hot plate where Mother cooked us hot oatmeal for breakfast. Dot made many trips from her house to bring us food and often took us around the corner to the Hershey shop where we could get sandwiches and soup. We all tried to talk about happy things when we were together around a table, but it was hard to ignore the wolves howling at our door.

Miss Bliss was a shut-in. I don't remember ever seeing her go out of the house. She spent her miserably moody days hunched over her static-filled radio with an old Pekingese curled up on her lap. Buddy and I tried to avoid her as much as we could when we came in from school, but she was always on the lookout. She hollered at us the minute we opened the door.

"Take off them dirty shoes," she would yell, flapping her arms like a marionette on strings. "It's hard enough keepin' this place clean without you kids trackin' in more dirt. And don't slam the door, neither. There's other people in the house so don't go makin' noise, neither. I keep a quiet place and people come here know that, so no shoutin' from you kids."

Oh, how I despised this old lady. I threw all my nine-year-old hatred toward her and her stinky old house and vowed never to live like this when I grew up. Oh, no. Not me, I said to myself. Although I knew my parents couldn't afford anything better, I hated them too, for taking us here.

There were many nights when I found myself gripped with a longing I had never experienced before— a crying of my very soul to be back in my blue bed under the big oak trees.

CHAPTER 2

The Dancing Cardinal

IN the cold light of the late November afternoon, Prospect Park looked forlorn and ordinary—not at all the pretty place I had hoped to see after such a terrible place like Miss Bliss'. We had been driving around for a half hour as Daddy searched the streets, squinting at the address written on a piece of paper Mother had handed him. He finally stopped in front of a deserted looking frame house—27 Moore Ave.

Mother peered out of the truck's window. "I've only seen it once before, late at night, but I think this is it. Wait 'til I go see if the key works." She disappeared into the shadows of the porch. In a moment she signaled to us. The door was open.

We all piled out of the truck like dust bowl migrants weary of traveling and in need of a comforting meal. I was trembling from the wind's sudden chill knifing through my thin sweater. I looked suspiciously at the gray two-story building with the piles of maple leaves in the front yard and the old yellowed newspapers scattered all over the porch. Some of them were still rolled up from how the newsboy had thrown them months ago. Nobody home, they said. The air of sadness in everything around us was far from welcoming. I let out a big sigh and felt the beginning of a sulk coming on.

"Now, Emilie Louise, none of that," Mother said. "You know we have to thank Aunt Ruth for allowing us to have this house for a while. It's a blessing." She kept looking straight ahead and gave me a little shove through the door. I felt she was trying to put on a brave face for us while hiding her real feelings. How could anyone love this place? I was thinking. But at least it was a place for us to live instead of that horrible old boarding house.

All we had with us was our clothes and our Teddy bears. Once again, we would be sleeping in unfamiliar beds, some as lumpy and bumpy as a road full of potholes. Again we would be eating from mismatched dishes and dull flatware. I counted on my fingers; one, two, and this made the third house we would have lived in since leaving my house of sunshine three years ago. I didn't even count the boarding house. That was an insult I could never forget.

While Mother did her creative magic in the kitchen and Daddy made clanking noises with the furnace in the basement, Buddy and I explored the musty rooms. When some lamps were turned on and light filtered into the rooms, and the radiators started hissing, the heartbeat of the house came back. Yes, I thought, this house has a soul. It wasn't too bad after-all. We sat down in the kitchen to bowls of steaming soup and toasted cheese sandwiches that warmed us and softened our disgruntled attitudes. Mother smiled at me. It was a tired and strained smile but it did help to brighten her sad eyes. Yes, this house was a whole lot better than living with Miss Bliss.

That night when Mother made up our beds with the musty sheets and blankets smelling from moth balls in Aunt Ruth's linen closet, I closed my eyes and pretended the bed was my blue bed and that the itchy blanket was my nursery rhyme quilt and that when I woke up in the morning everything would be fine.

The next morning sunlight streamed through the window and gave the room a much cheerier look. Curiosity tugged at me and I could hardly wait to go exploring. I shook Buddy. "Wake up and get dressed. Let's see what's outside."

We dressed in a hurry, took the stairs two at a time and bolted through the back door into the yard.

"Hey, Buddy," I yelled. "Come over here and see what I've found." There behind the garage was a small wooden shed, half-hidden behind some overgrown bushes. Although it was a bit ramshackle, I was filled with excitement as I looked at it and   I rushed to find Mother to get her permission to turn it into a playhouse.

"Oh, please, could we use it for a playhouse?" I begged. "It's only filled with old tools and stuff, but Daddy can move them away and I can clean it up so you don't have to. Please, Mother. Please? "

Mother seemed to have other things on her mind and was happy Buddy and I had found something to entertain us. That way we would stay out of her hair. Daddy obliged and in just a few hours, he had moved everything from the shed to the garage. Now the shed was ready to be turned into our castle.

Buddy and I washed the windows and swept the floor. We went scavenging and found some orange crates a neighbor was throwing out. Daddy was a wonder with tools and overnight turned them into a table and chairs. Mother donated a small faded tablecloth and a frayed rug she found in the basement. To me the crates weren't orange crates at all but new and shiny furniture, and the threadbare carpet Aunt Ruth had used for a doormat would be our magic carpet to fly to lands all over the world. The finishing touch was a beautiful crystal vase, really a jelly jar, which I filled with the last of fall's pretty leaves. When all was ready, Buddy and I moved in.

I was never happy in Aunt Ruth's house, but my little playhouse in the back yard delighted me. Inside that five-foot square I found a refuge from the outside world and my wildest fantasies came to life. Buddy and I played "house" for hours, sitting on our magic carpet, gorging ourselves with all the yummy things we could think of which we had set out in splendid array on our gleaming table. We were always rich in our playhouse. We were able to travel to exotic places, sailing around the world in private yachts or crossing new lands in special railroad cars and, of course, in our imagination our brother Charles, whose band jobs on the road took him away more and more, would be such fun on our luxurious voyages.

But there were times when we ran out of imaginary places to visit— restless times when the lure of investigating the mysteries of the adult world got us into trouble. One such time we had caught Mother smoking in her room. Her door was open and we saw her bringing a long tapered white cigarette to her mouth and then exhaling the smoke like a movie star. She never knew this scene had, unfortunately, planted an idea in our heads. We had seen people throw their half-smoked cigarettes out their car windows, and if we sat on the curb, we could quickly pick them up while they were still burning and finish them off. Now we were smoking, too, just like Mother.

One day when we had filched a pack of matches and were sitting on the curb taking turns lighting them, a lighted match fell into my lap and set fire to my new dress—a flowered one I loved that my sister had made me. Screeching at the top of my lungs, I high-tailed it into the house, slapping madly at the smoldering front of my dress. My mother was horrified. Never again were we allowed to sit on the curb but somehow, we got to those butts in the gutter anyway.

That winter the cold was ruthless. It crept through the ill-fitting windows and old doors and into the very guts of the house, where it settled like great icebergs in each of the rooms. The one warm spot was the kitchen where Mother kept the stove going all day. Most of the time we couldn't afford enough coal for the furnace but Daddy found pieces of once-fine furniture stored in the cellar, which he brought upstairs to burn in the living room fireplace.

This makeshift fuel was pale competition against Mother Nature's icy breath, but we were grateful to the furniture's original owner for providing this needed warmth. In the mornings when Buddy and I got out of our warm beds and stepped onto the cold floor we were jolted awake in a hurry and went flying downstairs to dress in front of the flames. Mother would have the kitchen stove roaring and hot oatmeal waiting on the table. It was a long walk to school and on those mornings the thermometer often dipped to twenty degrees and below.

I missed my friends and March School almost as much as I missed my first house. The school in Prospect Park did not have a cooking class—a big disappointment—as I loved everything about food and cooking—sparking a life-long passion—and the other classes were dull, too. The days went by with nothing exciting to look forward to and I dragged my feet to school each morning, wishing I were back in Easton at March School with my friends.

But Christmas was on the way and again Mother was gearing up, trying to dispel our despair as she dug deep into her store of tricks to keep us happy. It was very hard that year. Daddy's pick up jobs peddling toys and vitamin bars were bringing little money home—barely enough to buy milk and bread. Who knows how much he threw down on the bar for another beer, his battered ego desperate for some shoring up?

I kept hoping with all my little being that Charles would appear bringing his hugs and laughter. After days of waiting, I came home from school one day and to my delight, there he was—busy at work transforming the living room into a fairyland of miniature villages with little trains winding in and out as they puffed their way around the Christmas tree. I stuck to his side like a leech. I don't think he ever knew how much I adored him.

Although we didn't have enough money to buy a turkey, we did have a nice plump hen for Christmas dinner. As we sat down at the table, Daddy stood up and tapped his fork on the water glass. What was this all about, I wondered. Then he announced with pride in his voice that he had been hired as the manager of Upsal Gardens, a recently built apartment house in Germantown, Pennsylvania. As an added bonus we would have our very own rent-free apartment. The news miraculously banished the worry lines from Mother's face and sent Buddy and me dancing around the tree.

After a long siege of rawboned living, at last it was easy to smile at each other again. Now with a new job in the offing for Daddy, the air was more relaxed. Mother hummed when she put dinner on the table and Daddy stayed home to be with us. I guess the urge to drink was still there but for the time being he managed to put it down. Those nights before we left Aunt Ruth's house, I prayed hard that he would not give in and start hanging out again at the local bars.

I threw my suitcase on top of Aunt Ruth's old bed and started packing my few clothes. Halfway through, the thought of moving hit me and I lifted my arm and drew the number four in the air—our next move. Would this be our last, I wondered?

We saw the sign Fresh Paint as soon as the front door to our apartment at Upsal Gardens swung open. We stepped inside and my eyes popped. Oooh, I like this very much, I said to myself. The smell of new plaster and fresh paint said this was a brand new place—a pure smell so different from our other homes.

"Is this really ours? Really ours to live in? Is this where Daddy is going to work?" I asked, scurrying from room to room. My eyes didn't miss a thing. Sunlight poured through the large casement windows in the living room, lighting up the highly polished floors, falling on my shoulders like a warm shawl. Here were six big rooms in a brand-new building—all waiting to welcome our own things from the moving van.

At last when I saw my own bedroom made up with my own bed, tingles of joy went through me. I could hardly wait to unpack and claim the space as my own. There was a built-in dressing table that just cried for my creative hand in arranging half-used bottles of perfume, make-up and junk jewelry and there was a closet I soon filled with cast-off clothes. It was a little girl's heaven—perfect for make believe and I played dress-up for hours, pretending to be Bette Davis or Joan Crawford.

Most of my pretend collectables came from Mrs. Evans, a new bride, who lived down the hall. I was totally smitten with her. She was young and pretty and taught me the rudiments of make-up and the first lessons in how to dress. She listened to my prattle over many a bowl of chicken soup, feigning interest in every word I uttered and when I knocked on her door she always invited me in with a smile. Mrs. Evans filled a big, empty hole inside of me—one that I never knew existed, but Mother took to scolding me for visiting her so much,

"Why do you have to go and bother Mrs. Evans all the time?" she grumbled. "If you ask me, I'm not sure I would like you under my feet day after day. What is it that you find so interesting with her anyway? Can't you be satisfied with your own place?"

I felt guilty but I just couldn't tell her that Mrs. Evans was teaching me how to put on make-up or how she was opening my eyes to the world of fashionable clothes. Mrs. Evans was young and pretty with shining blonde hair. My mother's hair was turning gray. She was fifty-three years old and just too old for these things.

Buddy and I slid easily into the new schedule at the C.W.Henry School near Upsal Gardens. Although it was a lot like March School, it took me a while to feel like I belonged. I was homesick and I wanted with all my heart to be back with my old friends, practicing for a new play or getting ready to enter another contest.

But then one day, there was an announcement. Tryouts for the annual fall festival named The Bird Masque, would take place the next day on the school playing field. When my name was called to give my interpretation of the doomed cardinal bird, I pulled out all the acting tricks I knew. I fluttered and swooned and lay panting on the ground after the hunter's arrow had hit me. My dance won over the judges and I was given the coveted role. There I was—the new girl snagging the big prize. My parents thought this was like winning the Miss America contest, but even though they praised me, I tossed it off as though I knew all along I'd be chosen.

I had fallen kerplunk for the boy who was playing the hunter and for days my imagination had constructed a very romantic interlude between us—Romeo and Juliet went round and round in my head. I wanted with all my heart to impress him and I planned to dance so exquisitely that he would have to notice this talented little girl.

The day of the pageant arrived. People came early with their folding chairs and picnic baskets. The sky was a blinding blue and the forest glen, where the play was to take place, was rimmed with a riot of red and gold trees celebrating autumn in all its glory. The school children were dressed in colorful feathered bird costumes ready to tell the story in dance of the hunter and how he mistakenly shot the resplendent red bird. The music started and the dancing began. As the pageant unfolded, it came time for my entrance and I started happily hopping across the forest floor picking up imaginary seeds for my breakfast. The hunter arrived on the scene. He raised his bow. The arrow flew and found its mark. There was a gasp from the audience and then silence. With my imagination soaring, I became the injured bird in every cell of my being, flailing about but still dancing, sensing it was my last time, fluttering my feathered arms trying to fly, then falling back, hopping slowly, gathering my ebbing strength for another exhausted lift off, falling back on my wings again, this time sagging as the life force slowly left my weakened body and finally, with the audience weeping, I fell gracefully to the ground—stone cold dead at the hunter's feet. My killer hunter then picked me up in his arms and carried me to a bed of leaves in a hollow log. With overly dramatic gestures, he shed a few crocodile tears, gently touched my forehead, and walked away, his head bent low. By this time, my little girl romantic heart was about to burst through my red feathers. End of pageant—but not the end of my fantasy. I was so impassioned, I pictured my hunter coming back to lift me out of the log and bring me back to life with a tender kiss. So I just stayed in the log with my eyes closed beneath the cloudless autumn sky.

The audience of mothers and fathers had already folded up their chairs and blankets and were making their way out of the park but I hadn't moved. I waited and waited for my rescue. Nothing. I started counting. After a very long time, I heard my mother's voice.

"Harlan, here she is—she's still lying in the log. What are you doing in there, Emilie Louise? Get up, for heaven's sake. Everybody's left. We didn't know what had happened to you and we were starting to worry. Why in the world are you still lying in that log?"

Sheepishly, I climbed out and followed my parents to the car, dejected and deflated. My mother's scolding and disbelief went on.

"Harlan," she whispered. "Sometimes she acts so strange I worry about her." I heard her and got a feeling she was talking about Nana again. Was something wrong with me, I wondered?

During the height of that autumn's brilliant color and crisp air, Buddy and I found wading through the crispy crackle of fallen leaves such a joyful time—kicking them high and watching them dance as the fresh breezes sent them flying. The gardeners were always busy raking the leaves, and as quickly as they fell, they dumped wheelbarrow after wheelbarrow of leaves behind the garages in back of the apartments. We watched this pile of leaves grow bigger and bigger until the day it reached the garage roof. Then we hoisted ourselves onto the black shingles and got a running start, shouting as we leapt gleefully into the abyss. "Here we come, ready or not!" For that second when I was airborne I was free—flying just like a bird. Then came the landing on that huge leafy mountain, sinking down, down, down into the prickly bed of acrid scented leaves. Buddy and I, choking and coughing from the dust, scrambled out of the leaf pile to the clear air, feeling as if we had been knocked down by a big ocean wave.

In the middle of December, just before Christmas, a big blizzard snarled traffic and closed the schools for days. I had a bad case of flu so I couldn't enjoy the unscheduled holiday. I lay in bed like a sick puppy. Even my mother's never-fail medicinal miracles were not working and though she plumped my pillows with a cheerful, "Well, Emilie Louise, you are looking better today" I could tell she was fibbing. She had that worried look in her eyes when she shook out the thermometer and gave me another dose of Spirits of Niter.

One afternoon, she came into my room and told me to put on my robe and slippers—there was a surprise but I had to come to the window for it. Though my legs were shaky, I was curious and I inched my way along the wall to get to the window. Out there in the whitest snow I had ever seen, stood the biggest and most beautiful snowman and beside it was Buddy in his worn hand-me-down coat and Daddy's galoshes, stamping his feet and waving his arms to keep warm. He had made a card on a big piece of paper and the snowman was holding it. It said, "Get Well."

"Oh," I murmured. "He did this for me?" This unexpected show of love clouded my eyes. It was the best get-well card I have ever received. And it was at that moment that I felt like the luckiest girl in the world. I had everything any girl could want.

During those times in Upsal Gardens, Buddy and I were still close— almost as close as in the days when Rosie and Yanna used to sing to us, but once in a while my bossiness got under his skin and he paid me back for pushing him around.

One night when Mother and Daddy were leaving us alone for the evening to go visiting with the neighbors, Mother was full of instructions for us. "We're going to the Harris' down the hall. You know where they live, and we won't be late. You can listen to the radio for awhile, but remember bedtime is 9:30 and I expect you to turn out the lights then."

The minute the door closed, we started for the kitchen to raid the refrigerator. Not too much there. Then we went through all the cupboards, hoping to find a chocolate bar or some sort of candy. No such luck. Playing cards came next, but that soon bored us.

"Why don't we play hide and seek," I offered.

"Hey, neat! I know just where to start, so hide your eyes and count to ten and then try to find me," said Buddy, giggling.

I didn't know what he was planning, but I went along.

"Seven, eight, nine, ten—ready or not, here I come," I said, and started stalking around the apartment looking behind the furniture, under the beds, behind the doors, in the kitchen. I couldn't find him. Then I heard a snicker behind me—soon a muffled giggle. This time it came from the hall closet. I whipped open the door and saw nothing at first, then looked again. Mother's fur coat had suddenly grown sneakers with two skinny legs popping out of them. I reached in and flung open the coat and found my brother inside. He was laughing at me like a little hyena.

"Nannanayyanna, you couldn't find me, nannaayyanna, you couldn't find me." He taunted.

My temper flared. I didn't like being made fun of. I made a grab for him, but he ducked out of the way and started running around making faces and mocking me. I started chasing him, round and round the apartment, tipping over tables and chairs as we went in circles getting more and more riled up. All at once Buddy made a right turn, dashed into the kitchen, slammed the French doors behind him, and turned the lock so I couldn't get to him. By this time I was furious and close to tears.

"Open this door, you little jerk—Now!" I screamed.

"Nannanayyanna," came the answer.

That did it. I started banging on the glass with both fists and kicking at the same time, screaming for him to open up! Before I could think about what would happen, my bare foot went through a pane and shattered it to shards. Horrified, I stood there paralyzed, shrieking, watching my blood spurt everywhere.

Buddy unlocked the door in a hurry. At the same time the front door opened and in came my parents. Daddy, always the one to bandage our cuts and scrapes, quickly made a napkin into a tourniquet around my calf to stop the flow of blood. He carried me to the apartment building's first aid room where a nurse was always on duty. Glass particles were imbedded in half of my foot, but fortunately there was no major damage to any veins. The minute I saw the nurse in her white cap coming toward me, my tears stopped along with my shaking. I watched quietly as she carefully tweezed the glass out from under the skin and stitched up the large cut. It hurt like crazy but I gritted my teeth and told myself it was my own dumb fault and I was paying the price.

When Daddy carried me back to the apartment, I held onto him tightly. I nestled my face in his neck. My nose detected traces of talcum powder mixed with a whiskey smell—definitely Daddy's smell that curiously comforted me. Until tonight, I had felt invincible. But when the glass shattered, the *me* that I thought could never be vanquished also came apart in tiny pieces, giving me my first taste of humble pie.

Several weeks later Mother and Daddy were late coming home from a party. Hours after Buddy and I had gone to bed we awoke to noises from the kitchen. They were not the usual noises of accusations from Mother to Daddy. They were noises with other sounds we couldn't make out. We got out of bed to investigate.

We went into the kitchen and there was Daddy holding onto the counter, swaying back and forth, hardly able to stand. He was so drunk he was staring at us as if we were strangers. And my mother—my proper, fastidious mother, what was she doing? She was throwing up in great heaving splashes, vomit streaking her old black coat with grotesque chunks of what they had eaten and the floor was a pool of undigested spaghetti, disgusting white whorls swimming in red wine. Buddy and I had raced in on bare feet and now we were slipping and sliding in that mess before we realized what it was. I started gagging and so did Buddy. We just stood there staring. Mother's bloodshot eyes finally focused on us when she realized we were in the room. Leaning on the counter for support, she said in a strange voice, "Children, clean your feet and go back to bed."

I lay on my bed with my eyes wide open for a long time. My mother had fallen off her pedestal and I was very sad. I was also frightened for now I had no one to count on. I secretly trusted her to be the steady rock in our family but tonight she came apart and showed me she was vulnerable just like Daddy.

It wasn't long after that night we were told to start packing. Daddy had been fired and we had to leave Upsal Gardens. Buddy gave me a helpless look that said "here we go again."

"I'll start packing," he said with his head down.

I said nothing, but followed him out of the room. We weren't surprised. Maybe we had been conditioned but inside me a fencing match of emotions had begun that was to last for years.

CHAPTER 3

Life In The Celery Factory

A SOFT spring breeze ruffled my hair as I threw my suitcase in the back of the black pickup. For the fourth time in three years we were nomads. Hopefully, this time we might find a permanent oasis, despite my father's more frequent needs for a nightly watering hole.

Again, I watched a moving van take our possessions into storage—again I felt the pang of separation, when my blue bed disappeared into the truck's dark interior. And again, we had little more with us than our clothes. Somehow, this rattletrap truck had materialized out of nowhere for our trip to Ocean City, New Jersey. But in the back of my mind I felt Mr. Van Doren had something to do with it. I scrutinized the open backed pickup through mistrustful eyes. It reminded me of an old lady tapping her foot, impatient to leave. Buddy and I set to work, helping Daddy load boxes and suitcases in the back and then rearranging them into comfy seats for the trip. When everything was in place, Daddy got behind the wheel and then we waited—and waited. Mother was still scurrying about checking closets and closing windows. Finally she appeared in the doorway. Her face was pulled tight like something was sucking her skins from the bones and for a moment she looked ghostly and it scared me. She squared her shoulders and in one determined motion shut the door to Upsal Gardens. I heard the final click of the lock, telling me our brief hopes for happy times were forever sealed behinds the doors to those empty rooms.

As we lumbered down the highway to Ocean City, I could catch a glimpse now and then of my parents through the cab's window and from the martyred look on my mother's face I knew she took a dim view of this latest move. Daddy had a big job making the best of a bleak situation as he was so far into the doghouse there was no way out. But this time I wondered if my mother's fall from grace on that awful night had anything to do with Daddy's losing his job. I saw Mother take out her hanky as she turned her face toward the passenger window. She didn't speak for the rest of the trip.

In the truck's open back, where the wind whooshed our hair into a tangled mess, Buddy and I played hunters on a safari among the piles of boxes and suitcases. Now and then the anticipation of spending the summer by the ocean would go through us like an electric shock compelling us to shriek at passing cars, "We're going to the beach! Hey, aren't we lucky? We're going to the beach!" Of course, we didn't think beyond our visions of a whole summer of fun-filled days by the ocean. This was going to be like Christmas every day. We had no idea of the deprivation ahead.

Hours went by. The wind had finally forced us to huddle for warmth in a protected corner of the truck, beneath a pillowcase full of clothes. How much longer? I wondered. Just when I thought I would shrivel in the chill I suddenly smelled the ocean. I smelled that fresh, salty, clean air and knew we were almost there—wherever we were going. Buddy and I started jumping like two baby kangaroos.

"We're at the beach!" We shouted together. "*AT THE BEACH!*" We screamed with delight. But before we caught sight of any sand we pulled into a cracked tarmac parking lot behind a dilapidated white building silhouetted against a tangle of electrical poles.

"Stay here," Daddy said, as he got out of the truck. He straightened his shirt collar and hitched up his pants. "We'll be right back." He disappeared with Mother through a big brown double door.

Buddy and I were mystified. We waited impatiently, twisting our fingers, trying to get our hands warm. The door opened and Mother and Daddy reappeared with Mr. Van Doren. There was our old friend in his familiar gray fedora and big cigar, dazzling me with his diamond tiepin and flashing diamond pinky ring. I heard people call him "the Celery King" and when I thought of him wearing a crown of perky celery stalks, I always got the giggles.

What was he doing here? Was this his house? I hadn't seen those laughing eyes under his gray fedora since he drove away with Rosie and Yanna. I felt my heart go bump, bump. Were they here too? Maybe they were living with Mr. Van Doren in this big ugly white building, making him waffles and molasses crumb pies.

They all had big smiles plastered on their faces. When they told us this was Mr. Van Doren's celery processing plant and we all were going to work here, I turned up my nose. How could Buddy and I have fun on the beach and be cooped up here every day.

Mr. Van Doren lifted us out of the car and stood there, puffing away on his big cigar. "Well, look at you kids," he boomed. "You grew like beanstalks since I last saw you. Great to see you! You're going to love Ocean City!"

"Oh, Mr. Van Doren, do Rosie and Yanna live here?" I asked hopefully. He laughed and said, "No. they're in my house in Easton. You'll see them soon enough". He hugged both of us and then gave Daddy a piece of paper with directions to our summer cottage. I thought we would go inside the celery plant but instead Mr. Van Doren and my parents stood around, talking and laughing. "Are we going soon" I pleaded. "It's gonna be dark soon and Buddy and I want to get to the beach." My plaintive cry broke into their reminiscences.

"OK, kids, be on your way. See you tomorrow," Mr. Van Doren said, and waved goodbye. Daddy started the old truck and at last we were on our way. I could hardly wait to see our next home—the beach front cottage Mr. Van Doren had rented for us.

Well, sadly, my glorious expectations were dashed when our so-called beach house turned out to be an old, peeling two-story clapboard building. Sulking, I hauled my suitcase out of the truck and followed Mother up the rickety outside stairs. When she pushed open the screen door and stepped inside, I heard her sigh. "Oh, well, it's just for the summer and it will be fine."

How could she say it would be fine? It was a terrible, terrible place, worse than Miss Bliss's dump. There was an old moldy icebox, a spindly-legged sink and an ancient four-burner gas stove—all jammed into one corner with a splintery table and four mismatched chairs. An ancient yellow globe in the ceiling filled with the carcasses of dozens of flies was the only light. And this dreary cell of a room was going to be our home for the summer? I could hardly bear it. On top of all this, we had to share the bathroom down the hall with another tenant.

But the worst part was when I looked at the four army cots, with their worn striped mattresses, stacked one on top of the other, the awful truth hit me. We were all going to sleep together in this room! I shuddered. But Mother quickly took charge. Buddy and I swept and dusted. and Daddy rolled the shabby linoleum rug and put it out by the trash. Mother set to work taming the balky stove and soon we sat down at the rickety table for some delicious soup. When bedtime came, the cots were placed side by side and she did her best to make them comfortable with the limp sheets and worn blankets from the storage closet. I claimed the cot next to the wall, crawled in and turned my back on the others, hoping they wouldn't see my bitter tears. The longing for my blue bed and a room of my own was an ache that stretched from my stomach to my toes.

We all showed up for work at the celery plant early the next morning. When I walked through the door I was dumbfounded. The huge room in front of me was humming with busyness, but what nearly knocked me over was the horrible smell. It made my eyes water. I looked at the dozens of workers seated in front of the long rubber conveyer belt, preparing the celery for shipment to the markets.

The process looked boring and the humid air layered with cigarette smoke and the sour smell of sweat caught in my throat and made my stomach lurch. All my beautiful visions of sand and sea were gone as I stood there feeling sick with the stink of rotting vegetation and unwashed bodies.

My first impressions were not wrong. The first days at the plant were so dismal I had to bite the insides of my cheeks to keep myself from crying. There we sat—the formerly rich and elegant Woehrle family—in front of the slow moving conveyor belt. We were stripping the celery's useless outer leaves, tossing them in a water trough filled with rotted discards and then wrapping the remaining clean bunches in cellophane before securing them with rubber bands. By midmorning, the heat in the building was always above ninety degrees and the air was thick with mosquitoes and flies. As the temperature rose so did the stench from the festering celery trough. Also, festering inside was my fierce determination to never allow my life to sink to such a low as this. I discarded and packed. Discarded and packed. I talked to no one. Not even Mr. Van Doren as he cheerfully tapped me on the shoulder one day and commented how happy he was to see me.

One day less than two weeks into my employment my disgust exploded and with tears spilling all over my face, I started screaming. "I hate this place! I hate the way it smells and the way I smell." I stood in front of my mother with my face hot and distorted.

"You have to give me some money right now. Right now! To buy some Lifebuoy soap so I can take a bath and smell good again. Please!" I wailed. "Please. Please." My insides were heaving and I felt I was going to throw up.

Mother didn't say anything. She barely looked up from her work, but when she did, she reached into her apron pocket to give me a nickel. She told me to go home. I ran, choking and sobbing, past the judging eyes of the other workers, and through the brown double doors to the haven of clean salt air outside.

This was the swan song scene for Buddy and me to leave the celery factory. From then on, he and I were free agents roaming the beach all day long. My parents must have had anxious moments wondering if we were safe, but they had no choice but to stay on the job and endure the drudgery. It put food on the table and gave us a place to sleep at night. The one bright spot of living in our dingy room was its location. At a moment's notice, we could escape the room's dark clamminess by leaping over the back steps and running one short block to the ocean and the beautiful wide sandy beach, where we could fill our lungs with great gulps of fresh salty air and gratefully turn our little faces to the sun. We always slid into the back row of the calisthenics classes—two hilariously skinny kids mimicking the jumping jacks, deep knee bends, or whatever else the grownups were doing. For an hour so it was a fun game but we soon tired of it and went off to scavenge the beach hoping to unearth some treasures. We did this every single day in the white heat of July when time had turned into a dawn-to-dusk marathon. When the sun sizzled around noon we sought relief in the cool shade under the boardwalk. Finding our towels and socks with the precious dime Mother had given us for lunch stashed in the toes, we ran over the hot sand to the concession stand for a hot dog with mustard, sauerkraut and pickle relish.

When the sun started its downhill journey, we started for home, tired and sunburned and looking forward to a cool bath and a walk after dinner on the boardwalk with Mother and Daddy. They needed the diversion after a depressing day at the celery plant. Oh, how we reveled in the stroll on the boardwalk with them—breathing in the enticing aromas of popcorn, cotton candy and salt water taffy. I stared with envy at the people riding in the wheeled rattan strollers and was spellbound by the rhythmic therump, therump, therump of the wheels on the slightly concave ten-inch boards. For a dollar you could be pushed from one end of the boardwalk to the other by a boy gripping the handle and you could feel very special and not at all like the ordinary people who had to walk. Someday, I promised myself, I would have the money to hire one. I was always making lists of the "some days" and the "some things" I would have when I grew up. But for now, fresh clothes on a clean body that tingled each night from being kissed by the sun made me feel good enough, and the warmth of my father's hand as we walked in the cool evening was reassuring.

Working like peons eroded Mother and Daddy's spirits. Up until now they had managed a bright outlook as if our setbacks were just temporary, and just around the corner, things would improve. But many nights in Ocean City when they thought we were asleep, I lay awake, conscious of their conversations on the back steps. I couldn't make out most of the words but the tone was not a happy one. There would be long pauses punctuated by a bitter phrase I recognized. Their fear of what lay ahead coupled with an air of helplessness was contagious and turned the lumpy dampness of my cot into a stormy sea of dread. They sounded weary as though even talking was an effort. They sounded like they were tired of promising us things they could not deliver. They sounded so sad.

That summer I started designing dollhouses. Here in Ocean City, my daddy was home most every night as there was precious little money and certainly not a penny for beer. And he didn't have any friendly tavern buddies to set him up. One night, when he had finished reading the evening paper, I asked him if he could make me a dollhouse out of a cardboard box. His eyes lit up. He could do something for his little girl. He set to work and turned that box into a two story house with a roof and cut out little windows and a front door. He even partitioned the inside into three little rooms. I was thrilled. I hugged him tight and told him it was the most beautiful dollhouse in the world.

I went looking for matchboxes to fashion into miniature dressers and tables. I walked the streets looking for discarded magazines that would yield photographs of home furnishings I could paste to the walls and floors of my little houses—houses that wouldn't disappear overnight—ones where I could daydream and feel safe and comfortable and not be yanked out of my security to start moving again.

A strong yearning for real fabric curtains instead of paste-on ones came over me one day. I had been looking at Mother's raggedy dish towel and wondering if I could tear it from one end and make some draperies for my dollhouse living room. Then one morning, Buddy and I were walking past a news stand and I caught sight of a tray filled with coins for self-service—the honor system—you took your paper—you left the money in the tray. I stopped and stared at all this money.

Out of nowhere the devil's voice started shrieking inside my pounding head. *"Go ahead, take a nickel!"* it shouted. "They'll never miss it and think how real curtains would dress up your dollhouse."

I felt my face get very hot. I was about to steal. I stood very close to the change tray. Buddy was off looking at postcards and comic books. I looked around. Once. Twice. Nobody. Quickly my sweaty little hand darted into the tray and I grabbed a nickel. Dizzy with a nameless sensation I caught up with Buddy. "Hey, I just found a nickel," I said in a voice that didn't come out quite right. " Let's cross over to the Five and Ten and see if I can buy something for my dollhouse."

"Oh, you lucky stiff," he cried. "Where did you find it? Maybe, there's some more money. Show me where it was."

I dutifully took him back to a spot near the newsstand and pointed to the ground, but after his fruitless search, he gave up and we went across the street. By this time, the flush on my face had taken hold of my stomach and I was queasy. However, once inside the store, I found the fabric counter and half-heartedly bought a quarter of a yard of blue gingham. Later, when we reached our beach house room I sat out on the wooden steps and tried to fashion a pair of miniature curtains for the dollhouse, but the whole idea had lost its luster and the curtains didn't change the windows or make me happy. I wished with all my might I had not stolen that nickel.

A few days later we found sixty cents on the beach. It was a bonanza! On the way home as we passed the little newsstand, I nonchalantly dropped a nickel into the change tray. The sweet face of Sister Edith came back to me and I could almost hear her soft voice reading us the Bible stories. While I had repaid my debt, the hollow feeling inside of me was still there. The list of things I would never be grew by yet another number. I would never be a thief, I whispered to myself. Never ever would I steal anything, no matter how inconsequential it seemed.

During those days at the shore, Buddy and I were like Siamese twins. When it rained we hung out at the pier, side by side, checking the pinball machines to see if there were any games left on someone else's dime or ducking into the movie theater when the usher wasn't looking. The Depression might have been in full swing, but we didn't carry that gloom around with us on our daily jaunts in Ocean City. We had each other, the beach and the ocean and,that was all that mattered to us..

The summer began moving toward cooler days and life in that one room became more bearable.. Buddy and I could've gone on forever roaming and following our aimless routine like beach bums but the end of summer was upon us and it told us another change was coming. The jobs at the celery plant were about to end and Mother was determined to go back to Easton to register us for school. I could tell she was worried. We had no place to live, and Daddy needed a job back in Easton in order to rent a house for us. Our last resort was to put our hope and trust in Mr Van Doren who promised he would do all he could to help us.

The early morning air was chilly when we left Ocean City. I stood leaning on the bumper of an old pickup truck Daddy had borrowed from Mr.Van Doren, waiting while Mother made sure we weren't leaving anything behind. Small rivulets of moisture were making little deltas on the front windshield. I watched, fascinated, wondering which way the next drop would go—what path it would take on the way down—sort of like us I thought, wondering about our next home.

I opened my mouth, gulping in the air—taking in the familiar saltwater smell as if I could preserve it forever—and a deep sadness came over me. Oh, how I would miss the ocean and the never ending surprises it gave me. I would miss those days of meandering on the beach—the lost hours when we were free as the low gliding pelicans—when we were listening to the gulls screeching, and watching the sandpipers' marking the damp sand with tiny skittery scratches. I sighed, picked up my bag, and climbed into the back with Buddy.

Mother's tired face was ringed with damp curls as she fussed around before getting into the car, making sure everything was stowed in the truck to her satisfaction. Hovering over us, she gave us last minute instructions.

"Now children," she said, anxiously. "Here are blankets you can wrap around you, if you get cold, and don't forget to put on your sweaters right after noon. And here is a bag of sandwiches and apples and some water. I don't want you banging on the cab window saying you're hungry. It's going to be a long ride so no shenanigans. I mean it."

I saw that Mother's hands were stained a sickly green from chlorophyll from stripping celery day after day. She looked like she was about to topple over. It had been a hard summer for both Daddy and Mother. Buddy and I loved being beach bums, soaking up the sun, and were bronzed from head to toe. Whereas, Mother and Daddy, like the rowers in the old ancient ships, had faces as colorless as sand on a wet day.

Daddy turned the key in the ignition and gradually the old engine sputtered into life. The truck moved forward. We were on our way.

Wrapped up in the blankets and hunkered down amidst the boxes and suitcases in the truck bed we must have looked like two lost ragamuffins, begging a ride to nowhere. It felt good to be going back to our hometown— to Easton. We could tell Mother and Daddy were happy about it, too. For the first time all summer they were smiling. That made us feel more than very good.

"Mr. Van Doren found Daddy a job," Mother had announced earlier, a new lilt in her voice. "And, besides that, he has a friend who'll let us stay in his empty house until we can afford to pay rent."

Keeping count in my mental notebook, as the words "empty house" fell from Mother's lips, I jotted down that this house was house number six.

We finally reached the little hamlet of Seipsville just as the sun was starting to cast long shadows. Daddy steered the car down a narrow lane and pulled to a stop in front of a small Pennsylvania Dutch farmhouse. I felt a delicious excitement starting to dance inside of me. Eagerly, I scrambled out of the truck for a closer look. There, by the door, was a wooden sign fastened near the window: Circa 1830.

"Gee," I said to Buddy with wonder in my voice. "This house is over a hundred years old." No reaction, until I whispered in his ear, "Maybe it's haunted." That widened his eyes.

The hollyhocks by the front door seemed to nod hello, and when I stepped inside and looked at the wide-planked floor and the fieldstone fireplace, I felt I could almost reach out and touch the people who had lived here so long ago. It was a "small knowing," a little spooky, but wonderful to hold inside of me like a secret only I knew. I was falling in love with this house. And I could feel good things starting to happen here. Mother was right when she kept saying, "Rise above it." Well, I thought this move was a big step in the right direction.

This house charmed me in every way. It was built of fieldstone and had eighteen-inch thick walls that kept out the cold, and the wide windowsills gave Mother's red geraniums sunny growing places. On the cold, blustery days of fall and winter it was a special treat to lie in front of that welcome fireplace listening to the burning logs snapping and singing. I was not alone-friendly spirits were all around me. I could feel them sliding cheerily by announcing their presence with a cool breeze, a hint of fragrance, or the sudden rekindling of a dying fire.

Each night, when I climbed the narrow back stairs to my attic bedroom, I said a special "thank you" to our big, jovial friend, Mr. Van Doren. When I announced to Mother and Daddy that he must be our guardian angel,

Mother just laughed and said "Don't be silly, Emilie Louise. He's just our good friend." But I knew better.

After what seemed like many detours, we had finally come back home to March school and our old friends. Because our farm house was on the outskirts of Easton, Buddy and I would be picked up by the school bus at the end of our road. None of my friends had to ride the bus and there it was –that old familiar feeling of being just outside the circle.

It was a long bus ride and there wasn't time for me to join the other girls who gathered on the steps in front of the school exchanging the latest gossip. Because Buddy and I had to get up before dawn to be ready, we did have a chance to snooze or finish our homework in the morning, but on the ride home in late afternoon we were the last kids to be dropped off.

In winter when the sky had darkened, the walk home along the deserted road was a lonely one. We held hands all the way. Buddy and I were growing up and conversations were more difficult between a pre-adolescent boy and his slightly older sister. Our intertwined fingers said we were still close, but we soon ran out of things to talk about.

One cloudy morning in late spring, we set out for the bus stop with Daddy. As we trudged down the empty road, I looked across the brown fields, and felt a warm feeling of belonging to this farmland. The longing to be part of a clique had faded and I was learning to appreciate the landscape, especially on the days when Daddy walked with us. On that morning, the sky was dark and angry looking, not at all what a spring morning should be. And then, it started snowing.

"Wow," Buddy cried. "We're going to have a snowstorm in April."

"I don't think this will be much of a storm," offered Daddy. "This is called onion snow and it tells the farmers that it's time to plant their first crop—spring onions, or scallions. He reached down and touched the cracked earth. "Put your hand on the ground," he said. "It's warm, right? And it feels dry, but after this snowstorm, the snow will melt and moisten the dirt and the tiny onion bulbs will start to grow."

I put my hand down the way Daddy said to, and indeed the soil was warmer than I expected. Daddy bent down and patted the earth with his hand. This was a chance to ponder something with Daddy—something as simple as bringing onions forth from the earth. He had now given me my first lesson in how Mother Nature works harmoniously with all her children. I thought about this on the bus ride that morning and remembered as a little girl the wonder I felt when the rain fell on my face and when I looked deep into the velvety petals of a peony flower.

I found living in Seipsville full of new delights. I liked being a farm girl. I liked living in a historic Pennsylvania Dutch farmhouse. I liked the big sky and the wide-open fields. I liked the blustery days when the wild wind, unhampered by buildings or tall trees would sweep across the fields, whistling and whooshing. I liked the huge barn where Buddy and I would spend lazy afternoons daydreaming on the sweet smelling hay or sitting with our feet dangling over the edges of the second story opening, finally getting the courage to jump into the hay piled below.

I liked so many things about being outside, but when I would come home after an afternoon in the barn, and see my mother's tired face, I'd know that while I was playing, she had been working very hard cooking and cleaning and doing all the laundry by hand. When we could we helped her hang the sheets outside where the wind would catch them, flapping them to and fro and filling them with the sweet perfume of the fresh air. I can see the worn clothespin bag—it echoed her faded housedress. I don't think she had had anything new and pretty since the night of the stock market crash, when I overheard her saying she was scared to death.

In winter when the temperature dropped below zero and icy clothespins riveted the laundry to the line, Buddy and I struggled to keep the wind from snatching the frozen sheets from our small hands. It wasn't easy. Our fingers were numb and blue but we managed to get everything off the line and inside to thaw. Later that night, snuggling between those wind-swept sheets and breathing in the clean smell of outdoors, a wave of warm content swept me into dreamland. Even though I wore funny looking clothes to school, those sheets made me feel cared for and loved and that feeling was better than a new dress any day.

At that time, Charles was living with us after a long gig on the road, and he and Buddy shared a room over the kitchen. It was like a holiday because his light spirit chased away the heaviness from our days. Charles loved animals and brought home many abandoned kittens and pregnant dogs we found sleeping on our back porch some mornings. This set my Mother to fuming. Besides a few chickens in our hen house out back, she had no room in her heart for animals and she would storm on and on about how she had enough trouble putting meals together without feeding strays off the road. This battle flared whenever a new foundling came into the house. Mother usually won while Daddy turned a deaf ear.

One day I couldn't find a little gray kitten I had claimed for my own and the other kittens Charles had brought into the house were gone too.

"Where is my kitty cat," I demanded of my mother, suspecting she had taken it and put it out in the barn. "And what happened to all the other kittens?"

She turned to my father, who had just come into the kitchen and feigning a look of great sorrow, she said, "You tell her, Harlan." She turned to me. "You have no idea how little we have to eat and how hard it is for me to put a decent meal on the table. Milk is dear and even though kittens don't need a lot, you need it more. So please. Don't bring anymore animals into the house. I want that understood."

Until that moment, I never realized how powerful my mother was in persuading my father to do what she wanted—something he would never do on his own. He turned to me and told me matter-of-factly what she had done with the kittens. I screamed in disbelief.

"I hate you, you murderer! How could you drown those innocent little kittens? I will hate you forever." I ran sobbing upstairs to my bed under the eaves. I was heartsick, and, for the first time, I mistrusted Daddy's goodness. I hated that he had given in to Mother's demands. After crying miserably, I finally fell asleep feeling a chilly empty space, where only last night I had a purring ball of fluff warming my back.

One day Buddy and I came walking home from the bus stop to see a pile of steel cages in our back yard. Next to them were dozens of wooden crates filled with cackling chickens.

"What's all this for? What are you going to do with all these chickens?" we asked. "And what are those cages for?"

With a proud chuckle, my father told us. "Charles and I are going into the chicken and egg business, thanks to Mr. Van Doren. He is setting us up in business. With this new system, we can expect many more eggs from the hens. Penned up this way, they lay eggs twice as fast."

We watched in amazement as Daddy and Charles assembled the cages, and then shoved the poor squawking hens one by one into their little cells. Within hours "The Woehrle egg enterprise" was well under way and Daddy and Charles were patting each other on the back. Mother came out of the house in her apron, with a tray of cookies and cups of hot coffee. It was a welcome break and the three of them warmed their hands and passed the tray around, while they admired the new cages filled with clucking hens.

The idea of penning up chickens this way made me very unhappy. I finally spoke up. "Why do you have to put them in those tiny cages? I think you're being cruel!"

"More eggs this way," Daddy said, looking off into space and squirming. I could tell he hated my questions and that he felt more like me than he would admit.

"But they should be allowed to hop around and peck the ground," I said. "I remember when we had chickens at our old house they ran free and we loved them, and they delivered eggs easily. What was the matter with that? Rosie and Yanna had plenty of eggs for us to eat."

Charles turned away and then looked back at me again. His dug his hands deep into his pockets and shifted from one foot to the other. "Yeah, Emilie Louise, but we didn't have to sell those eggs and there were just enough for our family. Now we have to do what the experts told us to do because this is a business. We need more eggs, and we need them faster." This didn't sound at all like my tenderhearted brother, the one who would carry a three legged dog up the steps rather than let it sleep outside.

Eventually I got used to the chicken venture and so did the hens. They settled into their new home and the eggs kept on coming, dozens and dozens every day rolled down into a trough. Every morning before school, Buddy and I collected the eggs in our little baskets and took them into the kitchen where mother would pack them in egg cartons.

It was hard work for all of us, especially for Daddy and Charles to keep the cages clean, and even though we were all diligent about sanitation, and each had to do some of the poop scooping, the stench nearly choked us. But we had to put up with the dirty side of the business so we could have the benefits.

As the profits from the egg sales mounted steadily, we began to have an occasional piece of pot roast, or a new pair of shoes for us instead of having the old ones resoled. There was even some talk of a festive Christmas dinner when Dot and Dick could join us after church. Mother even hinted she might buy herself a new coat to wear so she *could* go to church. I can still see Mother as she stepped down from the back porch wiping her hands on her apron, heading out to check the hen house many times during the day. I guess she wanted to see that the hens had enough food and water, and make sure the cages were being cleaned.   If anything was not absolutely perfect we all heard about it immediately.

"There are only nineteen eggs in this basket," Mother said one day when I put down my stash. "There are usually twenty-four. Where are the rest of them?"

It was the third day in a row that my egg basket was light. Buddy's was also short of the normal count. Within a week instead of dozens of eggs to collect from the hens, we had only ten on one day and then four on the next. Something was wrong.

And then one morning on the day when it was my turn to collect all of the eggs before meeting the school bus, I came into the henhouse and saw one, and then two, and then three hens on their backs, their stiffened legs straight up like grave markers. My throat thickened with tears. The chickens were dying.

In a matter of weeks all the chickens perished. Daddy paced around the living room late at night running his rugged hands through his hair. "Mr. VanDoren said that when one chicken gets sick they all get sick. No use in trying to save any of them," he said. "They'll all be dead soon."

No more did we hear the cheerful clucking of the hens or have to endure the gagging smell of their droppings. Within six months of the beginning of the sick hen epidemic, every single hen had died and the empty hen house stood there- full of broken dreams.

Not long after the chickens were gone, Buddy and I learned we were moving again- this time to Porter Street in Easton. .Buddy and I did a little jig of happiness. Now we could walk to school again. But, then came a familiar feeling of sadness. I had grown to love this old farmhouse in Seipsville, and it would soon become home number six—a fond memory. Why was it when I began to love something with all my heart, it was taken away from me?

CHAPTER 4

The Little Black Purse

OUR new house squatted on the pavement like a big brown toad with warts. Oh, no, I moaned inwardly. I couldn't believe how ugly it was. How am I ever going to live in this woebegone place? How I wished I was a princess. Then I could kiss this toady house's front steps and turn them into a marble staircase with a handsome prince waiting at the top. It seemed to me moving from Seipsville to Porter Street was a step backward- not forward.

The inside of the house was even worse than the outside. The dimly lit empty rooms covered in dark brown paneling made me feel I was trapped inside a deep wooden box where I couldn't breathe.. Nothing about this place could make my heart sing—not even Mother's Pollyanna attitude as she pointed out the carving over the fireplace. I was so disappointed and mad at everything.

"Look, isn't it beautiful?" she exclaimed.

I nodded, seeing only the darkness.

The bitter cold days that followed had little luster. Because we couldn't afford to keep the furnace going at full tilt, we gathered in the kitchen, where the oven kept us warm. A working farm table with legs like the fat lady's in the circus was the center of our day-to-day happenings. On this table Mother put together nourishing potato soups, pepper pot soups or, if my sister Dot came to visit, tasty dishes from bits of this and that from the prime rib roast bones that she managed to sneak out of her in-law's kitchen. It must have been humiliating for my mother to accept these food scraps and I can imagine how it must have pained my sister to see us living like itinerants in one rented house after another. She couldn't help comparing our fallen state with the days of plenty in the River Road house. People still reminisce about the lavish wedding reception Mother and Daddy gave her.

We used our big kitchen table for every activity except sleeping. For our homework, for building model airplanes, for hot cocoa on snowy afternoons, for playing Chinese checkers, for making dollhouse furniture, and most important to Mother, to oversee our thank you notes for Christmas and birthday presents—a social ritual she followed faithfully. After the table was cleared, and the dinner dishes were washed and put away, Mother often sat down to unsnap her black change purse and count out its meager contents. In front of her she lined up faded white envelopes, rippled and worn from years of handling. All were penned in her fine cursive handwriting:

ELECTRIC COMPANY—MILKMAN—PHONE—GROCER

She could only put a few coins in each envelope. "But it keeps their good will" she told us, "and that's why we should always pay them whatever we can."

Daddy had not yet found a job, and I wondered why someone wouldn't hire a man as smart and as honest as he was. He certainly tried everything. I remember when we lived in Seipsville, he once ran on the Republican ticket for Recorder of Deeds, an elected position that paid a small stipend. He was trounced by his opponent—another defeat he couldn't take—so down to the tavern he went, hoping someone would buy him a beer. It had been very late when he came stumbling home and then came another screaming scene between my parents. I put the pillow over my head but I could still hear the row. Mother was really lit up with rage   I guess she was very disappointed with Daddy's showing at the polls. Maybe she thought his good name of years back would help him win. I heard the same accusations from her, yelling how Daddy was acting weird just like his mother.

"My mother has nothing to do with this," he shouted. "You think I'm crazy just like her?   Well, let's talk about you and the way you keep poisoning our children about me—telling them what a rotten father I am. You think I'm loony, huh?   Well you are wrong, wrong, wrong. I'm tired of hearing you say the same old thing and I can't talk to you. Then there was a loud crash and a scream. "Oh, now look what you've done, you drunken bum," Mother wailed. "You're a disgrace to this family— hobnobbing with riffraff at every bar in Easton—dragging our good name down. No wonder you couldn't get enough votes. Who would vote for a drunk?"

"Get out of my way," Daddy bellowed, followed by more noises— Mother's sobbing—the sound of a chair being overturned. – "You'll be sorry you ever said that!" he shouted and slammed the back door so hard it shook the floor under my bed. He was gone, but it was too far and too late to walk back to the tavern. He must have slept outside in the old pickup truck that night.

I hated these scenes with Mother and Daddy screaming at each other— calling each other horrible names. What I hated more was the silence between them for days after. These times set my insides to bobbing up and down like driftwood at sea. Living here in this house that reminded me of a warty toad was not a happy time for any of us.

But one Saturday morning brought a surprise. Buddy and I were sitting glumly at the kitchen table wondering what to do with ourselves when Mr. VanDoren burst through our back door, puffing away on his big cigar.

"Good morning," he boomed, and pulled up a chair next to us. "Hey, you kids. Wanna make some money?"

Our excitement grew as he told us his plan. It seemed simple. He wanted us to take orders for his celery in our own neighborhood on Fridays after school and then deliver what they had ordered on Saturday morning, door to door. And he would pay us a nickel a bunch! Wow! Working for Palmer VanDoren—the celery King of the East! This really puffed out our chests.

All it took to go into business with Mr. VanDoren was a big smile and the deal was cemented. From then on our little red wagon full of celery packages became a familiar Saturday morning sight around College Hill. The money we earned made us very proud to be part of the family. I offered Daddy some of my celery money hoping to make him smile, but he shook his head. He was growing quieter and more discouraged daily.

One rainy afternoon in November, Buddy and I came home from school to see our house in complete darkness – no light shining from any window. When we walked inside, there was a feeble glow from candles on the kitchen table, but the rest of house was as dark as midnight. Mother, Daddy and Charles were huddled around the table talking in low tones. Now what? I wondered.

"What's going on? Where are the lights?" Buddy and I asked. .

Mother turned her worried face to us and said, "We have no electricity. We couldn't pay our bill."

Dumbfounded, Buddy and I pulled up two chairs to the table and listened to what was being said, in great earnestness, by my brother Charles.

"We have to do it," he insisted. "I know it will work and I can do it."

" It's much too dangerous," Mother said, shaking her head. "I can't let you do this."

Do what? I wondered but didn't ask.

Daddy spoke up. "It'll be all right, Mother," he said. I saw how he held her hand, patting it gently. They do love each other after all, I thought. "I'll help Charles by holding the flashlight and that will give him two free hands to work with.

Mother shrugged her shoulders. Though she still looked terribly worried, she followed Daddy and Charles out of the kitchen and up the stairs to the front bedroom. Buddy and I tagged along, and hung back in the shadows watching and waiting to see what would happen. Charles opened the window and stepped on the roof. When he had a firm footing, he helped my father through the window. Hand in hand, they inched their way to the edge of the roof nearest the power pole. Charles threw a rope he had looped around his waist, out toward the pole just like a cowboy's lariat. He leaned very far forward and with a deft hand stretching to the pole, he tied the rope securely and then he wrapped the other end around his waist and made a complex knot. With his mechanic's tools dangling from his leather belt and a length of wire draped around his neck, he leapt forward and grasped the pole, wrapping his legs around its girth. Pulling on the rope, hand over hand, he inched his way up to the green glass connectors. My father held the flashlight's beam steady, but its weak stream was barely adequate light to see what he was doing. All I could see was my brother's sinewy shadow moving against the dark November sky. The wind had picked up and when a leaf plastered itself on Charles' face, I held my breath. He quickly shook it off. "Please, Charles, don't fall, please Charles don't fall—please be careful" I whispered. A long time went by. I think I was praying. Suddenly, light flooded the dark bedroom with a brilliance that blinded us all. We put up our hands to shield our eyes and then rushed to turn off the wall switches that were on when the power went out. Buddy and I whooped with joy. "The electricity is on. Yea, it's on! It's on!

How all this was accomplished was a mystery to me. All I knew was the fearful shaking inside of me gave way to calmness and a surge of love for my Daddy, who was sober that night, and my brother, who could have been fried like a grasshopper up on that electrical pole, but risked his life so we could have electricity.

Charles and his pick-up band were now playing on Saturday nights in a run-down bar and grill across the river in Alpha, New Jersey—the local hangout where you could always find a chorus line of guys in sweat-stained work shirts and mud-caked boots draped over the old mahogany bar. Saturday night entertainment hardly rose above a has-been piano and guitar combo. Faulty microphones and burned out stage lights could hardly inspire great productions but Charles, the consummate showman, had bigger things in mind. He had the idea of presenting his little sister in a song and dance routine. He had heard me sing many times, and a few years back after winning a singing contest and dreaming of stardom, I'd had a snit when I realized I'd never be as famous as Deanna Durbin. Mother and Daddy had told him how I ran from the room after a radio show where Deanna Durbin made a debut, crying my eyes out because someone had made it to the top before me. He thought I'd be thrilled to be offered a chance to appear with his band. When I heard this, I froze.

"No," I said. "It's a dumb idea and I won't do it. I'm not doing it."

He turned on his considerable charm. "Awe, c'mon kid. They've never seen anything like you. You'll wow them."

With stars in his eyes and booze in his belly, nothing could stop him from convincing me that I had to do it. I was in awe of his abilities, especially after he'd fixed the lights in our house. He was magic just like my Daddy, and I didn't know how to say no. It didn't matter that I had little training— just a few lessons from Louis Nardis, the town dance instructor—and that I didn't know how to project my voice above a quiet group in a small auditorium or classroom. Day after day, Charles put on the pressure and then after days of ignoring him, I finally gave in and said yes.

Two Saturday nights later, dressed in a top hat, white tie, and tails, and trembling like a new-born kitten, I climbed the few steps to the flimsy stage and stared out at a couple dozen half-tanked guys wearing work boots and mumbling to each other, while Charles talked gibberish into the mike. And then I heard Charles' band start playing the music for the recently popular "I'm Putting on My Top Hat" and I was so glad I had memorized all the words while listening to the "Saturday Night Hit Parade" on the radio. I took a deep breath and began sashaying across the dusty stage, little hip movements to the rhythm, trying to sing the song, now and then breaking into the few dance steps I had learned. When I ran out of ideas, I did an awkward cartwheel. I made up everything as I went along, my heart dancing wildly along with my feet. Mercifully, the song finally ended and Charles, fortified by a few more beers, came to the squealing mike and slurred into the mike, "Lesh give the little lady a big hand, whadayashay?"

I heard half-hearted applause as I fled to the ladies' room. I let the tears flow. My brother—the brother I had idolized all my life—had let me down me.

But the humiliation I felt was soon forgotten when good fortune smiled on Daddy. He was offered a job as program director of the local radio station.

Daddy came up with a good idea. He would present Charles Woehrle and his band for a half hour musical program featuring me as vocalist. Well, I felt this was going be much better than my last appearance. Instead of singing to an audience of barflies, I would be broadcast on the radio. Me? Singing on the radio? Just like Deanna Durbin? I felt touched by the magic fairy.

Daddy set to work to find a sponsor. When he took his idea to The Kuebler Brewing Company, they put their signature on a thirteen-week contract. Once again, our spirits were given a big lift. Charles hired top musicians and they were good—really good—and with his talent for arranging, the music they had was that "big band sound." When the boys gathered at our house for practice, my ear picked up the different harmonies in Charles' arrangements and I remember being thrilled with their sure timing—the whole band right on the beat. But it wasn't all musical fun. When Charles and his musician buddies were at our dreary house, another dark cloud hovered overhead. The beer flowed too freely. I can still see my mother sitting on the sofa, surrounded by music stands and instruments. Her face was a study in frowns as she saw Daddy tilting bottle after bottle to his lips. Being allowed to drink in his own home was rare, and he was like a kid on holiday but, like a kid, he could not say, "thanks, but I've had enough." For all the times the gang rehearsed at our house, the pleasure was always spoiled for me when, after everyone left, my father and Charles stumbled up the steps to bed.

For the next three months, at seven o'clock on Friday night, the show opened with my singing the theme song "Red Sails in the Sunset" and I usually had one or two songs during the half hour. At the end of the thirty minutes, as I softly sang the theme song.

My father read from his script, his head tilted and his hand cupped over his ear.

"And now, sadly, we have to bid you farewell," he would say. "Happy sailing 'til we meet at the same time next week. Good night from your friends at the Keubler Brewery."

I stood quietly during the fade out, watching the red "On The Air" light go off. The band members grinned at each other and me. We always agreed that it all went well. I did it! I remember Charles saying, "We have a good thing going, guys," and "You did great, Emilie Louise."

This was heady stuff. Now I was known as "Little Miss Beer Bottle" at school and at home, I basked in the glow of admiration from Mother and Daddy, especially when I added a few dollars to the little black purse.

On our final Friday show of a thirteen-week contract, Daddy was late for the pre-show rehearsal. Where was he I wondered? Was he hitting the bottle somewhere, when he had been sober for each performance since we started? When he finally walked through the studio door, he stopped and gave me a weak smile before clearing his throat.

"I'm sorry to have to tell you this," he said in his best radio announcer's voice, "but I just came from a meeting with the president of Keubler Brewery. They're not going to renew our contract." There was a moment of stunned disbelief and silence. Then we all groaned in unison, "Why?"

Daddy sighed. "Well, the accounts didn't show a significant increase in sales from their exposure on radio and it's expensive, so they weren't interested in signing on for another thirteen weeks."

In silence the boys in the band packed up their music and their instruments. The only audible noise was the sound of Charles disassembling his drums and the final click of the trumpeter's music case. "Good luck, Mr. Woehrle," they said with disappointment showing on their faces. "It was a great program and maybe you can find another sponsor."

It was a hope we all knew would not be fulfilled. The defeated look had come back into Daddy's face. In our dreary house on Porter Street; we began watching Mother's black change purse as it went from fat to thin.

Fall. Winter. Spring. The seasons came and went. We managed to get through despite the cancellation of the radio show. With spring's blessing of new life, our days seemed softer and less frenzied.

Daddy had a new job selling advertising with the local paper; the electric lights stayed on and there were no more embarrassing handouts left on the back porch. Now when Buddy and I did our homework at the big kitchen table, Mother and Daddy talked quietly on the back porch. Life had settled into a steady routine.

But one fine June morning that was filled with bird song, Mother announced that our Porter Street house had been sold and we had to move out. "But," she added, with a twinkle in her eye, "We are going to spend the summer camping at Lake Mineola."

Buddy and I looked at each other—eyes wide. Memories of the beach in Ocean City rolled in like waves.

"Camping? All of us?" we asked.

She nodded "Yes, all of us."

"Yippee," we shouted and made a beeline for the stairs to start packing.

When we drove away from the Porter Street house I stuck out my tongue and whispered "Good riddance, you big lumpy frog house. We were the best people who ever lived in your warty old rooms and I'm glad to leave."

Daddy had another old heap, a beat up wrecked Ford. I never knew how we got these cars, but we seemed to have no lack of junky transportation whenever we needed it. Often these wrecks were abandoned after we used them.

We began our journey. On the roof of this old jalopy, were boxes and suitcases holding clothes, pots and pans and other flotsam and jetsam we packed from the Porter Street house. Daddy took it slow and easy as any sudden turns would surely send something crashing to the road below. As we rambled down the road, streaks of brilliant sunlight sliced through the tall pines. The flickering light made me dizzy and I closed my eyes and started daydreaming about the lazy summer days ahead.

We made the normal two-hour drive in exactly four hours and Daddy finally pulled into a clearing of pine trees. There was a sign.

WELCOME TO LAKE MINEOLA CAMPGROUNDS.

Through the car window, I saw a flash of sand and shimmering water. There, in front of us, was a large lake dotted with miniature white boats and summer cottages, looking like dollhouses, on the far shore.

"Hey, Buddy!" I yelled. "I see a beach." Scrambling over each other to get out of the back seat, we ran down a path and on to a stretch of sand crowded with kids of all ages. We waved to them and heard them call back to us, "Hey, get your suits on and come on down. The water's great." Right away we knew this summer was going to be full of fun.

Daddy finally found the tent with our name written on a piece of paper tacked to the outside wall. Whoever would have thought that my next home would be a twenty by twenty platform tent with faded green sidewalls, and pitched roof to make it seem more spacious? I looked around and saw that on each little clearing in Camp Mineola the tents were same.

Shoved into one corner was a large table with four wooden chairs, a little stove and an icebox. A dripping faucet above a rusty iron sink told us there was running water and we had electricity—in the form of an outlet cord hooked up to the main box outside. We would have our radio to listen to Lowell Thomas and our programs. I had thought that our days in Ocean City were rustic but without a doubt this arrangement lifted my eyebrows. It was the embodiment of rudimentary housing. What surprised me was how happy Mother and Daddy were to be here. Daddy put his arm around Mother and they smiled at each other. It had been a long time since this had happened. Of late, there had been very few drunken scenes and whenever Daddy wasn't drinking, Mother was nicer and life was more to my liking.

"Let's take the table and chairs outdoors," my mother suggested with a lilt to her voice. "We can move them under the canvas fly and make an outdoor dining porch."

Since the tent barely had room for four cots and four trunks, the canvas fly created an outdoor canopy on one end that almost doubled our space. Every dinner beneath the sky turned the plainest hamburger into filet mignon. At night, it was a treat to lie snug in my cot, listening to the soft lapping of the water nearby, wondering what the loons were saying as they called to each other. Now and then, the hooting of the owls in the tall trees around us added a spooky touch to the darkness. And the cool of the night forest, instead the sticky heat of our Porter Street bedrooms, made me very glad to be here.

As nature's music was sending me off to dreamland, I could hear the faint strains of Harry James "Jungle Drums" from the jukebox down at the skating rink. . Boom—Boom it went, adding a bass note to all the hoo-hooooos, hoo-hooooos of the owls that came from the treetops—blending sounds from diverse worlds.

I marveled at how Mother and Daddy seemed to slide right into life in the woods. I remembered they told me they had gone camping in Maine when Dot and Charles were little so they must have loved living in a tent which included, I guess, how much they valued the homely chamber pot on chilly, rainy nights. Not for me. I preferred to take my flashlight and make the journey through the darkness to the communal bathhouse.

However, sharing the facilities with a gang of people I didn't know was not my favorite thing.

During the day, Buddy and I were in the water more than we were out on land. We splashed and swam until our skin turned blue and wrinkled and we had to seek the comfort of dry towels and the warm, sandy beach. But after dinner each night, we would walk down the road to the skating rink where all the kids gathered. The building was lit up with a thousand colored light bulbs strung along the roof, around the doorways and windows, and anywhere they could tack up a wire. From a distance, it twinkled with an irresistible invitation that said "Come. Here is where the fun is." It had everything a teenager could desire; a snack area with all the junk food one could think of, dimly lit corners for gossiping and giggling between teenage girls, and a veranda under the stars for dreaming a dream or two with a new friend. The gathering place was also a stage for us to try out the latest jokes and show our hairdos to one another. It was the perfect place for the boys to size up the girls and vice-versa.

I had begun to notice a budding femininity in my skinny thirteen-year-old body but it never got a whistle or a raised eyebrow while I was in my bathing suit. Nevertheless, I'd hoped to be noticed at the rink at night and perhaps, even meet a certain someone. There was no one in particular, but I thought that with my best walk and my best eyelash batting I would be able to draw the boys' attention away from a curly blonde siren who had an unusual feature of one brown eye and one blue one. Often after long hours of making idle chatter, running to the ladies room too often to apply another coat of lipstick, and trying to appear nonchalant, I would give up trying to get some male attention, and walk back to the tent alone conscious of an unfamiliar misery rising inside of me. I had no one I could talk to about this strange feeling. .

Buddy was oblivious to my unhappiness. He didn't have a clue about all the girl stuff that was tormenting me. I'm not sure I did either. Even though he had little in the way of material possessions, it didn't get in his way of having a great time with his new friends. I envied him and it came as a surprise for me to realize that my little brother was now the Pole star and I was his reclusive sister.

It was a different kind of summer—that summer of 1939. Mother was trying every trick she knew to find a place for us to live before school started and Daddy, again without work, was plodding the streets of Easton looking for a job. Every evening Lowell Thomas, the news commentator, reported grim happenings in Europe with the threat of war building each day.

However, a campground was hardly the place to feel pessimistic. It was hard to think of war when the sparkling lake summoned and when our new friends called us to join them we were only too glad to turn the dial off and leave the gloom inside the little radio.

Some nights Daddy came back to the tent very late and very drunk. By the time he appeared, my mother had worked herself up to a frenzy and could hardly contain herself—but because our tent was so close to our neighbors, she had to batter my father with low snarls instead of screams. I sighed. It was the same old movie and the same actors and I was tired of it. Ten years of this—ten years since Daddy's bank account went dry—ten years of drifting hither and yon, making do with very little, battling melancholy and his ever present need for the bottle.

Then one evening in the later summer, Daddy arrived home early, a serious look on his face. He had a copy of the Easton Express night edition under his arm. "I thought you would like to read this," he said handing the paper to Mother. She opened it and I saw the headline "Hitler Invades Poland." I knew right then there were big changes coming for all of us.

CHAPTER 5

Shiny Black Heels

THE night before we left Lake Mineola, thunderstorms pelted us with wind and torrential rains. By morning we were all damp and cold, and hardly speaking to one another. Doggedly we set to work clearing the tent and loading the car. Finally as the last soggy box was stowed under a make-shift, and not particularly waterproof tarp, we climbed aboard the aged Ford, grateful to get in out of the downpour. To our relief, the engine turned over and the cranky car crept up the incline to the main road. We settled ourselves for the slow ride to our new home—four very disgruntled people huddled in a small space, and all smelling like wet dogs.

The drive home was grueling. Daddy hunched over the wheel, peering out of the fogged windshield and trying to navigate an obstacle course of huge puddles along the roads. Mother in a nervous twit bit her lip and flinched each time the car shuddered and bumped as it took a blast of water. My mood was as stormy as the weather and I spent the entire trip feeling sorry for myself. Curled into a ball, I tried to nap, but the damp upholstery against my cheek did nothing to comfort me. I was sad we had to trade our carefree days by the lake for four plaster walls and a wooden roof to keep out the winter winds. And God only knew what this next house would look like. To me it was a bad omen that after weeks of cloudless blue skies it had to pour today—the day we were moving into 32 Cattell Street. One happy note was we would have our old furniture back and with it some sense of security. I had missed it, especially my blue bed. Dot's friend, who owned Lipkin's furniture store, had very kindly donated space in his warehouse to store it over the summer and without it, I had a funny disjointed feeling.

We pulled up behind the waiting moving van at 32 Cattell Street. Mother heaved a big sigh that told us she was glad indeed to still be alive after that treacherous drive and she immediately began ordering the movers around in her imperious voice.

"Stay in the car. I don't want either of you getting in the way." She said to Buddy and me.

I didn't mind waiting in the car. I suppose I was sulking, but hanging back gave me time to get a good look at our latest house—house number nine. It was a golden-oldie from Victorian days, every roofline flounced with carved lacy curlicues. I guess, at one time, the house was probably considered the latest in design, but age had grayed the pristine white clapboard and time had dated the architecture. Now it just looked weary.

Like Porter Street, it was a gray house, wrapped in shadows. As I walked around the gloomy rooms inside, my footsteps echoed and re-echoed with a sad lonely sound. Nothing in any of these rooms took my hand to say welcome. This house reminded me of an old maid wagging her finger at me saying no dancing allowed.

Mother tried her usual decorating tricks but this time she couldn't coax any life into this place. While she had arranged the living room perfectly, it lacked a spark of vitality. No one was comfortable on the faded velvet sofa and the piano was so out of tune we kept the keys covered so no one was tempted to sit and play. Strange, but somehow the dark windowless halls of this house became synonymous with my bilious green dress—an embarrassment that made me feel I didn't belong. As a result, I didn't invite anyone over and the room never rang with the happy chatter of my friends.

I was now a sophomore in Easton high school—a big social change from being a junior high student. The faculty at Lafayette College in Easton invited the young ladies from the College Hill neighborhood where Cattell Street was located to Sunday afternoon tea dances at the student lounge. At one of these dances I met Phil—five feet eight with fuzzy hair. He was no heartthrob but he was kind of cute and had an engaging smile. And when he took me onto the dance floor and I felt his inborn sense of rhythm, I knew we were meant to dance together. And did we dance! I don't think we missed a dance floor in Easton, where our feet flew to the Lindy Hop, the east coast and the west coast versions of the Shag and even got the cha-cha down perfectly. But our favorite dance was the jitterbug with all its dozens of interpretations. Our love of music pulled us together more and more and as a result, we built a warm friendship that lasted a long time.

The first time Phil came to the house, my mother, in her most charming voice, said, "How nice to know you. And what does your father do?" I cringed. I was always embarrassed when my mother started interrogating my friends.

"He's a doctor, Ma'am—a pediatrician in Allentown."

My mother was now more than enthusiastic in her welcome. "Oh! I am delighted to know that. Sons of professional men usually follow in their father's footsteps. Are you planning on going to medical school?"

Phil gave her a broad smile. "Maybe. I'm thinking about it."

"Oh, I hope so," she purred. "Well, enjoy yourselves tonight but remember, home by 11:00."

I was thrilled to be invited to this final dance at Eddyside—a local riverside resort where our gang hung out from May to October. Everyone I knew would show up tonight to hear one of our favorite big bands— Tommy Dorsey and his orchestra. For this closing dance, the pavilion shutters had been folded back, exposing three sides of the building to the soft evening air, and the glistening dance floor became a part of the brilliant autumn foliage and star studded night sky. The final festive touch was the addition of twinkling Japanese lanterns, dancing back and forth in the warm breezes. The magic was everywhere.

With our hearts beating in anticipation, Phil and I walked up the steps and stepped into the beginning of a beautiful memory.. I felt on top of the world. I wore an outfit of my own design—a simple white shirt paired with a navy and white bias cut skirt that flared out gracefully when Phil twirled me around. He said he loved me in that dress and when he complimented me, I knew someday, I could be a fashion designer, along with my singing career, of course.

We saw a large crowd standing in front of the bandstand listening to a new singer. No one was dancing. They all seemed spellbound by the vocalist; a very young and very thin boy with an enthralling voice. We stood entranced by his voice, which was smooth and clear-like no other voice I have ever heard before or since. The sweet sound of the clarinet accompanying him was a perfect background.

"Who is he?" I asked Phil .He shook his head. "I don't know-he must be just starting out."

A murmur went through the crowd as one by one they asked each other the same question, shrugging their shoulders and then passing along his name- Frank Sinatra. During intermission, Phil and I wandered hand in hand out of the pavilion, hoisting ourselves up to perch on one of the picnic tables. We chattered away about so many things. And then Phil leaned over. "May I kiss you," he whispered.

I nodded and closed my eyes, knowing I was about to get my first kiss and waiting to find myself in ecstasy. Phil leaned over and tenderly touched his lips to mine, lingering for just a second. "Oh, that was wonderful," he sighed. "I have never felt lips as soft as yours."

If I was hoping the stars would fall, it didn't happen. I kept my eyes closed after the kiss and tried to figure out how I felt. It was far from romantic. I giggled at the thought running through my mind- I just kissed a peach—dry and very fuzzy. As first kisses go, on a scale of ten it ranked a two. As inexperienced as I was, I knew my first kiss should've been more thrilling than this.

We made it home in time for curfew and the next day, though my mother never asked if I had a good time, she said with a satisfied look, "I approve of him. He has nice manners and a friendly smile."

My dancing dates with Phil were now every weekend.

The weeks turned into months and the fall came swiftly, bringing winter's grasp and a real decline in our living. Daddy was still picking up jobs wherever he could—as a handyman—delivering papers—clerking part time in a men's store — but he brought home very little—especially after stopping at the tavern.

Mother cut corners everywhere, even washing wax paper so she could use it again, and switching to lower wattage bulbs. As a result, the house grew darker and darker thereby creating a perfect background for her creeping emotional darkness. She hardly went out, preferring to hole up in her room most of the day.

I would come home from school to an empty tomb and feel despair hitting me in the face the minute I shut the door. I had to run upstairs and shut myself up in my flowered wallpaper haven. I was torn in two and floundering. On one hand, I felt great sorrow for my parents—a feeling that made me want to cry. On the other hand, I wanted to run away from all of this because I had no way of changing it.

It was obvious Mother didn't want to talk to me and gradually I stopped talking to her. The distance between us became as wide as the Arctic Ocean. She did manage to come downstairs at dinnertime and try to fashion a meal from pitifully little, but her movements were lackluster and her shoulders sagged, and she couldn't even manage a smile when Buddy told a joke. My only recourse was to escape into the world outside where there was light, and people laughed.

One night, after Phil and I had been dating for months, he said it was time for me to meet his parents. "Oh," I groaned, "Do I have to?"

"They want to meet you, Emmie, and I want to show you off." I wondered what was in his mind. I hoped he wasn't going to get serious—no thank you. I was not ready for that sort of thing. He was a good friend and nothing else.

Getting ready for Sunday dinner at Phil's filled most of my free time on Saturday. It took hours to launder and iron my only good white blouse, to get it pristine and white like it was spanking new. I'd added a good dash of starch to the wash water. I went over the seams lots of times with the iron, careful not to burn them. On Sunday morning, I took a bath, washed my hair, and used all the tools in my little cosmetic case. When Phil picked me up, I was turned out as neat as could be.

It was a long and extremely boring Sunday afternoon and I could hardly pretend I had a good time.

In the car coming home, Phil leaned over and gave me a squeeze.

"Thanks for doing this. It meant a lot to the folks." I tried not to show my relief that it was over. However, I wasn't sure where all of this 'Phil and family' was heading, after-all I was only seventeen. I knew that the only polite thing to do was to invite Phil to my house and endure a replay, even if a sirloin steak dinner like we had at his house wasn't affordable. I did know that we still had our good china, silver and linens, all packed away from our house of sunshine, and just maybe, maybe, my mother, whose long face and unhappy eyes seemed to say no to everything these days, might be able to say yes to this. I knew it was important to her that I associate with the right kind of people—like a doctor's son. I invited him.

At that time, I was too insensitive to realize how difficult preparing for this dinner must have been for my mother. I thought she was just being mean when she walked back and forth slamming doors and snapped at me when I asked her a question. Her first problem was keeping my father sober long enough to be presentable at the table. She did it, though she almost had to chain him to the bedpost so he wouldn't slip out to the tavern on the corner. The second problem was finding the extra cash for a pot roast and fixings. It must have taken a supreme effort for her to create and serve a meal with her usual grace. She must have been remembering the many lavish parties she used to host—where all that was required of her was the guest list and shopping list for Rosie and Yanna, ordering flowers, a trip to her favorite dress shop for a new frock for the occasion, and a day at the beauty parlor.

For Phil, she laundered all the linens, scrubbing them by hand on the old washboard. Then she took down the good china from the tall cupboard in the little-used dining room, and carefully washed each piece to make it sparkle. Certainly, the silver had to be polished. She did it all without my help. And then she still had to shop, and cook, and eventually clean up. At each turn I imagine she mourned the end of her shiny silver spoon life now reduced to faded sepia images in her scrapbook.

When Phil arrived, it was a sign to put our best selves forward. My mother amazed me. She snapped out of her woebegone role and was charming and gregarious, engaging Phil in interesting conversation and my father told some very funny stories. It was impossible to tell from observing this foursome, gathered around a beautifully laid table, that our family, once known as the glamorous Woehrles, was rapidly sinking into dangerous waters. We were all full of false cheer and gave star performances on that brisk Sunday afternoon, and when it came time for Phil to graciously thank us and leave, we closed the door on his back and lapsed into our former selves.

My room on Cattell Street was the only bright spot in that dreary house. Outside the window there was a tiny Romeo and Juliet balcony, and on the walls a leafy green wallpaper pattern sprinkled with white forget-me-nots. I spent hours on that balcony pouring out my discontent to the universe, praying and begging that something or someone would come and rescue me—maybe a handsome prince to reach up with a rose and gently spirit me away. I knew for certain it wasn't going to be Phil. He and I had drifted apart within months of our family dinners and neither one of us had any hard feelings.

It wasn't long after that Sunday dinner that I started making loud noises about wearing decent clothes. My sister Dot came to my rescue with two new dresses—my first real, store bought clothes in ten years. They were wrapped and sprinkled with magic powers and when I slipped these new clothes over my head, I entered the other world—the one where I believed my friends resided. The clothes turned me into the princess I was longing to be. I was blossoming from an awkward little girl into a self-assured young woman.

I guess my sister remembered how important pretty clothes were in her teen years, but mother seemed unable to realize I wasn't a little kid anymore, but a budding adult longing for her understanding ear. As I was growing up and started to assert myself more, Mother dug her heels in further and tightened her jaw more saying "No" to many of my requests. She was suspicious of my friends and my actions and I guess she thought she could control me with a tighter hold. Maybe in my sister's era this worked, but in 1940, these tactics were hopelessly outdated. "If only you could be more like Dorothy," became her litany and I grew to hate her when she said this. I wanted to scream it was unfair to be constantly compared with a sister who had everything she ever wanted when she was growing up. She never had to wear hand-me-downs or be ashamed of the way she looked. She never had to sleep in a freezing room or eat food from a charity basket. Couldn't my mother find a little praise now and then for who I was and the honors I was awarded in school?

My best friend Ginny lived next door to the Sigma Alpha Epsilon fraternity house at Lafayette College. It was in Ginny's big comfortable clapboard house that I found refuge, a place where I could relax and laugh. Both her father and mother were from Virginia and their Southern hospitality was in direct contrast to the grim outlook of my elderly Victorian parents. It didn't take long for us to make friends with the college boys next door and to our squealing joy, we found ourselves included in their fraternity parties. I had a mad crush on a boy named Ray who invited me to football games and fraternity get-togethers. It was during those ecstatic trips to the clouds with Ray that the discontent with my home and parents evaporated.

But back in my room on Cattell Street, I would flop on my bed and cry with frustration. I hated this house. I hated the gray colorless kitchen and I hated eating our meals there. To save on laundry, Mother had covered the table with oilcloth that at one time had a cheery pattern of yellow chickens, but now the yellow chickens were faded to a dispiriting mouse color and no matter how often Mother wiped this oilcloth, it was always sticky to the touch. And in the corners of this sad room, ghosts of countless somber meals whispered their sad tales to me. Perhaps Mother felt this too. Perhaps this is why she came to a dead halt here at 32 Cattell St. This room—the kitchen, which should be the heart of a woman's home—showed her weariness and despair. She had never replaced or tried to disguise the bare-bulb ceiling fixture with its metal chain waving back and forth, back and forth. It hung like Mother's tattered flag of surrender. The ancient appliances sometimes refused to work and the dingy walls and cabinets hadn't seen a paintbrush in years. There were big bare spots in the linoleum worn down by years of weary footsteps. But the back porch leaning precariously to one side was a fitting testimony to our sad lives. We were also leaning-leaning dangerously close towards the edge of a cliff.

After dinner one October evening the phone rang. It was Ray inviting me to the Harvest Ball. I was thrilled and told him I would call him back after I had spoken to my mother. I dashed into the kitchen babbling with excitement.

"No." My mother said with a set jaw. "I don't know the boy and until you bring him home and we have a proper introduction, you are not to see him. Is that clear?"

I was outraged—dumbfounded at her flat refusal.

"Oooh!" I yelled, "Why do you have to be so mean about it? The trouble with you is you don't even try to understand me, or anything I do! " I stamped my foot and then I went on. "Sometimes I wonder if you ever loved me. If you did, you wouldn't slam the door in my face whenever I want to go places. You want to hold me back because..." Sobbing and choking I went on with " you're so old fashioned that all my friends feel sorry for me."

Mother stood quietly, through most of this tirade. But when I said that my friends felt sorry for me, I saw her face tighten. And then her hand flew out—so fast I didn't see it coming—and she slapped me hard across my face. The blow came so fast it stopped us both in our tracks. She had never done anything like that before. I stood there, stunned and silenced. With that vicious slap, something inside of me started to shrink and close tightly like a vise against steel. With that slap, the fragile connection between us was severed and the last bond I had with my mother—daughterly respect— ended. This was the beginning of our very own ice age.

I fled, desperate to escape from this hateful atmosphere, and ran up the dark, squeaky staircase to my room, where I collapsed on the bed and surrendered to bitter tears. I hoped with all my helpless being that my mother was just as miserable as I was. The words *why can't you be more like Dorothy?* kept repeating themselves in my ears—over and over like a record stuck in its track. .

Every once in a while I'd hear the front door slam and I would hear "Anybody home?" and instantly the Cattell Street house shook itself awake. It was Charles! He brought the cheerful interlude our family hungered for. After weeks on the road bumming from one bar to the next, looking for a solid gig and a possible lead into a bigger venue, Charles would come home, hunt up Buddy, turn on the radio to a baseball game. Even Mother, who had not the slightest idea of what baseball was all about, perked up enough to learn the players and their positions.

Often on hot summer days, when the locusts were hitting their high notes and the refrigerator was laboring away with its loud hum, my two brothers, fourteen years apart, made a wonderful portrait of camaraderie. Sprawled out on the floor by the front door, where they might catch a passing breeze, they would drink innumerable glasses of iced tea and spend a couple of hours listening to the announcer's drone from Yankee Stadium. It was an afternoon of pleasure that didn't cost a cent, and it took them to a more exciting place than College Hill.

Slowly, with each passing month another layer of self-assurance was emerging from this girl/woman body of mine. And with this came exciting events outside my little world. My sister, always aware of the importance of social events, had an enviable social connection that came with her trousseau. This connection was still in good standing and made it easy for her to get my name on the "A" lists for the fashionable parties around town. During the Christmas holidays it was hard to keep my mind on school and most of the time I was in a pink cloud, delighted at being included in all the festivities. When the postman rang the doorbell and handed me another engraved envelope with an invitation to a dance inside, my heart jumped. I now had quite a collection of invites stuck in my mirror frame—fond memories of the ones I attended and anticipatory glee of those to come.

The most glamorous invitation finally arrived. This was the big event of the season — a black tie Junior Assembly held at the Saucon Valley Country Club. Dot and Uncle Dick took me to Laubach's department store to buy me a formal dress. It was pure ecstasy—a full-skirted white taffeta gown set off with rhinestone shoulder straps. The taffeta rustled exquisitely as the dress glided over my body, and when I adjusted the sparkling straps that looked like rows of diamonds against my pale skin, royal ancestral blood started flowing through my veins. The night of the ball, I stood in front of the mirror, enchanted by my own perfumed glow. I didn't see a gawky girl. I saw a mass of auburn curls surrounding a swan-like neck and the upwardly tilted chin of a true princess. The vision was dazzling and I was totally intoxicated by the new me. Bolstered with self-confidence, I approached my mother, and in an impulsive moment, I begged her to let me wear her one remaining diamond ring for this junior assembly. It was the diamond ring Daddy had slipped under her pillow at the hospital right after I was born. To my amazement, with no questions asked, she went upstairs and appeared a few minutes later and slipped the ring on my finger. "Have a lovely time," she said smiling. Was she saying she was sorry about the night weeks ago when she slapped me in the kitchen?

But the gaiety and lighthearted thoughts of dances and dresses didn't last for long. The holidays came and went and so did all the festive parties. It was January and another gruesome winter settled down on us like a heavy blanket. The Norman Rockwell calendar hanging on the kitchen wall had big black X's marking the passing days as time slowly tore off the pages one by one.

At school, I was in the center of things and giddy with my popularity. At home, I holed up in my room, hardly speaking to anyone—trying to sort out my roller-coaster emotions that came from living in two worlds— my flighty-as-a-bee one at school and my brooding, moody one at home. I was completely wrapped up in my own perplexities and totally unaware that the time had come to choose my course of study at school—a decision that had the potential to change the course of my life.

On the day when I saw the first robin hopping on our small patch of lawn, I learned if you don't pay attention, your life path could be decided by somebody else. Without consulting me, my sister Dot had gone to the guidance department at Easton High School and enrolled me in the stenography program, which meant I would be trained to be a secretary. It certainly did not include college, where all my friends were headed after graduation. I was furious. I went straight home after school and marched into my mother's bedroom. I tried to hold my temper

"What's the idea of switching my curriculum at school" I demanded. "Don't you know I'll be separated from all my friends—my gang here on College Hill since kindergarten? All of them are taking pre-college courses— but not me. Oh, no. Not me. All I'll be learning is boring stuff like typing and shorthand and I'll never be able to get in a college." I stood there, with my hands on my hips, shaking with anger." Mother looked at me, helplessness in every line of her face. "Emilie Louise, I am very sorry we had to do this. We can't begin to afford college for you—you must know that. So Dot and I talked it over and decided this was the practical solution so you would be able to get a good job after graduation."

So—it was clear who really decided to do this. Dot must have forgotten how she had all the breaks when she was my age and went to a fine college. Never mind that she squandered her opportunity for a degree by marrying Dick in her junior year. It didn't matter to her that I would never have a good education or experience college life in ivy covered walls. They didn't give a hoot about my desires. My shoulders slumped and I dropped my hands and mumbled "Well, at least you could have told me," and walked out of the room.

Now I was an outsider again. However, rather than share how awful I felt, like most teenagers I pretended I didn't care.

" No, I'm not taking algebra, or French or science."

"Why?" they would ask.

"Oh, I've decided not to go to college," I would say breezily. "I'm going to be a private secretary. I'll probably get a great job in Harrisburg. Maybe even New York," I bragged.

"Gee," they'd say, blind to the ache inside of me.

At times my resentment made my head throb, and I had to walk away when my friends started talking about going away to college.

I did have one English class with my college bound friends and I ate it up. Our teacher, Mr. Cooper, was a forty-year old Englishman and by the second class I was madly in love with him. His mellow voice as he read us the beautiful words from Tennyson or Wordsworth, took me to a wondrous place. And it was delicious agony to be so besotted by an older man who hardly noticed me. One day as class was being dismissed; Mr.Cooper stopped me and stood directly in front of me. I thought I would swoon. He took me by the shoulders and shook me gently. I felt my hair roots tingle.

"What is the matter with you?" he asked.

I had no idea what he was talking about. He went on. "You have such wonderful gray matter inside that head, behind that silly hairdo, and you don't use it. All you do is chatter with your girlfriends and now I hear from the office that you are not going on to college? How so?"

Caught off guard, I felt perspiration bursting through every pore in my body. I didn't dare confide my heartache to him nor tell him why so I just stood in front of him, shifting my feet clumsily, trying to think of something clever to say. But I was speechless with adoration. He looked straight into my eyes and shook his head in bewilderment and turned to join an entourage of adoring students in the hall—all hungrily waiting for a crumb of his attention. I became determined to show him what was really behind my silly hairdo, and proceeded to pull straight A's from his class from then on. It didn't matter what I did after I graduated, but when Mr. Cooper remembered me, he was not going to think of me as the hair-brained dummy. I made certain of that!

There were no familiar faces in my new classes but gradually I made friends—some with questionable reputations that lifted eyebrows. One such girl was Gloria who came up to me after typing class one day. I was intrigued by her savvy attitude.

"Hi," she started. "You live on College Hill, right?" With her hand on her hip, she cocked her head and gave me a long, surveying look.

I did the same and saw her short skirt and high heels - quite different from my knee socks and saddle shoes. She held my gaze, but continued with a friendly introduction.

"My name is Gloria and I live on South Side—you know, the other side of the tracks. You're on the hill with all the rich people. What are you doing in this class anyway?" she asked.

"It was my sister's idea, not mine," I said, my face burning. And then I stammered with my next answer, not sure if I wanted to be lumped with the rich people or belong with the kids I was going to spend another three years hanging around with. "We don't have the money for college."

"Oh," Gloria said, less antagonistic. She paused. "How about meeting me and my sister after school? We go to the Bluebird every afternoon. "

"Sure," I replied, already feeling I had made the wrong decision.

And that's how I became part of that *other* crowd—the crowd that hung out at the Bluebird restaurant—a dark corridor of a meeting place, where we drank Cokes spiked with aspirin for an extra adrenalin kick, and we learned how to smoke cigarettes simply to be cool. It was an unsettling journey into strange territory, but also an important part of my search for identity.

My mother would smell smoke on my clothes when I came home. "It's been dark for an hour," she would say in an accusing tone as I walked in the door. "Where have you been?"

"I was down at Hershey's having a coke with Ginny and Charlotte," I fibbed.

"It doesn't take an hour to have a coke," she would answer. "Don't think I don't know what tricks you are up to." She would turn and leave me feeling naked and ashamed. In times like these, I wished I had a Daddy who came home sober and had dinner with us—someone I could talk to. Some mornings he would appear in the kitchen while Buddy and I were hastily grabbing a bowl of cereal before we left for school, but there was never enough time for talk. The only personal times I had with Daddy were occasional Sunday mornings, when he cooked salt mackerel and home fries. He told me he loved this small bit of peace and concentration before everyone was awake. I felt he needed this quiet time more than the beer he had the night before.

I thought about seeking Buddy out for old time's sake, to have a good gab session and maybe share a few bits of our disparate lives. But he was out a lot with his pals playing ball or working the pins down at the local bowling bowl. And in times like these I longed for my happy-go-lucky Charles who still made me smile. But he was gone so much of the time that I wondered whether he was real or just a wish of my heart.

Fortunately for me, the dull classes learning the skills of an office worker were made bearable when I was given the leading actress role in the junior play "Charlie's Aunt." I couldn't wait for rehearsal times after school, where I could escape into the make-believe world of show business. I had no time to hang out at the Bluebird with questionable characters and my mother didn't dog me as if I were a petty thief on the prowl.

Once in a while she would ask me how the rehearsals were going but beyond that, she didn't seem to care. It didn't surprise me. Neither of my parents showed much interest in anything I did. But the last night of the performance, I saw them sitting in the audience with Dot and Dick and then they appeared backstage after it was over to congratulate me. I was so caught up in my glory I hardly acknowledged them. I don't even remember saying goodbye when they left.

The show was a success and received a glowing review in the Easton Express the next day saying,

> *Emilie Louise Woehrle charmed the audience, with her bright and spirited portrayal of Amy Spettigue.*

Going back to classes on Monday morning, where I was, once again, just part of the gang, was a hard bump back to the real world. My head was still in show business as I recalled the thrill of being called back by continuous applause for a second bow, and then on to the celebration party that lasted into the wee hours of the morning.

One glorious spring day as I was on my way out the front door of the school with another girlfriend, Dotty-Ann, an old March school classmate drove up in his old beat up jalopy. Dotty-Ann and I persuaded him to play hooky with us and we set out for the New Jersey seashore. As we chugged down the highway we sang bawdy songs and drank in the delicious wine of forbidden freedom on our way to Asbury Park. When we got to the seashore town, it was still in its winter sleep—boarded up and quiet—the beach deserted. We parked by the boardwalk, ran up the dune and watched the mighty ocean rolling in wave after wave. Over the winter, the sea had given up some of its secrets—we pocketed pearly pink shells and a piece of whitened driftwood for our lunch table where we shared cokes and sandwiches before starting home.

We were halfway up the main street when Bob's jalopy gave a huge grinding belch and dropped its transmission onto the pavement. It was stone dead. We tried to gather our collective wits and we disagreed whether we should call our parents or try to hitch a ride home. I opted for finding my own way. Bidding the others good luck, I started for the train station thinking I could find a way to go by rail. I was too scared to call home. At the train station I went up to the window and asked the ticket agent, "Can I go home COD like a package?"

The agent's eyebrows shot up and he pressed his face against the cage. "What?" You want to send yourself home COD?"

When I nodded, he burst out laughing.

"No, I'm afraid you can't do that. I guess you don't have the money for a ticket, do you?"

"No." I sat down on a bench and was about to cry when a man showed up and stood in front of me.

"Are you in trouble?" he asked.

I told him what had happened. Tears rolled down my cheeks while he listened. After giving me a pat on my head, the man walked to the ticket window and had conversation with the station agent. In a few minutes, the man came back.

"Tell you what," he said. "I stopped in here to buy some cigarettes, but I'm on my way to Harrisburg. I'll drop you in Easton, if that's okay with you."

I stared at him. He seemed like a kindly, middle-aged man. Nothing suspicious. And in 1939 when the entire nation was still trying to recover from the Great Depression, we all understood being short of cash, and hitchhiking wasn't unusual. Though I didn't know what to say and the thought that he might be dangerous did run through my mind, the ticket agent had seen me scrutinizing the man and he called me over. "Miss, I know this gentleman and I can vouch for him. He will take good care of you. Unless you have parents who can pick you up, what are your choices?"

I dreaded calling my Mother, so I got in the car and sat as stiff as a mannequin and just as quiet. It wasn't long before we were heading up the hill toward my house. The gentleman walked me to the front door where my mother, who must have been waiting for hours, anxiously flung it open. Anger flashed like lightning bolts from her eyes. Barely civil to my Good Samaritan, she grabbed me by my jacket and yanked me inside so abruptly and so hard I nearly fell over my own feet.

"Well, thank God you're home! You little tramp! " She slammed the door and continued on her tirade without even thanking my driver. "You are going to the convent first thing in the morning. Now get upstairs and start packing." She shoved me roughly toward the stairs.

There was *no* nearby convent to send me to, but I spent many a solitary hour like a nun while counting the forget-me-nots on my bedroom wallpaper, doing what Buddy called my convent time.

Though Buddy and I no longer had common interests outside of our family, I knew our unspoken bond of love would always be there. We both treasured the closeness we shared when we were toddlers and knew it was there forever. But I found words sticking in my throat when I started to tell him how I missed the fun we shared in the past and now I felt emptiness where once there was companionship. I couldn't tell him how I missed our little talks and secrets—missed the fun we had jumping into leaf piles and playing pretend in our marvelous dilapidated playhouse. I missed the swings and the bike rides, the joking and the teasing, even though sometimes it turned rough. And I wished that we weren't growing apart as we were growing up. But it was hard to tell him these things.

One snowy winter morning we couldn't go to school because the drifts were five feet high so Buddy and I both slept 'til noon. In our PJs and woozy from adolescent sleep, we finally wandered down to the gray lifeless kitchen.

"Hi," Buddy said grinning. "Some snowstorm, huh? Great to have a day off. " He poured some cereal in a bowl, added milk and sat down at the table.

"So what's going on with you?" I asked, between mouthfuls.

"Not much," he answered. Long silence while he attacked his cereal, swallowing in big gulps. I sipped my orange juice.

"I see you and that colored boy throwing the ball around in the alley. Is he a good friend of yours?'

Buddy nodded, chewing with his mouth open. Finally, he said, " He's new at school and nobody was talking to him, so I asked if he would like to come up and play ball someday?" Buddy shrugged and smiled, his adorable smile, the one I loved so much.

"We've sort of hung around together ever since. He's a nice kid. I like him a lot—a lot nicer than some others I've met who think they're hot stuff." He swallowed another spoonful of cereal. "I got him a job down at the Pomphret Club with me, setting up pins in their bowling alley."

I sat there with my brother and I wondered what he did with his free time when he wasn't working.

"Do you have a girl you like?"

"Nah—most of them think they're such hot stuff, too." He paused, looking at me.

"What are you doing outside of school?"

"Nothing much—the usual." I said.

"You sure don't spend much time at home."

That remark struck a nerve.. I wanted to tell him to mind his own business. Instead I said, "So why should I?"

He nodded. "Anyway, what's going on with you and Mother? Either you are yelling at each other or not talking."

Hmm, I thought. He doesn't know the half of it. "She's just hard to get along with. I notice you don't seem to have that problem," I said wryly. "Anyway, I'd much rather be over at Ginny's. There's always something going on there. Mr. Culpepper's the district head of the Boy Scouts. And, the SAE fraternity is next door. I've met some cute boys."

Buddy gave me a long, knowing look. "I hope they're nice to you," he said. He got up and left the table to rinse out his bowl in the sink. "See ya," he said and left the room.

I sat there thinking how Buddy's words had touched a forgotten tender spot inside of me. I felt a tinge of regret that I had not paid more attention to him lately and wished I had been more sensitive to his needs, whatever they were. Of course he *wouldn't* have a girlfriend. *How could he?* He never had more than small change in his pocket—certainly not enough to take a girl to the movies or have a coke at Weaver's drug store down on the town square. He was left out of the boy's crowd on College hill for the same reasons I was shut out of the girl's crowd. There were so many *me* things that got in the way of seeing his problems. At one time we were like two vines climbing a trellis together toward the sun. But now, we were reaching for different suns.

At the end of my junior year, I went on to fulfill a requirement of my high school business course. I was assigned an on-the-job position at Beck's shoe store in downtown Easton. The first week was fun waiting on customers and learning how to tally the cash register but then the hours dragged. So this was how I would spend my summer vacation? Working in a shoe store? I was bored already. I did have two weeks in August to look forward to—joining all my friends at Girl Scout camp in the Delaware Water Gap. Then in September, it was back to school—this time as a senior. To be top dog for a year in the high school sounded great, but after graduation, it was the job world for me. The thought of watching my friends planning for college life, after joyously throwing their motor boards in the air, was more than I could bear and I was just plain jealous.

I stood around Beck's most of the time waiting for the few and far between customers. On one particularly hot day when business had slowed to a crawl, my boss said, "We aren't going to do much business this afternoon so why don't you take the rest of the day off. I'll see you tomorrow morning, nine a.m." I could have kissed him. To have this chance to wash away my blues, as well as the stifling heat, at Eddyside, our stomping grounds on the Delaware River, was the best treat I could imagine. Luckily, I caught the next trolley to College Hill. At my stop, I walked four blocks to my house on Cattell Street. When I came in the front door, all was deathly quiet as usual. Mother was no where around. In my room I changed into shorts and a shirt, grabbed my sneakers and set off for Eddyside. Thirty minutes later I arrived at the entrance to Eddyside's low brick building that contained the concession stand, changing rooms and rows of lockers lined up like post office mailboxes. I found an empty dressing room, shed my sticky clothes and changed into my suit. I slipped the basket containing my clothes into a locker and turned the key. The sun was fearsome that late afternoon and I was more than ready to dive into the cool water.

Twenty-nine worn steps led to the sandy beach. Throwing down my towel, I ran into the water. It was gloriously cool against my hot skin. I happily bobbed and floated until I had cooled down completely and then swam rapidly to the wooden raft moored some sixty strokes away. Breathless, I climbed aboard and stretched out with a big sigh, feeling a lovely tingling sensation as the water on my body slowly evaporated. The raft was rocking gently to and fro and soon lulled me into a delicious cat nap. But it wasn't long before a splash of cold water jarred me out of my reverie.

"Yowie! Cut it out," I yelled, and rolled out of the way. It was Bill Gross, a long time buddy from March School. He leaned his arms on the raft. "Couldn't resist that, sorry. You looked too comfortable. How about some tennis? The courts are free right now."

Bill was such a nice guy and I loved his funny side to everything. "Sure, sound's great. I'll meet you up there in about half an hour. "

I dove into the water and swam to the beach where I retrieved my towel, threw it over my shoulders and started back up the twenty-nine steps. When I got to the top I saw a lone figure leaning on a cane in front of the concession stand. After a moment, I recognized him. It was Bob Betts, who had graduated a couple of years ahead of me in high school, and then gone on to Culver Military Academy in Indiana. I barely knew him, but the story of his near fatal accident was legendary. It seems he was in a baseball game and when sliding into third base on a tight throw, he collided with the third baseman's knee. Bob took a blow to his chest and passed out. He was rushed to the hospital. A very bright intern discovered Bob was hemorrhaging and immediately called Bob's father, who was a doctor, for permission for the surgeon on duty to remove Bob's ruptured spleen. The operation saved Bob's life. It was a story that made me pause.

I stopped in front of him. His face was pale but he was still very good looking. "Sorry to hear about your accident Bob," I said tentatively and pleased that I had remembered his name. "Uh, how are you? How are you feeling? Are you around for the summer?"

"Yeah, I am," he answered, "and thanks for remembering. "

I liked his eyes. They sure had a devilish look.

"I'm grounded for the whole summer – recuperating—before I go to college." Bob eyed me up and down before asking, "Where are you off to?"

"I have a tennis date, so I'm going to the locker room to change. Nice talking to you. Take it easy."

Slipping into my tennis shorts, I wondered why I had started a conversation with someone I didn't know. I'd only seen him once or twice, but he looked so lonely and forlorn. I felt sorry for him. I tied my sneakers, grabbed my racket and left for the courts.

My tennis match with Bill was into the second set when I became aware that we were being watched.

"Hey, do you call that tennis?" came a mocking voice from behind the fence. "It looks more like pitty-pat badminton if you ask me."

I turned around to see Bob Betts leering at me through the chain links. A little prickle went up my back. "Nobody asked you." I replied. "Yes, it is tennis." I then hit a savage cross-court shot that my partner missed. Good, I thought. That'll show Bob Betts that it's not badminton. Who did he think he was anyway, barging into our game and making a pest of himself?

When the game was finally over, and Bill and I were packing up to leave, Bob was still in the background kibitzing and hooting.

"Wow," he said, clapping loudly. "Congratulations. That was one of the best tennis games I have ever had the pleasure to witness. When are you planning to turn professional?"

I just kept walking.

That evening our doorbell rang. My mother was upstairs and I ran to get it. When I opened the door, there he was—the kibitzer, Bob Betts. I was perplexed and pleasantly surprised.

"Hi. Want to get a milkshake?" he said with an irresistible smile.

I admired his nerve and I was right about thinking I saw a devilish light in his eyes. It was twice as lively tonight as it was at Eddyside.

"I guess so," I answered. I invited him to come in and meet my mother, who had appeared at the sound of our voices. She looked warily at this strange new boy, but her expression changed the minute I said he was Dr. Betts' son.

"Oh," she said, warmly. "Of course, I know your father from way back when he assisted Dr. Fretz in operating on my son. But that was years ago. It's nice to meet you."

"We're going out for a milkshake. Won't be late. OK?" I said, leaving her no time to object.

"Fine. Have a good time," she said, as she closed the door behind us.

After a few stiff verbal exchanges, Bob and I relaxed and over several milkshakes, began enjoying each other's banter. When he dropped me off at my door, I was really befuddled. It surprised me but I had a really good time with him. More perplexing was the feeling that somehow I knew this innocent first night date was the beginning of a big change in my life.

The summer of 1940 was happy and carefree. Bob showed up almost every night in his family's station wagon.. We put a lot of miles on that Woodie, with its squeaky brakes—the late-night sound that told my mother I was home at last. We double-dated with Ginny and Jim and the four of us would take off driving half the night to take in a big band concert or a new play at Hunterdon Hills Straw Hat theater down the road a bit. We searched out carnivals, flea markets and circuses, and on many occasions drove to the seashore for a day of splashing in the ocean. My student job at Becks shoe store had ended and these were carefree, lighthearted days and nights—a slow gentle time for us to get to know each other. It was just what I needed to fend off my uneasiness about my future.

More often than not, the four of us would end up at Mud Run, the favorite after-hours smooching spot for our gang. Because I was an incurable romantic, I was disappointed when Bob's first shy kiss did not send me rocketing through the heavens. Although it had a little more pizzazz than Phil's kiss, I wondered why the swooning reaction I'd read about in "True Romances" never came and the night he said he loved me, it sounded more like a confession than a passionate declaration from his heart. As much as I imagined the dizzying feeling of being in love, it was just not there for me. In its place there was something else—something unidentifiable that drew me to Bob. I admired his keen intelligence and I wished to emulate him in many ways. He was the first person who inspired me to think beyond the superficial as he introduced me to a place where poetry and great literature and ideas dwelled.

But too soon, like all good times, the summer of 1940 came to an end and on the night before Bob left for Harvard we were quiet as we headed toward our hideaway at Mud Run. He eased the old "Woodie" into our favorite spot and turned off the engine. The night was warm, and it wrapped us with its rich earthy smells from the pine forest. As I snuggled into Bob's shoulder, I felt the soft September breeze from the open window gently pat my cheek. It brought me a certain kinship with the darkness—so alive with the songs of the insect world—songs that it made me a bit sad. There must be a million crickets out there, I thought, as their rhythmic chirping made me wonder what they were saying to each other. At least they were talking. Bob and I just sat there holding hands, each of us deep in our own thoughts.

"I'm really going to miss you," I said, finally. "It's going to be so different and we'll be so far apart." My voice trailed away as pictures of dull days and empty nights flashed in front of my mind. I was going to miss his wonderful smile, his companionship. And those tender romantic nights in Mud Run would be hard to forget.

Bob had been enthusiastically talking about beginning college life at Harvard but how could I share his enthusiasm when I knew there would be other girls—girls from Smith and Wellesley. I knew he would find them very attractive. My misgivings about Bob's bright future were beginning to taunt me, robbing me of sleep. I didn't sleep well at night. Would our summer of discovering each other just fade away or was our relationship strong enough to stand up to all the new temptations?   I felt the sting of tears behind my eyes.

"I'll miss you, too," he whispered and then encircled me in his arms and gave me a quick, soft kiss. He leaned back afterwards and said with a chuckle, "You know, I really wanted to go to Yale but when I had the accident, my application was pulled."

"So my Dad had some connections and pulled some strings. Bingo! He got me into Harvard at the last minute. Isn't that great?"

Great? I didn't think so. I could tell Bob was already thinking in terms of college and not really here with me in Mud Run. I couldn't match his excitement and wondered what to say as our last night together had turned into a discussion about Bob and what was on his life's horizon. Not mine. My life wouldn't be changing. I said nothing but listened to the crickets filling spaces between us. I tried t o appear enthusiastic, nodding and smiling, but it seemed Bob, who had lifted me to star status in his Universe, had found an new planet called Harvard and I was being shipped off to another galaxy. I felt diminished and unhappy.

He went on and on. "Did I tell you my brother Brooks is a senior at Harvard and is ranked number two on the tennis team?" He winked and gave me a little punch. "Remember the day we met and you pretended to be a top notch tennis player? You weren't so good. But you tried. It was funny."

Unsettling memories of that day came back with a rush. I bristled. Why did he have to bring that up?   "Well, really," I snapped. "I thought I was pretty good for having a rude, uninvited, audience jeering me from the fence. It was very distracting to play with a blow hard yelling behind me. "

"*Touché*!" Bob laughed and took me in his arms for one more goodbye kiss.

There was no deep feeling in this kiss. It was one my brother would have given me and I could tell Bob's heart just wasn't in it. .So, our romantic farewell evening, the one I had dreamed about for weeks, had fizzled with a loud whoosh. As Bob walked me to my front door, he must have sensed something was not right. I was usually walking slowly, but now I was hurrying to get inside where I could cry without him seeing me.

"I'll call you on Sunday nights, how's that?" he asked. "Every Sunday night. And then there are football weekends and you'll come and we'll have a ball."

I perked up. At least this sounded hopeful and those coeds with their eyes on Bob would have to take a backseat when I showed up for the big football weekends. Another squeeze from Bob and then he was gone.

I was downcast for days after Bob left, but then the telephone started ringing. Calls from the boys I had met at Lafayette College mixers, who were asking me to parties and dances at the school. My mother was highly annoyed as most of the calls came during dinner. So, she took the phone off the hook, which annoyed me twice as much. For the first time in my life, I was popular and I was collecting brass rings by the dozen on this dizzy merry-go-round. I was much too busy to miss Bob—much too busy to think about a boy who could only talk about himself when his supposedly best gal was in his arms

Surprisingly, a musical turn in my life came during a fraternity party I was attending. Someone put my favorite song on the record player and I started singing along with it. Soon my bosom buddies Charlotte and Ginny joined in and to our delight, we began harmonizing. Our voices melded as smooth as honey—a natural high, a rich low and in between and we were thrilled with our sound. We practiced every moment we could.—even during free time at school. A teacher heard us one lunch hour and asked us to sing at an auditorium program. This was our big debut as the Girlfriends—not as polished as the Andrews Sisters, but pretty close.

Ginny's father knew a world renowned orchestra leader and choral director, Fred Waring, and Waring was eager to snap up young talent for his national and international touring company. He wanted us to audition. On the night before the tryout, I tossed and turned with the anticipation of traveling with his big band. I would be famous like my mother and father had been and maybe I could even get Charles a job as a drummer with Fred Waring's band. In my head, I designed gorgeous sequined gowns and invented knockout hairdos and I could see the three of us, The Girlfriends, dazzling huge crowds, who had waited hours in line for tickets.

Our parents didn't like the idea, and one by one they firmly put an end to all our daydreams. Secretly, I was relieved to stay put in Easton for the moment. As much as I wanted to be famous, I remembered when my brother came home in a frightful state from a road tour. He was, according to Mother, half dead from no sleep, too little food and as I listened at the top of the steps to Dorothy and Mother talking late into the night, addicted to drugs. I wasn't sure quite what that meant, but my skin crawled when I remembered his slack cheeks and putty tinged skin, his lifeless eyes, and his inability to laugh for months with Buddy and me, no matter how much we tried to pull him into our games. No. That life was too scary for me.

I barely managed to balance my studies, even the commercial ones. My head-turning social life had me skipping from one swirling party to the next, and although the promised phone calls from Bob came right on schedule every Sunday, they were not the high point of my week. I think he sensed it. But the low point for me was continually receiving Ds on my report card. After each bad grade I'd buckle down and pull it up to a B or an A again.

With each passing week of that school year, my new social life was pushing Bob, and his elitist intellectual superiority, and our summer romance, into a hazy background. A new interest, the boy who played the lead in Charlie's Aunt, sought me out one day during our lunch hour jukebox soiree in the gym. He was a fabulous dancer and we twisted and wiggled to the latest Glen Miller records until our knees shook.

The few times I'd danced with Bob, it was like dragging a lead doll across the room. He had no rhythm and no bodily sense that he was stepping on my feet most of the time. I'd smile sweetly at him and squelch my disappointment about his clumsiness on the dance floor. I guess dancing was frowned upon by his no-nonsense Methodist mother.

One Sunday afternoon after a soda shop get-together with my friends, flirting with the college students, Bob phoned with more excitement than I'd ever heard in his voice before. "How would you like to come to Boston for a football weekend?"

I stood in the dark hallway, the telephone plastered to my ear, feeling joy singing in every fiber of my being. Pictures flashed through my head—moving pictures of ivy covered buildings and football stands filled with cheering students and their dates, snapshots of after game parties and fun. "Oooh! That sounds great," I answered, controlling the amount of enthusiasm and then laying it on exactly as if I were Scarlet O'Hara. "I've been missing you terribly and hoping you would ask me to come see you."

"That's great," he said. "I've checked the schedule."

He knew I would say yes. I could tell from his voice. A trickle of guilt washed over me thinking of how little I'd thought about him lately.

"There's a train at one-thirty five from Easton on Friday afternoon which will bring you to Back Bay station around six o'clock. I'll meet you there and take you to the hotel—the one where the college has rooms for the guy's dates." He said all of this in one breath ending with "How about it? I have it all planned."

"Oh, yes," I answered. "And thanks. It will be wonderful to see you." I hung up and started to believe everything I said. That I missed him a lot. This was it. This was Bob! This was life!This is what I wanted, forever!

Of course when I told my mother, I could see her mouth set in the no position before I even finished the itinerary.

"Absolutely not!" she exclaimed. "I am not going to allow my daughter to spend a weekend at a boy's college without a chaperone."

"But the weekend *will* be closely chaperoned. Bob reassured me completely." And indeed he had slipped into the conversation one line about chaperones. "Other visiting girlfriends will be at the same hotel. Boys are not allowed beyond the lobby at any time."

My mother's rigidity began to come down as she narrowed her eyes, scanning my face to see if I was telling the truth, and then she said she guessed it would be all right under those circumstances.

"Yes." I said. "Those are the rules. "

I ran to my room and counted the bills and change I had saved from my job at the shoe store. There was enough to buy a dress and one pair of shoes. I just had to look wonderful for Bob. I pleaded with my sister to take me on a shopping trip to Laubach's Department store.

"Please, please," I said. "I have to look good for Bob. I need something wonderful to wear for the weekend at Harvard." So, Dot took me to Laubach's and we picked out a princess-style gray wool coat, a red pleated dress and shiny high-heeled black shoes. Back home in my room, I stood in front of the mirror in my room, surveying myself from top to bottom and I sighed with pleasure. I liked the way I looked—a little like Ginger Rogers when I saw her as Kitty in the movie "Kitty Foyle ".

I had never taken the train to New York's Pennsylvania station and I was shaky with nervous anticipation. To calm my fears, I hung on to Daddy's hand and jabbered nonsense until the uniformed conductor yelled *All Aboard!*" I gave Daddy a quick hug and kiss and carefully climbed the metal steps in my new high heeled shoes. The conductor showed me to my seat and where to stow my luggage just as the train began moving.

I pressed my face to the window and there was Daddy waving to me and I kept waving back to him as the distance between us slowly widened. Through the glass, I saw how weary he looked. The catch-as-catch-can pick up jobs he had at factories or bars, (I never knew where) and the cash and handouts from his good friend Mr. Van Doren, had not been kind to his self esteem but his deep brown eyes and gentle touch still reflected his old fashioned courtesy. Sober, he was kindly and fun. But when he drank, he turned into a monster.

As the train rolled across the New Jersey flatlands, now blazing with autumn colors, I brushed off a tingle of apprehension and tried to settle myself in for the ride. I was nervous and worried about everything that could go wrong, especially afraid that I would get on the wrong train and arrive in Chicago instead of Boston. By the time the train pulled into Pennsylvania Station, my carefully applied red nail polish was chipped and scratched from my picking at it.

A friendly porter guided me to a taxi stand. "To Grand Central station," I announced with authority, even though my legs felt like Raggedy Ann's and little rivulets of sweat were making their way down my back. After a hair-raising, but mercifully short ride, the cabby screeched into the unloading curb. I somehow managed to give him the correct change. "Well," I said to myself, "I made it this far." I took a deep breath and I walked into Grand Central Station where my breath stopped. I wasn't prepared for the magnificence of that huge hall and couldn't help stopping mid-step to gawk at the crystal chandeliers and the pale blue domed ceiling depicting the galaxy sprinkled with stars. *This was the big city, all right!* And suddenly, I understood what a country mouse I was standing here among hundreds of people rushing this way and that —people who all knew what they were doing and where they were going. No sight has ever caught my small town girl's awe again in the same way. I stopped to ask directions half a dozen times before I finally found the right track number for Boston and, with a big sigh of relief, put down my suitcase in the upright position and sat down on it to wait until boarding time.

I was twenty five minutes early and the train wasn't on the track yet, I looked around, feigning nonchalance while butterflies rose and fell in my tummy. Not far from where I had planted myself, I saw two girls, obviously college girls, sitting on their suitcases. All of a sudden something clicked.

Bob had told me his roommates' girlfriends were coming for the weekend and that we would probably all be taking the same train from New York. I walked over to them, dragging my bag, clumsily.

"Are you Nancy and Jean?" I asked.

Their mouths flew open and they jumped to their feet. "Yes, I'm Nancy," said the short haired blonde.

"And I'm Jean!" The one with the auburn hair piped in. "How in the world did you know? Out of all these people, how did you know who we were? I can't believe it!" Jean shrieked. We all started talking at once and we kept talking all the way to Boston.

When we stepped off the train, it was madness and confusion. The train had been loaded with people all coming for the big football weekend, all laughing and shouting to one another, clearly old friends coming together for noisy reunions.

All of a sudden I felt shy. Everyone around me seemed to know each other. I looked around and wished the wind coming in from the Harbor would pick me up and take me far away: My clothes were all wrong. I wasn't properly dressed for a college football weekend. The other girls were wearing expensive tweed coats with matching skirts and pastel colored sweaters adorned at the neck by single strands of pearls, undoubtedly real and handed down from their grandmothers. Compared to these stylishly turned-out coeds, I stuck out like someone from another land. I felt poor and out of place. Just as my lip started to quiver, some part of me remembered my first day at March School and I squared my shoulders and resolved that for this weekend I would pretend, no matter how much effort it took, that I was a coed. I may be dressed differently, but my clothes weren't hand me downs and they were certainly fashionable elsewhere.

At first I didn't get the affected college girl demeanor even half right. My first head turning gaff started at the train station where, after spotting Bob, I squealed at the top of my lungs, "Honey!"

Faces turned. Eyes questioned. There was Bob coming towards me, hunched down in his coat, obviously embarrassed by my behavior. But my humiliation didn't last long. All my misgivings gave way to the thrill of simply being in Boston, the place where Paul Revere started his ride and where our country began.

On the first night Bob and his friends, including Jean and Nancy, all drove into town for a lobster dinner at Bookbinders, a famous seafood restaurant. I put on a blasé attitude as I let my oysters-on the-half-shell slither down my throat like this was nothing new. But inside, I was tickled and squealing right down to my very toes in my silly shiny black high heels.

The next morning the boys gave us a first class tour of the Harvard campus. We gazed in awe at the famous glass flowers in the Fogg Museum and sat quietly in the back pews for a moment in the Holden Chapel, built in 1744. I gaped like a tourist at historic ivy covered buildings—the students lounging on their steps, books piled beside them. I felt my heart yearning for this life Bob had been entitled to. I keenly felt the loss of my family's legacy which would have allowed me to experience all this first hand as a Radcliff student, rather than as somebody's girl friend.

Strangely, Bob's didn't act like my date. Over the weekend, he often left me to small talk with strangers while he clowned around with his buddies drinking himself into a stupor. He and his friends all had nicknames like Wallwork, The Whale, The Chief. I could hardly remember who was who. Bob's nickname was Boone—I never knew why but I sensed this persona opened a door to another part of Bob giving him the green light to throw off the shackles of propriety and act a little crazy. I asked him why the nicknames. "Hey, we all have them and you need one, too. How about Punchy? You sure acted like you were punch drunk when I picked you up at the station." I flinched. It was hardly like being given a dozen roses. I was beginning to think Bob was embarrassed by me and sorry he had asked me to come for the weekend.

That night, though alcohol was forbidden on campus, the boys found a way to have plenty around and Bob, just as my father, didn't know when to quit. During dinner, when we were all laughing and having a great time, he disappeared and never came back. The minutes became hours. The boys went to look for Bob and came back to tell us they had found him passed out drunk on a staircase. They managed to get him back to his room and into his to bed. This ended the evening with a dull thud. Nobody wanted to do anything but go back to the hotel and I wanted to take the next train home!

As we walked in the chill of the New England night, my chin went higher. I felt the Pennsylvania Dutch perseverance in me rising. I said little but I was damn mad. It was clear that even though Bob had all the advantages of the privileged, he was sadly lacking in the social graces I expected. His bad manners were much worse than my innocent *faux pas* of wearing the wrong clothes. I couldn't wait to go back to Easton where I belonged—where my popularity was soaring. I would leave Bob behind in his hallowed halls and I would dance with boys who knew how to dance and who told me the clothes I wore were peachy keen!

Early in the second evening of the visit, during a dinner dance, an unexpected episode in the ladies bathroom sent a signal to me. It began with a remark I overheard while I was washing my hands. Two friends were confiding in one another as they stood at the mirror reapplying their make-up. They paid no attention to me.

"Jim said the boys were all set, but I'm scared. Remember the last time and how many got caught? They were on probation for months so I'm not too keen on it," whispered a girl with an auburn pageboy. She followed her opinion with a tremulous question, sounding like small girl. "What are *you* going to do? Are *you* going along with it?"

"Oh, why not?" said the other girl with confidence as she snapped shut her compact and dropped it carelessly into her purse. "We're here to have fun. Don't be such a spoil sport. Okay?"

I watched her give a daredevil head toss and stride out of the ladies room, her high heels clicking emphatically on the tile floor. The other girl leaned on the sink, still looking scared.

My mind was flying around. What were they talking about? I dried my hands and went back to the group. When there was a lull in the laughter, I took Jean aside.

"OK, what's going on? I know this is my first time on a Harvard weekend and maybe I'm naive but if you know something that I don't know, let me have it. I heard something in the bathroom about the boys knowing how to get around the rules at the hotel?"

She giggled and then leaned over and whispered in my ear. "The boys are planning to sneak in after hours and spend the night with us."

I felt the blood rushing to my face. "Oh, really? Is that so! Well, I haven't heard this from Bob so I don't know what he's planning." Inside, I was churning. What was I going to do? Is this what the weekend was for? Is this what's expected of me—sharing a bed with Bob because he invited me here? Was this what other girls did to be part of the group? I felt like I was sinking into quicksand and wished I were home.

I was nervous all evening long. Sure enough, when we all decided to call it a night, Bob took my arm and steered me away from the others. He snuggled against me, pressing his body close to mine. "Hey, Punchy, how about we spend the night together. We all know how to get into the hotel without being seen so there's no need to worry." He was lightly twisting a lock of my hair between his fingers and then he held me away to look at my face, pulling me back again for a better than average kiss. He seemed to know a lot more about romance now than when he was saying goodbye to me in Easton.

So, I mused, getting angrier and angrier, - *this little caper is nothing new for you* — just- just *another weekend party girl, a sucker for a practiced move.* My head started pounding and I felt a little sick. I turned and gave Bob a long look

"Sure, honey—you can spend the night. I'll make up a bed on the floor for you."

He stared at me and then burst out laughing. "You must be kidding. You are, aren't you?"

"Nope! You're welcome to spend the night on the floor any time you want. Final offer. Take it or leave it."

Bob steered me to the desk by my elbow and shifted nervously as he checked me in for the night with the matron at the desk.

After a rather perfunctory kiss on the cheek, I climbed the stairs to my second floor corner bedroom and closed the door behind me. It had been a long day and night of partying. I sank on the bed, exhausted. Despite reeling from so much new information, as soon as I put my head on the pillow I drifted off. I wasn't asleep for more than a minute when I heard a soft knock.

"Punchy, are you in there? Let me in."

I shook myself awake, padded across the floor and opened the door.to see Bob anxiously waiting. I gave him a sidewise smile and shoved a pillow and comforter into his outstretched arms. His mouth hung open in surprise. It was obvious he'd been expecting *me* to submit to his charms.

"There's the floor—pick your spot." I went back to bed with great self-satisfaction and turned out the light. Within seconds I heard Bob's snores wafting up from the floor.

On Sunday when it was time to go home, there were no hugs or kisses from Bob. Taking his cue for the impersonal goodbye, I boarded the train and waved offhandedly. As the train whistle blew, Bob was already engaged in some sort of horsing around with his buddies—rough childlike shenanigans that reminded me of the way Buddy used to act with his friends   It was a relief to feel the train start to move away from Boston.

Nancy and Jean were catching different trains so my ride home was lonely. Unhappy thoughts chugged along with each mile as I tried to understand why the weekend fell flat. I did a lot of thinking and as the train grew closer to my destination, I realized I had been thrown into an arena where I was outclassed. I didn't like this feeling. My mother had always reminded me I had good blood in my veins. Maybe so, but that was not enough to feel equal to those with the latest clothes and suave demeanors coming from trust funds in their names. With all of my sunny spirit trying to break through the clouds, in the end I felt eclipsed by something outside my familiar planetary system and I wanted to chuck it!

But I was only seventeen and dwelling on the unfair things in life was not my style. So it was back to school the next day. The weekend of being the odd one in Boston faded fast as the telephone started ringing for me again. Invitations and requests for my company did wonders to salve my bruised ego and made me forget about Harvard college football weekends— for the moment.

When Bob phoned the next Sunday, the call lasted all of two minutes. He didn't ask how I was or what I had been doing. He sounded flat and bored I made the usual small talk with him, all the while dreaming of the up coming weekend, when Ginny and I would be double dating for the big football game Saturday with Lehigh. My date, Ray, had an irresistible charm and this promised to be a far better weekend than the last. I finally hung up.

It was as if Bob had sworn on the Bible never to miss making his Sunday night call to me. They were as regular as his heart beat. One Sunday night, however, I was not home and my Mother took the call. "He sounded a bit irked," was all she said

Monday night he called back. "I tried to reach you last night and you weren't home," Bob said testily. "Where were you?"

"I went down to Hershey's to have a Coke."

"Yeah, and with who?"

"Just some of the gang. Isn't that OK? Do I have to stay home for four years?"

" At Hershey's? Having a coke, I bet," was his sarcastic response.

"Is there something wrong with that?" I asked innocently, while feeling guilt wash over me like dirty water.

"I don't like what I hear is going on there—that you are dating Lafayette guys. Aren't we supposed to be going steady?"

His statement startled me. I was certain our romance was over and I also wasn't even sure I liked Bob any more. He had acted like a jerk.

"I wasn't aware that we were going steady. You never asked me. Am I supposed to guess these things? You certainly didn't act like I was your steady when you said goodbye to me."

Bob countered like a lawyer. "It sounds like you don't want to go steady. Is that it? I get it. Are we on our own now, free to go out with anybody?"

"If that's what it sounds like, then that's what it is," I said softly. I was pushing the envelope, testing it a bit further with each phrase.

"OK, Punchy. You got your wish. See you around." And with that Bob hung up.

Oooh. This was not what I had expected. I knew I had made him squirm but I really didn't think he wanted to break up. I stood staring at the phone, while questions raced around in my head.

The tables had turned too fast and now I felt rejected. I put the phone back on the cradle and closed my eyes while trying not to feel scared. I already missed him. Perhaps I was not being fair. Maybe I couldn't play all ends against the middle and get away with it. Maybe I didn't even know who I really liked enough to go steady. Did Bob and I really care that much for each other?

I *did* know that I wanted him to stay in my life so I went upstairs to my sanctuary to write him a long letter and try to get back into his good graces.

Dear Bob:

I'm sorry I made you mad. I am not sure what really happened. Maybe we need to

talk more. I do know I already miss you.   Emmie

Bob called on the following Sunday, and it was as if our tiff had never happened

He was gushing with affection and asked would I like to come to Boston in two weeks for the big Yale game ."Of course I would," I chirped. This time my mother gave me the green light without my having to tell her the chaperone arrangements.

I arrived on time at Back Bay Station and saw Bob waiting to greet me without his buddies. That perked me up. I had his full attention on the way to Cambridge and we laughed and joked about his funny old car and what was planned for the weekend. He dropped me at the hotel with no mention of our last meeting here.

The big game thrilled us with a last minute touchdown win for Harvard and the rest of the weekend was frenzied activity that swept me along in all the excitement. We all drifted from one celebration party to the next and although there was too much drinking at the game and Bob fell asleep in the back of the car coming back, he didn't desert me this time and go off with his drinking buddies. He was with me but he wasn't really there. It's hard to explain.

We were on our way to yet another party—this time at a boathouse on the Charles River—when we took a different route from the others and found ourselves on a picturesque path on the river's shore. We strolled in silence, letting the fresh breeze from the water brush off some of our party veneer. Finally Bob asked, "What is it with you, Punchy? You don't seem to be happy to be with me anymore. What's going on?"

I stopped and turned to look at the water and the crews practicing in their shells, holding my face toward the sun as it was dropping on the horizon. I was trying to find the words.

"*What is going on?* Well, Bob, you tell me? Because this is the second time I feel like I'm being ignored on a weekend where I've made a trip to be with you, specially. Maybe I expect too much—like expect you to treat me as if you're really glad I'm here. But no. You're busy horsing around with your dateless friends, getting drunk and falling asleep. Last night in the lounge and today in the back of the car on the way home from the game." I felt my eyes brimming. Oh my, I didn't want tears. I choked them back.

I looked up and saw Bob's bewildered face. I swallowed and went on. "George is always by Jean's side. The same with the other couples in the crowd, but you seem more interested in getting laughs from everyone else with your jokes. You forget that I am even there. You ignore me!" By this time I was throbbing with anger.

Bob shook his head and stuttered. "Gee, Punchy, I didn't know you were bothered. I thought you were having a good time."

"Well, that shows how insensitive you are. Maybe on the outside it looks like that, but I'm hurt by the way you act around me. I just don't feel the same way about you now as I did last summer because you're never really talking to me. "

Again, I looked out at the Charles River, thinking how beautiful it was, sparkling in the sun like a thousand dancing diamonds. I turned to Bob.

"I think we had better go our separate ways for a while and not take each other for granted."

For the rest of the weekend Bob and I hardly spoke. He dropped me at the train station on Sunday with a blank face as though I were a package being dropped off at the Post Office.

"See you around, Punchy," he said and put the car in gear

All I could do was watch as he turned the corner and disappeared behind a building. I knew it would be a long time before I ever saw him again and I didn't know if I was sad or relieved he was out of my life.

Back home, after I had recovered from the breakup and nursed my flagging self-esteem back to health, I started dating Phil again. I would hear Bob was in town every now and then over a holiday but our paths didn't cross for many months. But one Saturday when Phil and I were having hamburgers at the local hangout, Bob walked in with Dotty Ann, the friend who had gone to Asbury Park with me on my playing hooky jaunt. My heart did a funny whoopdedo and Bob and I looked at each other, wondering what the other was feeling. We were polite but I saw that Bob's mouth and chin were bright red from Dotty Ann's lipstick. I had to turn away and pretend to be incredibly interested in what Phil was saying. To my surprise, I felt rejected by Bob and I didn't like it one bit.

The last months of my senior year were bittersweet. I had a big part in the musical "My Maryland" and our trio, The Girlfriends, was in demand and wherever we went, we had an eager audience. There were the graduation parties and tearful goodbyes, and when the celebrating was over and twelve long years of school were truly behind us, it was a sobering moment. The time had come to put away childish things and look ahead.

It didn't help my moody outlook to learn that our Cattell Street house had been sold to Lafayette College. It seemed we just couldn't find a permanent home and nine different places in ten years gave me a deep yearning for a more enduring residence. I decided the nomadic life was not for the faint-hearted and I was beginning to understand my mother's frequent tears.

But the gloom didn't last long for the next night Charles bounded up the steps hand in hand with Marion, the fetching brunette he had been seeing for quite some time. His wide grin and her glittering diamond engagement ring told the joyful story. After everyone had calmed down, he told us he had just signed a contract on a building with four apartments and there would be room for all of us. This was stunning news. Our housing problem was solved in a most delightful way.

For us, leaving the Cattell Street house seemed to throw off a bad curse that had plagued our family for ten years. In our new quarters on Hamilton Street, we could feel life relaxing. Daddy now had a new job as a Pennsylvania State Health Inspector and for the first time in years he was bringing home a very welcome paycheck. I was so happy to see how this gave him back his dignity and a sense of importance. Also, he was making an effort to control his love affair with the bottle. And my mother came out of her shell and began a career in politics. Before long, she was known as Mrs. Republican of Pennsylvania. So, after a stormy decade that threatened to destroy all of us, life started to hum and Mother and Daddy began to know happiness once again in their lives.

And I was fleeing the nest to begin a new chapter in mine.

CHAPTER 6

Betty Boyle's

WITH a little tug on my heart, I put my dancing saddle shoes in the back of the closet and slipped into the new shiny brown pumps of a government working girl. To join the secretarial pool in the Department of Internal Affairs was an exciting opportunity, and the prospect of being on my own gave me a mile-high feeling. I had a job! I was grown up. And I was a little scared. While my friends would be going off to Bennington or Sarah Lawrence, my journey was taking me to a big city and a different kind of life. At first I was downcast that I wouldn't have the college experience. But I soon discovered the thrill of cashing a paycheck each week was a very happy experience. Mother had been wringing her hands about my being so far away from home in the wicked city of Harrisburg. However, a friend of Daddy's found me a room not far from the government office buildings in Betty Boyle's boarding house. Betty, we were told, supervised her brood, as she called her boarders, like a drill sergeant. As it happened, Daddy's new job as a State of Pennsylvania Health Inspector required that he check in at the office in Harrisburg every Monday and Friday so I had built in transportation with him to and fro from Easton.

The Sunday night before I left for Betty Boyle's, I packed my bags and a few knickknacks and put them near the front door to remind me that come Monday a new life was waiting for me in Harrisburg. Early the next morning while Daddy packed the car, Mother hovered over me making sure we hadn't forgotten anything.

She pressed a box into my arms. "Here's a thermos of coffee and some fresh doughnuts," she said with a little smile. She looked as tired as her faded bathrobe, and much older than her fifty-nine years. But her positive spirit shone through her sleepy eyes when she placed a kiss on my cheek. I felt her cool lips on my skin. "Now be sure to call when you can and let me know how things are going."

She was trembling and I knew she didn't like my leaving one little bit. I tried hard to appear bright and eager and self confident but inside my stomach was doing acrobatics.

"Goodbye, Emilie Louise," she said softly. "Be good."

It was an easy two-hour trip, with little traffic so early in the morning. Humming along in Daddy's car, a Pennsylvania State black coupe, I was uplifted by seeing the smudges of lavender gray mist beginning to drift and swirl in the new day — revealing a roofline or a hilltop -a painting by nature. How I loved early mornings! And this one was so special. I felt warm and safe being with Daddy. He had never lost his ability to talk to me like I was an individual. We stopped half way in the little town of Hamburg, half way to Harrisburg, for a wonderful breakfast of Pennsylvania Dutch scrapple and pancakes.

Back on Route 22 to Harrisburg, we passed through one small farm town after another, where I saw milkmen leaving bottles on front porches and housewives sweeping yesterday's dust from the front walk. Peeking into the lives of these townspeople filled me with an exhilarating sense of communion with others that gave me a tremendous lift.

As Harrisburg came into view, I realized it definitely had a character of its own. It was an old city of row houses dating back to the later half of the nineteenth century. In its heyday, it had been a thriving port on the Susquehanna River and may have been quaint then but it was now a solid mass of identical four story buildings, each twenty-five feet wide with a maple tree opposite the front steps.

On that steamy July morning, Daddy pulled the car in front of Betty Boyle's boarding house at 221 Briggs St. I held my breath. I always did when we moved into a new place, wondering what would happen if I sensed it was an inhospitable house full of bad feelings. I remembered I had always managed to survive but today was a different sort of test. Today I would be on my own and I was starting to get sweaty palms. But when I took a good look at where I would be staying, I was relieved to see the house was simply another anonymous row house just like all the others. It was not scary looking at all and I felt my nervousness start to leave me. Daddy placed my luggage and few belongings on the stoop and promised to be back soon to escort me to my new job. I squared my shoulders and rang the bell.

When Betty Boyle answered the door I put a big smile on my face.

"Yes?" Betty said, peering through her thick glasses. "What do you want?

I quickly explained I was the new girl and was starting my job in the Department of Internal Affairs that very day and would it be OK if I just freshened up a bit?

"Oh," she said. "I hadn't expected you until tomorrow, but come in and I'll show you where you'll be staying. I don't have a single for you right now, so I've put you in a double room with Nancy."

Betty picked up one of my bags and closed the door behind me. On the way upstairs, she told me how each floor had one bath shared by four girls, the hours for dinner, how you made your own breakfast, etcetera and all of the rules in the house. When we came to the middle room on the third floor, Betty opened the door.

"This is Nancy's room. Her roommate moved out so you can stay here until a single comes up. They've all gone to work so the bathroom's free." She disappeared for a minute and came back with fresh towels.

"These are yours," she said curtly. "Pick out a place to hang them so you can keep track of which ones are yours. Before you leave, I'll give you a key to the front door. There are a few rules I insist everybody follow." Betty put her hands on her hips. "There will be *no* men visitors in the rooms. *No* staying out after 11:00 PM. And," she continued, this time shaking her finger at me, "you must carry your key with you at all times! Have I made myself clear?"

"Yes Miss Boyle," I mumbled.

As I listened to her heavy footsteps disappear downstairs, I looked around the room. It was cozy, with memorabilia everywhere. Framed photos of family and friends, places and pets covered the tables and walls. Flowered chintz curtains hid the pull down shade, and the final touch was a pair of dolls sitting prettily on matching pillows. I decided I liked Nancy just from her décor.

After I washed up and got dressed again in clean clothes, I waited for Daddy. He finally drove up and I got in the car. Now I was very nervous. He reached over and patted me on the arm. "I want you to know how proud I am of my little girl. You will do just fine in your job and remember I will pick you up here on Friday and we'll drive back home together and you can tell me all about it"

After we parked in the government employee's lot, we went into the building and took the elevator to the fourth floor where we stepped out into a cavernous hallway. It was beautifully paneled in rich, satiny wood, reflecting the light from a dozen chandeliers.

"Pretty classy," I whispered to my father, who squeezed my arm in return.

We opened the heavy carved doors to the office of the Secretary of Internal Affairs and introduced ourselves to the receptionist who announced us through the intercom. In a few minutes the office manager appeared, looking like the stereotype of the old-fashioned spinster matron. Drab clothes, hair pulled back in a bun, rimless glasses, no make-up and no smile. She introduced herself as Miss Brown and told me to take a seat in the waiting room. My father shook her hand, thanking her for her time, hugged me and wished me luck. I watched his retreating figure go through the door. I was totally alone in a strange new world.

By this time my freshly ironed dress was sticking to me like a wet shower curtain. I was suddenly overwhelmed, convinced I would not be able to do this. But after Miss Brown showed me my desk and introduced me to a smiling girl at the desk next to mine, I stopped shaking and got to work typing my first letter. It was a disaster, as were the many drafts that followed that first day. My euphoria, along with my self-confidence, had deserted me. I had to hang on to this job but not if I filled the wastebasket with ruined paper.

After a week I began to improve and my letters were whirling into the typewriter rollers and out again, pretty much pitch perfect, but I still hadn't laid eyes on my boss, the Secretary of Internal Affairs.

"Miss Woehrle," Mrs. Brown said to me one day, scaring me half to death. "Secretary Adamson would like to see you. Please get your steno pad and pencil and follow me."

"Yes, Miss Brown," I murmured and quickly returned, my pad clutched tightly against my galloping heart. This was the main event — my chance at recognition. I prayed I wouldn't stumble over my feet. She opened the door to Secretary Adamson's office and ushered me in, closing the door softly behind her.

I was not prepared for what stood before me. Secretary Adamson was handsome. Six feet or more with curly brown hair, crinkly blue eyes set in a young friendly face, and a smile that was dazzling. I stood there for a second unsure of how to approach him. He got up from his desk, smiled and came to shake my hand.

"Welcome to Harrisburg and the Department of Internal Affairs," he said. "Sit down and tell me all about yourself."

I talked for at least fifteen minutes and he listened, my stenography assignment forgotten. I told him about my mother and father's stardom, my lead roles in the school plays, my love of dancing and fashion design and my disappointment that I couldn't go to college because the depression had cut into my family's finances. Finally, Secretary Adamson stood up, said he had an appointment and that it was a pleasure to have such a lovely girl in the stenography pool. He led me to the door and kissed me on the cheek. I was dumbfounded by this charming man and especially his kiss.

Two days later Miss Brown came to my desk. "Secretary Adamson would like to see you."

I took my steno pad and went in. I came out again with no notes, only this time I'd been talking with him for about twenty minutes. I noticed he had a way of drawing out the tiniest details about my life.

After this, visits to his office became a regular part of my day. Sometimes they only lasted for only five minutes while others were often lingering with lovely back and forth conversation. I never wrote one word on my steno pad. However, I felt special and cared for. I felt like I was the only stenographer who was interesting enough to have Secretary Adamson's attention.

One unusually gray August day, Miss Brown stood prissily in front of my desk. "Secretary Adamson would like to see you. I think he wants you to sing at our Labor Day party and wants to know if you would be available. I'll let him fill you in on the rest." I followed her as she led the way to his office door. For some reason she didn't look pleased. Well, for me this was a pleasant surprise. Miss Brown ushered me in and closed the door behind me. I noticed the draperies were pulled over the windows and Secretary Adamson had turned his desk lamp to low. I stood by the closed door and waited.

"Miss Woehrle. May I call you Emilie?" he asked.

"I guess so," I said, slightly unsure as to why he would ask. He was my boss and could call me anything.

"Did Miss Brown tell you I would like you to sing at our party? I remember you told me you sang. It would be a pleasure to hear you, and then I hope you will favor us with a couple of selections. We will talk about how to go about it a bit later, closer to the actual event. "

"Oh, I would love that," I said. My voice trilled.

Secretary Adamson got up from his desk. "But first, why don't you come over here, next to me."

I took a few steps and found myself standing beside him. He put his hands on my arms and pulled me closer. He had never come near me before and I was stunned. I think I tripped over my own feet.

"I want to see what it is you're hiding under that big sweater. I think what you have under there must be lovely," he whispered.

"Oh, my God," I thought. "I don't believe this." I stood there like a wooden Indian, mute and scared, while the Secretary's hands lifted my sweater and began exploring the unknown territory.

"Lovely," he whispered. "Just as I imagined."

Adrenaline shot through me like a hot iron. I remember gripping the edge of his desk for support as he leaned harder into me. I wished I had the nerve to slap his face and leave. But he had the upper hand. I knew he wasn't worried that I would kiss and tell. I had already told him too much and he knew that keeping my job was more important than reporting what he was doing. He had expertly delved into my situation and he knew I couldn't give up the money. But how far did he intend to go with this dangerous interlude? I felt as if I was sleepwalking as he led me to a couch against the wall where he gently laid me down on the leather cushions. I felt his six-foot frame climb on top of me, squeezing the breath out of me. I was conscious of his hands exploring my body and his moaning, begging me to return his hot kisses. Panic rose in me and I tried to scream, but no sound came from my mouth. And then I began praying. Abruptly, Secretary Adamson sat up and backed away. I took advantage of the pause, jumped to my feet and fled his office. Of course, I bumped right into Miss Brown who took one look at my disheveled appearance and immediately shot through his door into his office.

"Oh, boy, this means trouble," I said to myself.

For the next few weeks, business was brisk in the office of Internal Affairs and between the endless stream of visitors and the paperwork left in their wake, the secretarial pool stayed late on many days. But there were no more summonses for me to take my steno pad and enter the inner sanctum. I began to relax. It was obvious that Miss Brown had taken charge of the Secretary's appointments. And I had also figured out I was just another one of his playthings, something to liven up his day.

However, as soon as the workload lessened, Mr. Adamson started asking for me again. I skewed up my courage ready to go in and slap him hard across the face—all the while envisioning my bankbook and the growing balance printed in green ink on a yellow page. My freedom was there in that small book—freedom that came from putting up with the awful truth of this plum job.

Unhappily, the sordid scene we had the very first time replayed itself dozens of times—me, on the sofa beneath his writhing body and beseeching kisses—his large hands under my sweater—black panic choking me. And just when I thought my prayers would never be answered, he would abruptly get up and ask me to leave.

For weeks, whenever Miss Brown would call my name, I felt the terror begin. I felt every eye on me as I walked from my desk to Secretary Adamson's office. I wondered if the other girls were wondering why the secretary always asked for me and not them? Or maybe he was already finished with them? Maybe the new girl was always his target? I dreaded these encounters and longed to tell somebody—to get help from someone—but I didn't. Even though I was caught in an unbelievable situation, I was determined to stick it out and not run home crying. I needed a miracle badly.

My prayers were finally answered. Miss Brown called me to her desk one day and told me they needed a secretary downstairs in the Research Department and she had recommended me for the job. She smiled at me warmly and it was obvious she had been through this scenario with Mr. Adamson before, and knew just what to do. I thanked her a lot and cleaned out my desk immediately. On my way to the Research Department, which was not half as attractively outfitted as the office I was leaving, I said a grateful goodbye in my heart for Miss Brown.

My bosses in the Research Department were kind gentlemen and welcomed me like I was their daughter. The Research Director would now and then ask me to do a special report for him, which sent me running all over the capital building gathering certain data he needed. This made me feel very important. His assistant, a jolly bear of a man, saw to the everyday administration of the department. While the Research Department was not one of the hot tickets in government jobs, here I was safe.

It was four o' clock a lazy December Sunday afternoon at my boarding house—time when Betty's brood, as she called us, would gather for coffee in the living room and listen to the regular Sunday afternoon New York Philharmonic broadcast. A gentle snow was falling outside but here in Betty's comfortable shabby living room we sprawled on the old stuffed furniture, enjoying the music and the warmth of each other. Suddenly the beautiful strains of Mendelssohn's Midsummer Night's Dream ended. There was dead silence. Then we heard.......

"We interrupt this broadcast with a special news bulletin. Pearl Harbor has been attacked by Japanese aircraft and warships. At last count, seventeen ships were sunk. Hundreds of our servicemen are dead or wounded. President Roosevelt will be speaking to the nation. We repeat: Pearl Harbor has been attacked by Japanese Aircraft and warships. Stay tuned to this station for the more news."

The music resumed but we didn't hear anything. We sat slack-jawed in silence.

"Where is Pearl Harbor?" someone finally asked.

"I think it's in Hawaii."

"We'd better stay here and listen to the President."

I leapt out of my chair and ran to the phone to call home. Several girls were standing behind me wanting to do the same thing. I was surprised I got through. My mother picked up on the first ring.

"Emilie Louise, isn't it horrible?" she cried. "We are at war!"

The telephone took a beating that night. There were dozens of calls to families, asking for advice. We all needed their reassuring voices. I can remember how we talked way into the night over the dining room table and smoked too many cigarettes. We did a lot of crying between endless phone conversations that went well past midnight. Betty brought out the bottle, no longer shy about her drinking. We all agreed she had a good reason.

Monday was bedlam at the office. I stood by watching while many of my co-workers emptied their desks and tearfully gave their friends a goodbye hug. The gravity of being at war meant that many men would be joining the military and many women would have to fill their places in what would be war related plants and offices. A hush hung over the building that afternoon as the offices were closed early and the lights were turned out. I walked back to Betty's feeling very much alone.

Soon after that fateful Sunday, Betty's boarding house brood dwindled as most of her boarders went back to their hometowns. Even though both my brothers were not going to be drafted—one was too young and the other too old—I knew they were going to enlist. I agonized about what I should do, especially since Mother and Daddy would be consumed with worry over both of their sons.

As much as I wanted to jump into action I put all thoughts of joining the newly organized Women's Army Corp out of my head. Two sons in uniform were enough for one family's war effort. I asked my mother to contact her friends about finding me a job in one of the many manufacturing plants tooling up for the war effort in the Easton area. A secretarial position in one of these plants was sure to open up. I waited in Harrisburg, stayed on my job, and went home on weekends.

With five girls left in Betty's brood, each one waiting to figure out the next step in her life, we talked of nothing but war and hung onto the tiniest details we overheard, embellishing and willing them to be encouraging. But it didn't work. Instead, the news seemed to worsen with each passing day. Months went by while we doggedly went off to our jobs every morning with hope in our hearts, only to have it squashed by the grim nightly news.

Valentine's Day was approaching and images of Bob came creeping into my thoughts of late. One night, I had a sudden urge to write him to see how he was doing. I had no hard feelings left, only good memories and some confusion. So, after quickly saying goodnight to the girls, I went upstairs to the back room where there was a little writing desk, a chair and a lamp. I sat down at the desk, and after a few moments of contemplation in the tiny room where there was no distractions the letter practically wrote itself.

Dear Bob:

It's been a long time since we have seen each other and tonight I am thinking about all the good times we shared and wondering what happened to break us up. I've missed you terribly and would like to know if you feel the same way. In a few days it will be Valentine's Day. I guess I am being romantic, but I am remembering the past Valentine's Days when we were together and how much they meant to me. If you would like to see me, write back. If not, just tear up the letter and forget I wrote it. It will be ok, though I am thinking fondly of you.

Punchy

In the morning I took the letter with me to work. It would give me a little time to see if I really wanted to mail it. I didn't get very far on my walk to the government building. With no hesitation, I dropped the note in the first mail slot.   .

When I came home from work a few days later, a letter postmarked Boston was waiting for me. I blinked in disbelief. There hadn't been enough time for Bob to receive my letter and write back. I tore it open.

"Dear Punchy:

By the time you receive this it will be Valentine's Day. Will you be my Valentine? I miss you. Hearts and flowers, Bob."

My heart did a little flip. I couldn't believe that we had both written love letters on the same day. Two days later when he received my letter, he called me. We were bashful and awkward and there were long silences between very few words.

"May I come to see you in Harrisburg?" Bob finally asked.

This was totally unexpected. I hadn't even considered he would come to see me from Boston.

"Fine with me," I answered.

"This weekend?" he asked.

I gave him the number of the Harrisburg Hotel, which was hanging on the wall near the phone, and hung up. I was shaking like a leaf. I sat down on the chair, staring into space for a long time.

On Friday at four ten pm, Bob's plane was touching down at the Harrisburg airport. I was at work but in my mind's eye, I saw him coming out of the plane into the terminal, hailing a cab and giving the cabby my address. I raced home after tidying up my desk. I was feeling like a bird on its first flight, the self-confidence I had acquired since being on my own gone—poof! Just like that. And my veneer of the sophisticated secretary had cracked wide open, revealing the gawky, small-town girl I had left behind in Easton. I tried to regain my equanimity while changing my clothes and putting on makeup, but it wouldn't come back on queue. *What was it about this man?* With anyone else, I was self-assured, never questioning whether I had on the right dress or too much make-up or whether my behavior was acceptable. But Bob always shot holes in my cocksure balloon.

It had been more than a year since I'd last seen him alone, and my uneasiness grew and I began to wish I had never agreed to his visit. I flitted from one thing to another hoping to speed up the clock. What time would he call? What time would he get here? Would the day ever wind down to evening? I remembered he had said something about dinner.

Betty, who often hovered nearby was out buying beer for a party she was throwing and I sat by the window waiting, wondering if I was too silly in thinking we could recapture the wonder of those summer nights long ago. When the phone rang, I jumped as if I had touched a live wire.

"Hello?"

"Hi, Punchy, it's me. I'm here in my room at the hotel and ready to come over.

The hotel was just a short walk away and I gave him directions to Betty's house. I started to pace. My watch said 5:33 then 5:34. He should be ringing the front door bell in about fifteen minutes. By then I hoped to calm my galloping heart. I looked at my watch again and it was 5:37 and the bell rang. I think my heart stopped. I ran to the door with a silly smile on my face, but there, of all people, stood a little Brownie Scout.

"Hi!" she said, brightly. "Do you want to buy some Girl Scout cookies?"

"Sure," I said. I dug the quarter out of my change purse and took the box from her. I was about to close the door when Bob came bounding up the steps behind her, wearing the same infectious grin that had turned my heart over so long ago. He hesitated, I stepped backwards and so did he, and then he came forward and swept me into his arms. I breathed in his familiar scent, his Old Spice after-shave, and his favorite Half and Half pipe tobacco aroma that clung to his coat. It was back to our summer romance in seconds. Kisses and hugs. Gazes and caresses all on the door stoop.

I led Bob into the living room, letting my eyes feast on his smiling face and how his thick brown hair spilled over his eyes. With his tweed jacket and scuffed penny loafers, I couldn't remember anyone ever looking so good to me. Standing there with Bob in front of me, the world seemed unreal and words did not come naturally. As I took him on a tour and showed him how life was lived in a working girl's boarding house, I was suddenly embarrassed by the sagging sofa, the shabby slip-covered chairs, the untidy tables piled high with magazines. I showed him the dining room with its long table set for dinner, and the well-worn kitchen, the lunch dishes drying in the drainer. I watched him taking it all in and wished I had not brought him through the house.

There was no one around when we left so we locked the front door and started walking back to the hotel where Bob had made reservations for dinner. Swaying together, arm-in-arm we savored this walk. We were both still silent, only listening to the sounds our shoes made on the sidewalk. I think we laughed once or twice as we stepped over a large crack in the pavement and onto each other's toes by accident. This was the stuff of romantic novels and though we were behaving as if spontaneous reunions happened every day, beneath my nonchalance there was a feeling of disbelief and an ominous sense that the War had already begun to threaten us.

The dining room at the hotel didn't open until seven and so we decided on a pre-dinner reunion drink at the bar in the lobby. Every bar has that special table in the far corner. The one where the man and the woman sit and twirl their cocktail glasses, gaze into each other's eyes and make promises to last a lifetime. Our table was waiting for us. We made our way over to the darkened corner and sank gratefully into plump cushions.

"Two Johnny Walker's and soda," Bob said to the waiter. In this clubby, friendly meeting ground Bob and I would start to repair our broken romance. After a steak dinner and a bottle of wine in the dining room, we went back to the bar again and by now our tongues were flapping like loose sails, as we were telling each other our stories. The feelings of loss and loneliness we had both harbored for so long came spilling out, unchecked. We held hands. We sighed and we cried. Over and over again we kept saying how wonderful it was to be together again.

We camped out in that bar until the bartender finally had to tell us to leave. Reluctantly, we pulled ourselves together and paid our bill, thanking him for putting up with us. By now, he knew our whole story.

"That's OK, kids. Better go home and get some sleep," he advised us in a kind way. What he was really saying was you two have been hitting it pretty heavily for hours and it's time to quit.

He ushered us out and closed the door. We stood there looking at each other. We didn't want to go our separate ways.

"I have a bottle in my room. Can I persuade you to come up and have a nightcap?" Bob asked. "You can sleep on the floor," he teased as he kissed my forehead. "Just in case you don't want to go home."

I knew, even before he asked, that the night wasn't over and by accepting his offer to come up to his room for another drink, I would become the one being lead, no longer the leader. In the seconds that followed his question I had to make a very important decision. Did I love Bob enough to throw aside the moral teachings I had grown up with? It was clear that this was the man I wanted to spend the rest of my life with and so I allowed myself to be taken into his camp. I had been given a second chance and this time, I would not let him go.

It wasn't just one nightcap. It was one too many. We filled the hours with tender talk and tender embraces that led to expressing our love for each other in uncharted territory for me. Submission was sweet, but afterward came the shadow of regret. My mother's words came back to haunt me. "Remember," she said, "You are the captain of your own ship." Well, tonight, I had made a commitment—to be with Bob for whatever life dealt us. I was no longer independent Emilie Louise Woehrle. Tonight I had taken the big step and traded her in for the new role as the future wife of Bob Betts. Would it fit?

I lay awake in the dark snuggled next to Bob, struggling with the enormity of the gifts this night had given me and feeling emotions kneading me like so much dough. Sleep was out of the question. So I nudged Bob and whispered that it was two in the morning and I had to get back to Betty's or I'd be thrown out. I tried rousing him. I tried shouting in his ear and shaking his head. I tried cold towels and tickling his feet. Nothing worked. He was out cold, in a stupor. I flopped down on the edge of the bed and held my own throbbing head, feeling so enervated that all I wanted to do was to fall down next to him and go to sleep. But I had to get back to Betty's.

Finally I gave up and left on my own. As my footsteps slowly took me through the dark, deserted streets, the ghosts of everything past and present were right by my side, some laughing, some reprimanding, some sympathetic. I had just given myself to Bob and yet inside I felt like a small alley cat put out on the street for the night. I did not question why Bob had not been able to bring me back to Betty's the way I imagined a prince would bring home his hard won princess on a white horse. I pushed that thought aside.

Finally, I reached Betty's house, bedraggled but relieved to be back in my familiar world. And then, after feeling around in my pockets, I realized I didn't have my key. I could hear Betty's admonitions, her warnings, her sergeant at arms orders and I was terrified. The first time I tried to ring the bell, my hand shook so much I missed the button. I tried again and this time I heard it ring.

It felt like a long time between my ringing and finally hearing someone fumbling on the other side with the dead lock. The door opened and there stood Betty, breathing fire, all red-eyed, gray hair falling around her nightgown. She broke into a furious tirade.

"Where the hell have you been, you little slut. You've kept me awake half the night worrying." She hauled me inside and slammed the door, pushing me hard.

"Upstairs, you no-good street walker! We'll see about this in the morning."

The next day was Sunday and, without planning to. I slept in. I was hung over and disoriented and I didn't get downstairs until late morning. No one was stirring. When I got to the living room, it was empty except for Betty, spread out on the couch—looking very unwell—worse than I looked. I hung around, waiting for the moment to tell her what happened last night. When she finally opened her eyes she groaned. "Oh, it's you. I'm disgusted with you. I have never had the likes of you living here and I hope I never have to put up with another one like you again. You disgraced me and yourself, you know." She closed her eyes and turned over, her hiked up nightgown giving me ample view of her generous backside.

I turned away. "OK, I'll move out," I said. "I don't want to be here anyway if you refuse to understand why I was so late." I took a deep breath and spoke sweetly as if I were Cinderella after the ball. "Last night, Bob asked me to marry him."

When Betty heard the words "marry him," she huffed and hauled herself off the couch and went upstairs to bed. She never brought up the subject again.

Later I met Bob at the coffee shop for a late breakfast. He looked tired but happy, as I'm sure I did. We had a long quiet time over innumerable cups of coffee, staring into each other's eyes and into our future together until it was close to the time for him to leave for the airport.

"Bye, Punchy. Remember, I love you," he said, as he put money down on the counter for the breakfast.

Brilliant sunshine pouring through my window woke me earlier than usual on an early spring day. I took a deep breath of the fresh, fragrant breeze. Nobody was stirring in the house, so I showered quickly and had time to press my favorite brown and white check cotton dress..

I felt I was in a bright new world as I walked, the four blocks to the office- feeling a joy so big that it bubbled up from the very bottom of my five-foot-five inch frame. My head was in the clouds, as I recalled last night's phone conversation, the same as so many others since Bob had come to see me in Harrisburg. "I love you, Punchy," Bob whispered over the miles and the words, "I want to marry you," sang in my head like a Debussy Nocturne. How could I concentrate on anything but Bob? .

It was like a circus trying to make a phone call at Betty's on Sundays. All of the girls took advantage of the Sunday phone rates and the certainty that everyone would be home waiting to talk to them. Hot wires, we called it. When I finally maneuvered a place in line, I could feel everyone listening to my conversations with heads cocked and ears tuned. By now, the whole story of my romance was out in the open and they loved to tease me.

Bob wrote that he had the weekend of April first free and did I think I could make it to Boston to select my engagement ring. April first? That was April Fool's day. We both laughed at this, but I agreed. Mother went into bubbly congratulations when I called her with the news the day Bob proposed, and when I said I was going to Boston for a weekend, I'm surprised she didn't send me a negligee, though money was still tight. My dear boss gave me his blessings when I asked for time off.

"Well, it's about time that fellow did right by you," Betty harrumphed, when I shared my plans with her. I wished she could've been more of a softhearted woman to lean on than she was.

Each time we spoke my mother asked questions about the wedding date and I knew that the kind wedding my mother had thrown for Dot was out of the question. I said we would talk on the weekend. I hadn't been home in months and I wanted to see my friends so my plan was to go to Easton before heading to Boston.

I caught a ride home with my father, happy to have two hours together, alone. We hadn't seen each other since Bob's visit to Harrisburg turned my life upside down and I was itching to share my joy with Buddy, now a restless senior in high school. I knew he was planning to enlist right after graduation and it hit me hard in the gut to think of him going overseas. Of course he wanted to emulate his big brother Charles who had been snatched up the minute he appeared at the Navy recruiting station. His knowledge of electronics made him a natural for teaching SONAR, the sound of navigation and ranging, at a submarine school in Florida. I wondered idly if he had ever told anyone about tapping into the power pole outside our Porter Street house.

Daddy was a sympathetic sounding board, always ready to listen to the latest gossip at the office, or what was going on at Betty's Boarding House and always able to offer some insight into why people behaved the way they did. His sensitivity and gentle nature slowed me down and I could think straighter when I was with him.

I threw my bag into the trunk and climbed into the front seat beside him. I gave him a kiss and thanked him for giving me a ride. "Well, I guess Mother told you Bob wants me to come to Boston this weekend for an engagement ring. I know he plans to write to you about this but hasn't had a chance yet. It's a big step for both of us and we hope it's the right one."

Daddy was busy negotiating Friday afternoon traffic and didn't say anything. As he concentrated on his driving, I had a chance to take a good look at him and was heartened by his fresh appearance. No stubble on his chin and no stale beer smell. His job as Health Inspector for the state was restoring his dignity and bringing back the daddy I loved. I gave a little thank you prayer.

When we were finally on the highway to Easton, I settled back and took a deep breath. "First off, I am going to be as honest as I can, Daddy," I started. "I've thought a lot about why I want to marry Bob Betts and asked myself a lot of questions. The best reason is that Bob Betts is in a class by himself—different from the other boys. No one I've met has come close to him. You know what I mean." I paused and looked out the window. Daddy still hadn't said anything in response.

"Daddy," I continued after we passed through the last traffic light in the City. "This isn't the hot romance I always dreamed of. I want you to know I've had a few of those—you know—the kind when you go around in a daze, crazy out of your mind in love. But those never worked out. They're like falling stars"

Daddy smiled and took his time before speaking. "I think I know what you mean.. We've all been young, once. But what is it that you're *really* trying to say to me? You don't have to cheerlead Bob. We like him very much. What's bothering *you?*"

The question surprised me and I felt defensive. "It's hard to describe. I guess, in a different way, I *am* in love with Bob. I'm in love with his mind, with his sense of humor, with the way I feel when I'm with him."

Despite his silence, I knew Daddy was listening to every word. I looked at him instead of the road in front of me and asked, "Does this make sense to you?"

Daddy slowed down and pulled over to the right lane. I kept on talking. "You have to admit Bob is handsome and has a terrific personality and with his keen mind, he'll go far. But it's deeper than that. He's such a wonderful human being, Daddy. He has all the right things in a man. Things I want to share for my life—to father our children. And, you know what?" I kept going as if I were nominating Bob for public office. "This may surprise you, but Bob inspires me to stretch my mind and think."

That made my father turn and look at me with a questioning look on his face. For a minute, the image of that night in Harrisburg made me pause. No, I was not going to stain the glowing portrait I had just painted of the man I was going to marry. Not even for myself.

My Father was much smarter than I was. "If Bob is half as wonderful as you describe, you two ought to be the perfect pair," he said, and gave me a broad wink. "Because you are a very wonderful girl and he's the lucky one, too."

"Daddy," I said with assurance. "Bob's my ticket to the world I desire and I want to marry him. I think he was meant to be in my life forever, and I know we will make a winning team."

My father smiled and nodded his head. He understood what it meant to be able to change the course of your life for the better.

CHAPTER 7

Stope Hammers And The Girl From Amsterdam

THE next twenty-four hours between Harrisburg and Easton were a blissful blur. Somehow, I found myself again on the train headed to Boston and Bob and settled . down for the four-hour trip, this time with beautiful butterflies of happiness perched on my shoulder.

When I got off the train, Bob was wearing a smile that could have lit up Times Square. We fell into each other's arms as if it had been a hundred years rather than six weeks. Bob headed the car to downtown Boston to Thomas Long Jewelers. It was early in the day so we had the manager's full attention. After we explained that we wanted an engagement ring, nothing extravagant but a clear white diamond, we were presented with black velvet trays, tray after dazzling tray. We both liked a unique emerald cut diamond. Bob picked it up and ceremoniously slipped it on my finger. It fit perfectly and I held my hand out in front of me to look at it.

"Now will you marry me, Punchy?"

I nodded. We kissed me in the middle of the store and he said he would love me forever. At that moment the stars in my eyes outshone all the diamonds in the store put together.

Dinner that night was a two-person candlelit affair of the heart. No big party. No loud people wanting to impress everyone. It was warm and comforting to have this time to ourselves. Tomorrow was time enough to get together with Bob's best friends to celebrate and when I got back to Easton I knew the chaos would truly begin. After dinner when I had gone to my room, as that soft knock came on my hotel room door, that beautiful ring on my finger was the key that opened it wide.

As the train to Easton slowed into the station I saw Mother and Daddy on the platform, wearing big smiles. "Let me see your ring," Mother asked urgently.

Obediently, I held out my hand.

She looked closely. "Why, it's all lines," she said with a trace of disappointment.

She had never seen an emerald cut diamond before. It was too trendy for her. I thought she was hopelessly old fashioned.

In the car on the way home, Mother was breathless with plans for an engagement party the following weekend. She had arranged with the social editor of the local paper for prime coverage of my engagement announcement. I smiled. Good for Mother. She was enjoying this turn in my life immensely. For so many years she and my sister Dot had tried to slot me into acceptable spaces in Easton's society and always had been disappointed by my lack of interest in such frivolities. Now it looked like they were going to get their wish. The Betts had a name worth bandying about. I smiled, thinking how the good blood Mother insisted was running through my veins had paid off for her, and now she wouldn't worry that I would run off with some no-good lout and ruin the family name.

Mother had quickly run to our local jewelers and picked out a silver pattern for me. She brought a fork home to show me, all excited with her find. "Isn't this beautiful, Emilie Louise? It was by far the loveliest they had in stock so I brought it home to show you, hoping it was what you wanted."

What could I say? It was nice, but I had no chance to see any of the others in stock so I had no comparison. "Fine," I said. I had to think of how Mother took charge of Dot and her wedding preparations, selecting everything. That's what women like Mother did in 1941, and I had to remember that my linens, the crystal and the china and eventually the caterer and the flowers, was extremely important to Mother. I knew this made her feel young again when she had planned Dot's wedding years ago. She had endured years of deprivation and now that her rebellious daughter was finally getting married, she was on top of the world. I let her pick anything she liked.

Ken Kressler, one of my mother's friends, had arranged an interview for me on Monday at Ingersoll-Rand in Phillipsburg, New Jersey. I was hired on the spot. Daddy took me back to Harrisburg for the last time, where I packed up my stuff at Betty Boyle's and said a complimentary, if not relief-filled, goodbye. I was moving back with Mother and Daddy on Hamilton Street, but I *was* moving on. I could not say that for the few women that were left there, and certainly not for Betty whose cases of empties at the back door every Sunday were increasing as the war escalated.

After the initial engagement fanfare, Bob and I saw little of each other between his graduation and his being shipped out overseas. He had gone directly to Officer Training Camp in Ft. Sill, Oklahoma as soon as the war broke out and he was reassigned to top secret overseas duty. I had no idea where he was going as the fighting overseas raged. I didn't allow myself to think of the future—it was too frightening. Instead, I thought about our life after the war was over and dreamed beautiful pictures of us in our first home.

I moved into the extra room in Mother and Daddy's new apartment. I liked this building that Charles bought. It had none of the unsettling darkness of our former house on Cattell Street and my little room overlooking the back yard and green trees was a perfect nest for a fledging that had returned. When all my belongings were in place, I felt warm and protected. And having Mother and Daddy around soothed some of my worries about Bob.

It happened that our nice neighbor next door also worked at Ingersoll Rand and offered me a ride to work every day. I was now a part of a car pool where we passengers all chipped in with money and gas coupons to buy gas. Being one of the hundreds of thousands holding up the home front gave me a sense of unity but it was far from glamorous. I had a lackluster job working for a company that made rock drills, the hard-working drones of heavy equipment to move earth and believe me, I failed to become fascinated by stope hammers, jackhammers, and the like. But even if I wasn't " Rosie the Riveter" helping to assemble a wing on a fighter plane, I knew what I did was a link in the vast chain of supplies streaming overseas and even though I wasn't carrying a gun, I felt I was standing right next to Bob defending our country.

My office was in a converted factory building, built of brick and stark as a jail. I typed and filed, typed and filed. Once again, I had a boss with a roving eye. He thought he was irresistible and one day he teasingly threatened to catch me in the storage room.

"Just try it," I challenged.

He knew I could run faster than he could, and I was no longer afraid I would lose my job. I had job skills that I knew I could use anywhere.

By November the days were long, gray and dreary. At first, after Bob was shipped out, he wrote often. Then not so often and finally there were great spaces between letters. I knew he was on the move with General Patton's Third Army, so I paid close attention to the broadcasts from Lowell Thomas every night, but very little was said to raise my spirits. Many times, when I was alone in the office, I stood at the window, watching the men loading machinery by forklift into containers for shipment overseas. Back and forth they would go in ballet like rhythm, rain streaming down their yellow slickers, and I would wonder where all these jackhammers were going—wonder whether they were going to Bob's outfit—wonder.

After weeks of not hearing from Bob, and with my stomach in knots, thinking the worst, a letter arrived. It chilled me to the core. It was beautifully written, but by a man who was telling me if he came home he might be someone else- someone I didn't know.

"Emmie:

Sitting here in the crisp autumn afternoon, with the fertile countryside of eastern France spread out below us like a gigantic terrain board, I discovered how much the war has changed me. Instead of clinging tenaciously to life that every threat, even of a hard tackle in a backyard football game makes you bunch up inside, I found that I was sitting there listening for the sound of the shells to tell me whether to duck or not. I wondered whether anything would seem vital and urgent and important when this is over. Then again, this may all be the basis for a firmer understanding of things, which sometimes a complicated education tends to dull. I think that I shall understand men much better and know them for what they are worth.

Over here it does not matter who you are or where you come from but what sort of man you are. And it has given me confidence to bear up in the company of many of the fine specimens I have worked and lived with. Some have blossomed out into thoughtful, courageous, unselfish men who do not put themselves above all else. It is an unusual and unexpected thing that has happened but I know that I understand things much better. I hate this war! We all hate it. It changes us and even though we shall readjust when the time comes, we who have seen and felt will never be free from the memories. The people who will talk about the war and glamorize it in their reminiscences will be the ones who have not known its horrors."

This didn't sound like the Bob I knew. I shook my head and put the letter aside, depressed and wondering what lay ahead of us.

During those years at Ingersoll-Rand, I made many wonderful friends. We valued each other as comrades in battle. We gathered in the cafeteria every noon, needing to laugh at the latest jokes and, of course, to exchange some juicy gossip.

Fortunately, our local farmers were still providing Easton with Pennsylvania Dutch fare; pork and ham, spring and fall fresh vegetables and I looked forward to my mother's excellent cooking each night. She said she loved hearing me come home, slamming the front door and saying, "Oh, what is that delicious smell? What's for dinner? I'm starved."

Once a week was girls' night out. We saved our money and went to the local grill for dinner, where we could have a drink, and sit around and gossip for hours. And then there was a bridge night, another excuse to get together and act a little goofy. These breaks lightened our fears and kept us from becoming crybabies. The Faculty Club at Lafayette College opened a canteen for the servicemen stationed there. The College Hill girls were asked to be hostesses at tea dances to mingle with the boys and make them feel welcome. Hopefully, a night of music in the company of some pretty girls and pleasant conversation might take away some of their loneliness. Naturally, when my mother heard about this, she had a holy fit. She felt that since that I was engaged to Bob, I shouldn't be seeing other men, let along dancing with them. For me, it was a welcome pleasure in a lean social life but she made it sound dirty.

Slowly, however, it became more and more difficult to find the ordinary things we took for granted. We carefully darned our dwindling supply of silk stockings and wore last year's coat like a badge of honor. We learned to listen to the ground waters and would ferret out which stores were expecting a shipment of our favorite thing and then gladly stand in line for hours to purchase it.

Each week we went to the Post Office where we picked up our ration coupons for sugar, butter, coffee, tea, gasoline, shoes, and dozens of other items—just enough coupons per person for that particular time period and no more. Hoarding was frowned upon. We learned to tolerate the new wartime butter substitute called margarine—an unreal blob of white goop that we mixed with a pellet of yellow food coloring. We used it in cooking but when it came to spreading the stuff on toast, the neighbor's strawberry jam was so much better.

The War Department initiated a bond program to raise money and it was an immediate success. Everyone wanted to be part of the effort and we could buy stamps for as little as twenty-five cents or a bond for as much as a thousand dollars. Dot and her friends started making corsages of flowers fashioned from war stamps and soon I was busy helping them. Each stamp was carefully wrapped in cellophane, twisted to resemble a flower petal and then tied to other flowers to make a corsage. We collected cellophane from all our friends who smoked and I can still see that huge box full of donations. It was rarely empty. Every Saturday, we set up a little booth in the town square and sold our creations. We were always sold out. The idea was so successful that the florists began fashioning bridal bouquets, and Life Magazine carried a cover picture of a bride carrying a war stamp corsage. We beamed with pride knowing we had contributed thousands of dollars to the war effort.

I have never felt so much a part of this country as I did during that time. People were united in a new way that had never happened before or has happened since. As the weeks turned into months and the news broadcasts brought only bad news, we were robbed of sleep and were only kept informed by newspapers photos of our soldiers slogging through boot-high mud or on snowy winter marches in bitter winter storms.

Three years later, in the fall, our hopes began to rise as the power of the German onslaught began to weaken. In the last six months of World War II, we were beginning to hope the outcome was near. On May 8, 1945 the glorious news came of our victory in Europe. Though it was only one part of the war equation, it was a significant triumph. We were certain Japan would come next.

During the celebrations I was certain I'd hear from Bob, but I didn't, and weeks went by.. I was just about to call the Betts house and ask if they had heard from him when he called. He was breathless. "I'm at Fort Dix, in New Jersey, and I hope to get a thirty-day leave and come home. But I can't talk, Punchy. There's a line of guys waiting for the phone, so I have to get off. But listen, you have to answer right now. Will you marry me as soon as possible? I have a thirty-day leave when I finally get out of here. "

"I g-g-guess so," I stuttered. That was all I could say before he hung up.

In the silence that followed, my mother, who had been sitting nearby, with her sewing in her lap, pricked her finger. "Ouch! What did he say?" She tried to sound nonchalant.

"Bob has thirty days before he has to go. Somewhere? I don't know very much, but he wants me to marry him right away—I guess in those thirty days—as soon as we can arrange it. That's what he said."

My Mother and I looked at each other and grinned. The long wait was over. I was about to become Mrs. Robert Betts.

But it was July before I heard from Bob again. When he finally called and my Mother yelled for me to come to the phone, I took the stairs two at a time. It was a miracle I didn't fall.

Before I could even utter the word "hello," Bob gushed, "I think I have a ride to Easton with some guy's parents in few days. Oh, gosh! I'm coming home, Punchy. I can hardly believe that we'll be together again. Soon."

Tears of joy and disbelief spilled over and my young heart quickened as I thought of being held in Bob's arms again. I saw his brown hair falling over his forehead—his radiant grin. He was coming home at last. It was really happening.

"Oh, it's so wonderful to hear your voice," I said, thinking of the frightening inferences in his letters to what was happening to him in Europe.

"Punchy, I have a lot to tell you," he said, softly. "I'll see you soon." And before he hung up, he added with zeal, "We're going to make a wonderful team—for life."

For two days I hung over the telephone, waiting. I went to work. I came home to sit on the porch, looking up and down the street every few minutes for Bob. I pushed food away from my place at the table. I slept fitfully and smoked endless cigarettes. Just when my patience had given out and I was contemplating calling the Betts and asking them to pull out all the stops to find their son, a car drove up in front of the house and out stepped an unfamiliar looking United States Army officer.

"Goodbye, and good luck," I heard him say, and the voice sounded exactly like Bob's.

I think I stopped breathing. Was this Bob? It didn't look at all like the soldier I kissed goodbye two years ago.

The stranger walked towards me with outstretched arms but I remained standing as if I had been incased in wax. My face felt curiously frozen. I couldn't believe this soldier was Bob, my husband-to-be, my lover, my friend. The radiant grin I had dreamed about so often was now a sad smile pasted on a thin face And his once devilish eyes had a strange faraway look of painful memories. When I saw how his uniform hung limply on his thin body a shudder went through me. I wanted to cry. After a moment, the soldier stepped forward and gently wrapped me in his arms. His frail body was trembling like an injured kitten.

"Oh, honey," he whispered. "I'm home. I'm so happy to be home." He held me tighter and I began to believe that yes, this was my Bob. Still I had not warmed to his touch.

"I know I look like hell warmed over but I'm back—I promised I'd be back—took longer than we wanted. But, Punchy," he went on, "we have a lot to talk about." And then he kissed me, softly, tentatively. It was a kiss from someone not quite sure of himself, almost as if we'd never kissed before. We stepped away from each other, bewildered and embarrassed. In the silence that followed, a million thoughts raced through my wooden-puppet head. I didn't know who I was.

"We have to talk about the wedding," he said. "I'll be going away again soon. I felt my knees buckling but I managed to take Bob's hand and lead him to the settee. "Here," I said, "sit down and I'll get you something to drink."

He sank wearily into the wicker sofa. "Thanks," he said softly. "That would be great." He seemed too tired to even speak. I was slightly dizzy and unable to focue on this dream-like scene.

Mother had heard Bob arrive and came bustling out of the door smiling and gushing greetings to Bob. It was a perfect moment for me to excuse myself and head for the kitchen. I could hear Mother calling to Daddy who was tending his garden. When he came there was a lot of conversation among all of them. I was having a terrible time collecting myself, thankful I was alone for a minute.

I finally got the tea made, the ice in the glasses and the lemon on a plate. I straightened up and carried the tea tray back to the front porch. Everyone was chattering and everything seemed pretty normal—except it wasn't. What in the world was the matter with me? I put the tray down on the table.

"Well, Bob," Mother said finally, "I can't tell you how happy I am to see you safe and sound. We have heard from Charles and Buddy and they both hope to be home shortly. We have so much to be thankful for," she said, dabbing her eyes with her handkerchief." With that, she nodded to Daddy and rose from her chair. "You two have a lot to talk about so we'll see you later."

After they went into the house, Bob and I sat looking at each other in the steaminess of that July afternoon. I remember how embarrassed I was by the perspiration rolling down my face, the sweat stains under my arms.

We squeezed the lemons in our tea, relishing the frosty feel of our glasses, and fiddled with the tall silver tea servers, wondering what to say when our hearts were crying out to be heard.

Finally, Bob cleared his throat. "You know I couldn't write you a heck of a lot from Europe—nothing that gave you any information, you know...where I was, or with the names of anything. Everything I wrote was censored. I felt like all I did was say I was still alive."

"Oh, but those words meant so much to me," I said. "Especially when you told me you were finished with your tour of action and going on to Nice. "

"I was *pulled back* from action, and sent to Nice for other reasons."

What was he saying? Was we he telling me he was a spy? He went to Nice as a spy Oh, come on, Emmie, I said to myself. You've seen too many movies. I spoke up. "I'm so glad you were out danger," I said, lamely, my mind spinning.

He smiled ruefully. "After a bloody encounter, they awarded me a commendation for heroic action but what I had been through did weird things to me. I was sent to a rehabilitation hospital in Nice. I didn't know it but I had battle fatigue pretty bad. All I wanted to do was sleep forever........" His voice dropped off as his mind instantly flashed back to that hospital

"And my superior officer had to get me away from action, so I could get myself back together again." He paused, looking down at his feet. I sat twisting my hands wishing I could run to my bed and pull the covers over my head.

I wondered what he meant by battle fatigue. Just what was it, exactly? I remember his V-mail from Nice but nothing about a rehabilitation hospital. A wave of uneasiness chilled me like the tea going down the back of my throat.

"I remember you wrote you had been reassigned and your new duty was aide de camp to a general—I think his name was MacKelvie—after you left Nice."

"Correct." Bob clipped. He stirred his tea, nervously. "I don't know how to begin ......but there is something I have to tell you before we can go on, before we can talk about anything, even our wedding."

I sat up straighter, and put my iced tea down, my fingers dug into the wicker beneath my seat. I watched him picking at his ragged nails.

"I was so lonely—very lonely. I had been at the hospital for about two weeks when my buddy and I were given a pass for a night out. We hated the smells and the sights in that hospital. We didn't feel ill and we hated being in the company of some of the guys who were just not going to make it. They were going mad or dying from injuries that couldn't be fixed. So, like two hicks from the States, we slicked up and went to town for dinner." Bob was staring at the heat waves rising from the macadam street.

" I'll never forget the softness of the air that night," Bob continued. "Italian families were in the town square playing with their dogs and kids, and the outdoor cafes were jammed with people having a good time. It was hard to believe that just a few hundred miles north, there was a bloody war going on—that people were dying as they were laughing." Bob put his head in his hands.

When he could talk again, he said, "We found a little restaurant by the harbor, a place full of American soldiers. Some guys we knew already had a table and waved us over. We had a couple of beers, and then I dug in on the cold shrimp, and I remember my mouth watering over some home baked rolls. After a while I felt someone was watching me. I looked up and saw a very pretty blonde across the table. She looked half-starved—almost emaciated. Northern European, I thought to myself. She kept staring at me. It was disconcerting at first. After a while, she leaned over to ask her date something and I heard him say, 'Sure, why not?' I thought they were going to ask me to join them for a beer. Before I knew it she was sitting next to me. I looked across the table and got the OK sign from her date. She told me her name and her English was pretty good, so we didn't have a language problem. She asked me some questions about myself, where I came from, why I was there. She told me she was a refugee from Holland and through friends had managed to get to the Riviera with her child, where they would be safe. Her funds were running low so she was forced to take any job she could find, including selling herself and she offered me her services in exchange for some money to feed her child. I wanted no part of that." Bob was matter of fact up until this part of the story but then he slowed down and was having trouble going on.

I think every cell in me stopped working.

"This should be the end of the story, Emmie, but it isn't. I felt very sorry for her. I did give her what money I had on me, promising I could get more the next day." He picked up his glass and sat staring across the street at a green lawn where many past days he and Buddy had gleefully tossed a ball back and forth. Was he remembering those days- comparing them to the horror of his overseas days?

"I saw her the next day and I gave her the money. And then the day after that I saw her again, and we met again the following day. I was so grateful just to be alive and in the company of living and breathing humans," he hesitated. "And....I guess you know..."

I said nothing. It was a while before he spoke again. "The inevitable happened. And this is what I had to confess, Emmie, had to have you know, and had to beg for your forgiveness. I feel rotten about what happened, but I also feel good that I helped her buy food for her and her child. I wasn't just a soldier helping nameless faces. I helped. I know I did.

"It's bothered me a lot but I had to tell you before we started making wedding plans. I'm *not* completely ashamed, but you *had* to know, because you would've found out." I would have found out? How? And probably I never would have known but intuitively, I knew Bob wanted this off his conscience so he dumped it on me. I was the priest in the confessional booth and he was desperate for my blessing.

By the time he had finished his story, he had put his head in my lap and I was stroking his forehead, saying, "I understand how it could have happened. I don't blame you. You were on sick leave and had problems yourself that maybe she took away for awhile and..." Yet, there was an ugly monster inside of me howling and kicking and screaming.

Was Bob so obtuse? Didn't he realize that by telling me such an intimate story he was dealing me a blow I would never get over? I would have been better off not knowing. There were some things we should never talk about, I thought, and some things we should always keep on the table. Which ones should they be?

I had to ask the next question. "What was her name?"

"Inger," he said.

"Oh," I answered. What did it matter? What I was wondering was did she look into his eyes when they made love—wondered if Nice was humid and did she sweat the way I was sweating—did she moan and call out his name—did she..........

The rest of the evening was like finding our way through thick fog. It was painful for me and though Bob never said anything, I could tell he was lost, too. We finally bid each other goodnight with another cardboard embrace.

I turned to go into the house, sick at heart, wondering how I was going to relate to this changed Bob, and the role he had bestowed on me—the all-forgiving, understanding, scrubbed-pink-angel-of-mercy, *his* girl-next-door. This was not me. He didn't know the girl I had become while he was gone. He wouldn't recognize me as part of the home front—one person among millions who bravely signed up to learn thousands of bewildering tasks required in our war plants—the women who wore pants and punched time clocks and carried tuna fish sandwiches in metal lunch boxes—who worked the night shifts cheerfully. Some of us even wore hard hats. We were proud women giving what we could to the war effort, earning our own way, growing stronger each day knowing we could handle life on our own. Now suddenly, with Bob's appearance, the girl I had become was slipping away. Deep inside I knew I was about to lose something that meant a great deal to me. I knew that when Bob slipped that wedding ring on my finger, my former self was doomed and would disappear—maybe never to return.

Only five years had passed, since we first met but it seemed like a century since we were those starry-eyed teenagers in the pine-forested hideaway of Mud Run. If we agreed to go ahead with our wedding, when Bob and I would be standing in front of the minister saying "I do," would any part of those young lovers we had once been be standing there with us?

Way into the night I tossed in my bed. I took each memory aside to examine it, trying to remember my feelings. In my head, I knew I loved Bob. But my heart would not speak. Much as I commanded it to tell me what to do, it remained shutdown. Before turning out the light, I took a long look at Bob's picture on my nightstand. I saw how much the war had taken of his verve and his looks. Maybe in time the dashing Bob with his bright teasing eyes would come back to me, but the damage to his psyche had left an ugly scar and I knew then if anyone could help him recover, I could.

For a whole week I went through the motions of doing my job at Ingersol-Rand. I spoke to no one about my reunion. Friends hugged me and greeted me, but my mind was elsewhere. Mother had taken me into her room and presented me with the little black purse I had come to know so well from our meager days. It was stuffed with bills. She said she had been putting aside a little each week for over two years in anticipation of my wedding day. She said she couldn't afford a big wedding but the money she'd saved would pay for a dress and trousseau and a small but tasteful reception. I wasn't going to disappoint Mother. I would marry Bob.

By the time she finished presenting me with the money, we were both crying. I couldn't believe she had done this and I tried to tell her how much it meant to me, but she brushed aside my stumbling thanks, saying that we'd better start planning a trip to Wanamaker's in Philadelphia to find the wedding gown of my dreams and a few other things for my trousseau.

All week long Mother was dashing from one chore to the next, accomplishing wonders. We had only six days to prepare and Mother had already begun to book the florists and musicians and the hall at the Easton Hotel. We went to Philadelphia and bought a dress and the rest of my trousseau.

I worried about Mother as her face was covered with red splotches. I knew she had high blood pressure, but it was no use talking about it to her. She always changed the subject.

Daddy and Bob had begun to take their coffee together on the porch in the early mornings and Bob was now calling Mother and Daddy, Lil and Harley. I could hear the easy drone of their conversation, sharing baseball stories or one of those jokes women never get or maybe Daddy was giving Bob some father-in-law advice—first night stuff, and all. I smiled to myself, refusing to let anything that had happened recently get in my way.

Mother had reserved the small ballroom at the Hotel Easton for the wedding reception. She was thrilled when she told me she was able to hire three elderly musicians to provide the music. Elderly? Well, I wondered if the music they played would be old, too. I groaned when I heard this.

On top of this Mother had decided against serving alcoholic beverages in deference to Bob's parents, who thought liquor was the devil's own drink. While I had known this when I first met Bob, it never occurred to me that my life would begin so seriously with a cello, a violin and piano playing some unfamiliar dated music and my friends having to stand around with no way to loosen up and have a good time.. Much as I wanted to challenge my mother, I said nothing. I let my mother do what she wanted. The image of the worn bills she had carefully saved in her little black purse and given to me with such love and tenderness made my heart turn over. This was her wedding more than mine. Me, the child brought by the stork at a most inopportune time in her life, would now bring her some pleasure.

The day of the wedding dawned with a heavy hush. I had fallen asleep quite late and was just aware of the light coming into the window, when I felt Daddy's gentle hand messaging the back of my neck and slowly, the cobwebs lifted from my head. I opened my puffy eyes. What a night it had been, staring into the darkness for hours, full of anxious thoughts, doubts coming at me from every corner. Today is supposed to be the biggest day in my life. Where is my joyful expectation?

Daddy sat on the edge of my bed. "Are you awake?" he asked. " I've been out on the porch since sun-up trying to read the wind direction from the CK Williams smokestack. The wind is coming from the southeast so that means fair skies. No rain in sight. But, Emilie Louise," he said with humor and concern. " I'm afraid today is going to be another hot and sticky one. The thermometer already reads 89 and it's still early."

I yawned and sat up, pulling the blanket around my shoulders. I looked at my father, the Daddy I remembered from childhood, who would push me on the tire swing and take me to the market on Saturday mornings. His face was now lined from years of too much worry and too much booze, but it was still very kind. "Daddy, tell me," I said, " I need to know. Before you and Mother got married, how did you feel?   Did you have doubts?"

Daddy laid his hand on my shoulder and smiled, He nodded yes.

"I'm so afraid I'm making a big mistake, I said. Bob isn't the Bob I remember and this is making me crazy. Remember the day we drove home from Harrisburg and I told you all the reasons why I wanted to marry Bob? Daddy, I feel like I'm going to marry someone I really don't know. It's not Bob, and it's scary." I paused and looked out the window at the early morning haze. A little voice inside of me was saying, "You know you have to honor this commitment. It would break Bob's heart if you backed out."

"I think you have a bad case of the wedding jitters," Daddy said, tweaking my nose. " Bob is a strong person and it will take a while, but he'll overcome his bad memories. And it will also take time for you to know each other. What you had at one time is still there. And, yes, I did wonder myself, before Mother and I wedded, whether it was the right thing to do. It certainly was, because if we hadn't gotten married, you wouldn't be here. So there," he ended with a chuckle. "Now, I will leave you alone so you can get dressed."

He closed the door softly. I rolled over in my blanket cocoon.

The apartment was abuzz with activity when I appeared in the kitchen. "No thanks," I said when offered breakfast. My stomach was twitching and I felt like I was floating down a stream, unable to touch either shore. The coffee helped settle things and I remember people coming and going; beautiful flowers, piles of wedding gifts. It looked like Christmas morning in July.

"Oh, Emilie Louise, your gifts are beautiful," my mother gushed. "Look at this lovely crystal pitcher. It's Waterford, the best you can buy." Her eyes sparkled and I smiled, hiding the turmoil inside of me. I couldn't spoil this day for her, either. She had worked so hard to arrange a church wedding and reception—not a big splashy affair but far better than one in a musty courtroom in front of a wheezing justice of the peace.

Hours later, when I finally slipped the white satin dress over my body, I felt I was taking on a new skin. White was the symbol of surrender, I remembered. My thoughts turned to Bob. Was he as apprehensive as I was? Happy but scared. Was he as uncertain of the future as I was?

At five minutes to four I came to attention standing in the church vestibule, listening to the organ player banging out "Oh Promise Me," and waiting for the pause that followed.... then the first strains of Mendelssohn's wedding march.

This is it, little girl, I said to myself. My legs felt like jello as I took my father's arm and we started down the aisle together. Daddy was so proud— so happy his daughter was getting married. I saw my mother in the front row, a big smile on her face. I wanted to feel that same burst of joy I saw on her face, but it wasn't bubbling up. I pasted on a smile. Today I was an observer in this play. This was what I said I wanted. Well, not completely. I had to admit to myself there were some missing pieces from my dream.

A war had orchestrated this wedding. Today, both my brothers were on duty in the Navy—Charles, my older brother, was still in Florida, and Buddy was somewhere out in the huge Pacific Ocean My sister and her husband, Dick, who had contracted TB, were away in a cure cottage in Saranac Lake, New York, and many of our friends were with their husbands at faraway Army bases. No. This was not as I dreamed. The day was sadly diminished.as I realized everyone who mattered was absent.

I heard someone promise to love, honor, and obey. Was this me? When the minister said "and you may now kiss the bride," we obeyed like two awkward children. I could feel Bob trembling as he touched me. Yet, for the first time in a long time, I felt a kiss that was gentle and full of promise. Passion? How can people be passionate when they are pulled as tight as kite strings on a windy run? Maybe the passion would come later. I had read somewhere that it might. As soon as we were joined together in holy matrimony, we began to exit the church and we didn't have the faintest idea of what was ahead of us.

CHAPTER 8

Let's Have A Drink!

WE heard the photographer shout, "Stop right there!" And he held us captive with his flash bulbs for too long . Bob's face was one huge scowl. I knew all he wanted was a Bloody Mary to take the edge off his annoyance at so many instructions and no time to relax.

"C'mon, honey," I urged him, despite my own unease. "Where's that famous grin of yours? These pictures are the "forever after" ones for the scrapbooks—pictures our kids and their kids are going to look at and wonder if you were really happy on your wedding day. He gave me a sick smile.

"OK," I said. "Say cheese," and I squeezed his arm.

By the time the picture taking was over, we were both dripping with sweat and out-of-sorts. Daddy's weather prediction was right on the mark. It was miserably sticky and hot.

James, Bob's oldest brother who carried jokes around in his breast pocket, drove us to the reception regaling us with some really corny ones he'd memorized about newlyweds.

"James, will you cut it out, please" Bob finally shouted. "It's hot enough without having to listen to you."

Oh, boy, I wondered if Bob was going to make it through the reception. If only I could get him that Bloody Mary!"

Mother met us as we entered the ballroom. There were little knots of people standing around, waiting. "Is the newly married couple ready to come and greet everybody?" she sang in her best hostess voice.

We were and we circulated, shaking hands and greeting our parents' friends. The chamber ensemble attempted to fill the huge room with glorious sounds but the empty spaces where our friends should have been merely echoed their feeble strains. Our parent's guests were politely sitting in chairs lined up against the walls, nibbling little sandwiches and sipping non-alcoholic punch. It took a serious effort, but I smiled and reassured my mother her party was lovely. Everything was fine-just fine..

I watched her having a wonderful time, moving from one group to another, laughing and conversing with her friends. My father looked over at me a few times and winked. The temperature in the room must have been way over ninety degrees and fans in every corner were helpless against the onslaught of the oppressive heavy heat.

Suddenly, a great crescendo on the piano came forth for the cake! The musicians played their best rendition of "The Wedding March." Bob put his hand over mind and we cut the first slice, broke it in half and gave each other a piece. Flashbulbs blinded us. Loud applause from the guests and then the strains of our song "East of the Sun and West of the Moon" came from the elderly trio of musicians. I was amazed that they knew it. Bob took me in his arms, bowed his head, as was his style and we shuffled around the floor with everyone watching. At that moment I was embarrassed for him. Of all the things he had to face today, I think this public display of his lack of dancing skills scared him the most. He was only too happy after circling the floor to hand me over to Daddy, whose rhythm and grace was a welcome relief.

Sometime later after changing my clothes in the bride's changing room and thanking my mother, again, I went to the top of the hotel stairs where I threw my bouquet over my left shoulder. I doubt there was anyone there young or agile enough to want to catch it.

On our way to the Princeton Inn, and the start of our honeymoon, the stiffness and frantic pace of the last six days, fell away and I began to relax.

"Do you feel married?" I asked in a teasing way.

Bob sighed and yawned at the same time. "How can I answer that?" he said. "I've never been married so I don't know what 'being married' feels like. That's like saying 'do you like your artichokes with a butter sauce or hollandaise' when I've never eaten an artichoke."

At first I was a little hurt by his answer, until he said in a louder voice," I know right now I am the happiest guy alive and I am looking forward to a lobster and a good bottle of wine at dinner—and then, to our first real night together. Is that a good enough answer?"

As the question lingered in the air, I felt as if Bob was a little irked with me.

"I'll take it. It all sounds just wonderful," I said, hoping I sounded enthusiastic. I think I was waiting for a profound discussion on this momentous thing that had just happened to us. I chided myself silently. *Get out of the car, and act grown-up, Emmie.* But, I didn't feel married or grown up. I felt like a very small child who was play-acting.

The Princeton college students employed by the Inn were stumbling over themselves when we arrived, all trying to be efficient. In a short time, our car was whisked away and we registered and were shown to the bridal suite. We were shown a bottle of champagne chilling in a silver bucket on the mahogany pie-crimped tea table in front of the window. Very nice, and so very special!

We couldn't wait to get out of our clothes and stand under a good hot shower—to come out and cool off as the water evaporated on our skin. It gave us both a sense of new birth. We had been miserably sticky and cranky for too long. Bob, being a gentleman, offered me the bathroom first. We were both painfully shy. After we dressed, Bob popped the champagne and we sat in twin wing chairs on either side of the fireplace, making up toast after toast to each other and our magical life ahead. When we started to sing popular songs and the bottle yielded not another drop, Bob announced, "Time for dinner."

We made our way—rather unsteadily—downstairs to the dining room, which was beautifully decorated in English chintz and Queen Anne furniture. *Someday,* I thought, *we will have a house like this one.*

Bob ordered lavishly from the genial waiter assigned to our table. "We'll have a bottle of Sauvignon Blanc, to begin with, and then two Caesar salads and two lobsters."

The Sauvignon Blanc arrived quickly but by the time we were served the lobsters, our appetites had waned.and we ate little, absently toying with the silver forks and claw crackers. We lingered a little too long over dessert and a little more wine. Neither one of us wanted to make the move to go upstairs to our suite and behave like the newly married couples of Bob's brother's snickering jokes.

"Good night, Mr. and Mrs. Betts. It was a pleasure to serve you," the young waiter said, as Bob and I could stall no longer, and the staff clearly needed to clear the dining room out. It was almost midnight.

"I think it's time for us to really celebrate this marriage business. OK?" Bob said.

My answer was a silly smile. As we left the dining room, the college boy bid us a good night. "Please let us know if there is anything else you would like," he said.

Bob squeezed my hand and we started for the staircase, our hearts beating double-time and our heads woozy with wine.

If I expected a movie directed love scene, I was sadly mistaken. From the minute we shut the door, it was a replay of the Three Stooges. Bob started clowning around—a throwback to that Harvard boy who fell asleep on the stairs—kidding and laughing over who was going to use the bathroom first and which side of the bed did I want. Of course he was nervous and embarrassed and I was a little bewildered by his behavior, but I felt I had to match his mood even in our marriage bed. Our being intimate again was not the same as our first time in Harrisburg, when we really pledged ourselves to each other with great tenderness. That had been two years ago. Tonight, the romance I'd felt then had been replaced with a new feeling I couldn't identify. Two years had brought changes and I knew I was no longer the scared little small town girl. As I finally sought sleep, an uneasy thought kept coming back to me. What was Bob like with Inger? Was she the siren and me the little brown mouse?

"First nights, even on Broadway," I said to Bob in the morning, as I was dressing, "are fraught with stage fright, miscues and blunders. You should have seen my first performance of Charlie's Aunt."

Bob kissed me on the cheek and laughed.

We giggled through breakfast and I realized I liked sitting at the breakfast table being a married woman. It felt cozy, even if it didn't feel sexy, yet.

We packed our bags and called the desk to check out. Overnight a chill wind had blown away the sticky weather and now scudding gray skies glowered at us. The weatherman was forecasting a Nor'easter just as we were scheduled to spend a few days of our honeymoon at the seashore. As we parked the ancient Packard in front of our seaside hotel and peered through the mist, we saw a drab, poorly constructed three-story wooden structure.

Seaside Heights

We were puzzled. The brochure had praised this hotel with superlatives. But instead of "graceful veranda furnished with white wicker and flowered cushions, seaside blue hydrangeas leaning on window boxes overflowing with petunias," there were worn wooden steps leading up to a porch devoid of such beauty, and two sad-looking very thirsty potted palms on either side of the entrance. We hauled our bags out of the car and entered a quiet and empty lobby. Bob hit the desk bell. Ding !

"Anyone here?" he shouted. No answer. Another couple of dings brought a perspiring middle-aged man.

"Sorry to keep you waiting," he said, with an embarrassed smile. "We're kind of short staffed and I was pitching in with the cleaning. Didn't hear you at first—vacuum cleaner, you know?" So much for the advertised full staff of uniformed attendants.

Bob signed the register and I peered over his hand and saw there were very few guests entered there. Good. That meant fast service in the dining room.

"Can you tell me the hours in the dining room?" I asked him.

"Oh, the dining room is closed" he said. "It's only open for special occasions. Good thing the war is over. Maybe the folks who used to come here will come back, but up until now, it's been mighty slim pickings for guests. Especially couples—all of the boys were away. But there's a good diner just down the street where you can get anything you want, anytime. The owner's name is Mort. Tell him I sent you and you'll get a free coffee."

Ah! No fine dining either. I guess we weren't thinking realistically, forgetting how the war stripped our lives of many pleasures we took for granted. But being in Seaside Heights had one certain pleasure that we both looked forward to—being next to the ocean. Here I could make squishy sounds walking in the sand and marvel at the waves outlined in lacy foam, drawing thin circles at my feet. I could revel in the surf's pounding roar and delight in the stiff legged skitter of the sandpipers. Here was a chance for us to unwind and begin to understand what forces led us to be Mr. and Mrs. Bob Betts, cementing their love in Asbury Park in late July, 1945.

"Let me show you your room," said our man of all trades as we followed him to a Lilliputian space with two tiny windows at the end and a miniscule bathroom to match the rest of the accommodations. I tried not to show my disappointment. It wouldn't help to whine when these were the facts, and I had what I'd prayed to have—Bob next to me.

The first thing we did after we put our bags down was open the window for that famous ocean breeze. We stood there with our eyes closed, taking in the calm hypnotic sound of the ocean.

"What on earth was that?" Bob said, as an odd and very loud noise like raspy breathing, wafted in the window along with the ocean's sound. He maneuvered his lanky body close to the window.

"Oh, I forgot to tell you," said our new friend looking a bit uncomfortable. "The American Lung Association was having a fund drive and asked us if they could park a man in an iron lung on our street. How could we refuse? So we said okay and he's been here for over a month"

"But he's parked right under our window," I whined..

Our man of all trades shrugged his shoulders, smiled, and left.

It turned out that even our clothes didn't fit into the miniature closet and the towels in the bathroom were so thin you could read a newspaper through them, as my father was fond of saying when fabrics wore thin. When I said it to Bob, he picked up the newspaper from the rickety table and put the towel over it, holding it up to the light.

"Yep," he said. "I can read the headlines." We burst into raucous laughter. After all it was hard not to see the funny side of our fairytale honeymoon, which, moment by moment, was taking on the Puckish air of a " Midsummer Night's Dream" and giving us a lot of chuckles when we envisioned telling the tale to our friends.

The sky was darkening when we walked to the recommended diner. It was warm and cheerful, with a cook who made bountiful soups and crusty home baked rolls—exactly the comfort food we needed. We settled in a booth and ordered the day's specialty- beef stew, which was delicious. We loved being together here in this hospitable diner and were not eager to leave. Not only were we slightly jittery about our expected erotic liaison, but the sound of that poor guy in the iron lung was depressing background music for our supposedly romantic interlude.

We topped off dinner with homemade apple pie and lingered over coffee on the house, as promised by our hotel manager.

"Let's take a walk on the boardwalk," I suggested as we headed to the beach, glad for another reason not to go back to the hotel. On the boardwalk, a cold ocean wind cut right through my white princess style spring coat, making shivers dance up and down my back. Someday, I vowed, I would learn how to dress. But tonight, that wasn't important. It didn't even matter that my carefully done hair was now hanging in damp disarray from the moisture laden fog. I was too happy to care.

We strolled up and down for a long time, stopping now and then to hold each other closely in the wonder of being together, and whispered the love words stored away in our hearts for so long. After my gloveless hands turned stiff from the cold, we headed back to the hotel.

Our second honeymoon night was a bit better than our first, though it was a sleepless night for all the wrong reasons—opening and closing the window, in and out of bed, horsing around like sixth graders but managing to have some surprisingly lovely sex now and then. For most of my generation sex was a rocky path because we knew nothing about the male body and he seemed to know little about mine. But, and I think this was the saving grace, Bob saved us from being completely embarrassed with one another by his relentless silliness. Fortunately I was fast letting go of my little girl visions of a tender love scene with my movie idol Ronald Colman, and I easily fell into the craziness of *our* reality, laughing and joking along with Bob. Clearly, I had not married Ronald Colman. Clearly I wasn't in any movie I had ever seen.

The rain and fog in Seaside Heights was a disappointing and dismal backdrop for romance so we decided to go home After bidding goodbye to the innkeeper, we said a silent adieu to the other guest—the man in the iron lung—still there—still waiting for donations.

"Never mind, Punchy," Bob said with an engaging smile as we drove away, "we'll have our real honeymoon after we end this damn war on all fronts."

August 14, 1945 dawned clear and cool filled with sunshine and bird songs. I remember so well how we piled into the old Packard for our trip to Indiantown Gap, where Bob was due to report today. He had on a fresh uniform and looked fine—ten times better than when he first came home. I was so grateful that the past thirty days had restored some of his mental and physical health. He put on his overseas hat at a rakish angle to match the forced smile on his face and rallied us by saying "Okay, gang, let's get going. I have to sign in by noon according to what it says here," and he waved his orders in the air. "The honeymoon is over," he quipped.

Dr. Betts hoisted himself into the front seat next to Bob and Mrs. Betts and I climbed into the back. Bob eased the car out of the driveway and turned left toward the Cumberland Mountains and Indiantown Gap and we settled down for the trip.

Silence settled over us. We turned on the radio to take our minds off our fears and were listening with half a ear when suddenly an excited newscaster interrupted the broadcast. The voice cracked with emotion: "Ladies and gentlemen, we have just been notified from Washington that the Japanese have surrendered. The war is over!"

The news stunned us but immediately, we were filled with hysterical joy. Bob was shouting "Hallelujah! Amen Yeah! Yippee!" Dr. Betts started pounding Bob on the back and Mrs. Betts covered her face with her handkerchief. I was in tears.

"Thank you Lord," I whispered.

The four of us had been in the lowest frame of mind one minute and in the next we were shouting praises to the powers that be for bringing the horrors of the last four years to an end. I kept saying over and over, "Buddy and Charles are coming home!" I looked at Bob in wonder. He was not going to the Pacific. He was not going to leave me again. Our happiness lit up that car like a blazing meteor and it was a miracle Bob kept the car steady on the road.

When we arrived at the base in Indiantown Gap it was jumping with wild excitement. All of the stiff protocols of army demeanor had vanished and the boys ran willy-nilly into one another whooping and waving their hats, hugging and laughing, crying and shouting. I kissed Bob goodbye with hope and a promise that he would ask for an immediate medical discharge based on his history of extreme battle fatigue. He felt confident it would be honored.

Bob's release orders sent him to Ft. Jackson, the mammoth US Army staging area for returning servicemen, in Columbia, South Carolina. The midsized city could hardly handle the huge crush of visitors relating to activities around the base. Hotels and motels, rooming houses and emergency housing barracks were soon filled to capacity and I resigned myself to staying in Easton while Bob went through the agonizingly slow process of getting out of the army.

Soon after Bob had arrived in Columbia, he brother James called me saying he had found us a place to stay with some friends of his. What a wonderful break! With a song on my lips, I packed my bag and was on the train to Columbia the next day. It was a long day and night with no sleeping arrangements so by the time the train got closer to Bob, my excitement had dulled. The intense heat inside the car and having to sit up all night could have turned me into a whiny, sweaty, totally unglamorous new bride, but fortunately, my seatmate helped the hours to fly by.

He was a small, charming man, keenly interested in life, and full of enthusiasm about his new job as a liaison officer between Washington and the Philippines. We talked non-stop about *his* life and ambitions, then about *my* life and *my* hopes for the future. He introduced himself as Ferdinand Marcos. Many years later when his notorious troubles as a dictator were plastered all over the newspapers and TV, I remembered our chance meeting in 1945 and I silently wished him well.

Mr. and Mrs. Howard and their four lovely daughters were delightful and did everything they could to make us comfortable. It was my first exposure to the famous Southern hospitality and I loved it. Their home in the suburbs was a spacious brick Georgian Colonial endowed with all the grace of that period. It sat prettily among a luxurious stand of Southern pine trees. Our room was large and airy, stretching from the front of the house to the back with many windows overlooking blooming azaleas. It had a private bath so I knew this must have been the master bedroom. How thoughtful of them to give it to us for the time we would be here.

For six weeks as the army began to dismantle that huge machine that supported the war, we lived in the land of drawls and magnolia blossoms, enduring endless sultry days of waiting while the Army sifted through the records of thousands of soldiers and we northerners adapted to a pace so slow it seemed to go in reverse. The easy life of the south was good for Bob and he began to relax. However, his charm during the day was darkened by his tormenting memories at night. Many nights Bob had nightmares, thrashing and mumbling and crying out from a deep sweaty sleep.. Sometimes his hands closed around my throat, while he shouted obscenities. Wresting away from him, I struggled to rouse him.

"Bob! Bob! Stop it! Wake up!"

When he awoke he had no idea of what had happened. There in the quiet of our graceful southern bedroom Bob's hideous nightmares erupted, leaving us breathless as if we were being chased by man-eating tigers, cold sweats banishing our sleep for the rest of the night I timidly suggested that he talk to me about the things that were haunting him. But he shook his head and said no. I backed off.

In all the years we were together, Bob never uttered a word about his war experiences.. He kept those memories bottled up. Luckily, just as our long Southern days and fitful Southern nights were becoming unbearable Bob was released from the army.

He came in the front door one steamy afternoon crowing, "Get packing, honey," "We're heading home."

CHAPTER 9

The Fifty-Two-Twenty Club

OUR soot-covered train whistled and clanged as it inched its way into Easton, finally arriving at the platform with a loud sigh. As the doors opened and a tangle of weary ex-soldiers with wives and sweethearts in tow spilled out, I looked around and felt a sting behind my eyes. I had been away only six weeks, yet as I stood there, I felt like an emerging chick pecking its way to the light. I was seeing all the old familiar things in a new way—the funny old stores on the main street, the monument in Circle Square, the Arcade market, along with the First Reformed Church's white steeple pointing its finger straight to God. A bittersweet cloud drifted briefly over me. My life as a single girl was over– Part One—memories penned on the opening pages of my scrapbook. The pages in Part Two— My life as Mrs. Robert Betts—were blank, staring at me, waiting to be written. What would they say?

The station platform fairly pulsated with joyful family reunions. The laughter and tears in this momentous homecoming scene was an emotional high for me, and I swallowed hard to keep from bawling. Finally, through the bedlam, we spotted our parents waving and smiling at the edge of the crowd. Gathering ourselves and our bags, we inched our way through the people and into their outstretched arms. Their hugs and kisses were like cool waters to our tired spirits.

Somehow, we all squeezed into the old Packard and Bob carefully carved a way through the maze of cars and people and out to the main street. We were alive with excitement and everyone was talking all at once. Daddy told me Charles had already been mustered out of the Navy and was on his way home but Buddy who was on the battleship New Jersey in the south Pacific, would have to wait until the ship was ordered back in port. But they were both OK. I could see the relief in the eyes of both my parents. I knew the worry they had lived with over the past two years and they looked very tired.

"What about Brooks, Dad?" Bob asked. "Have you heard when he will be home?" I could see Bob was anxious to hear about his favorite brother. "The last letter we had from him," Bob's mother answered, "was from South America and although he didn't give a date, he did say it wouldn't be long before the Ferry command would start relieving the boys of duty—no more need to shuttle planes back and forth to Europe." She, too, was worn out.. "And Johnny wrote that his outfit from Germany was being re-deployed and he hoped to see us soon," she added. So Bob and his brothers were all miraculously spared. How can we thank you enough, God? I silently prayed.

By this time, Bob had parked the car in front of Mother and Daddy's apartment and helped Mother and Daddy up the steep front steps. "We'll be back in the morning and have a good long talk," I said, waving a kiss as we pulled away. Next stop Bob's home.

Dr. and Mrs. Betts' apartment was in a wing off to the side of the Betts Hospital, yet far enough from the grim day-to-day activities there. The atmosphere was really bad for a battle-weary soldier who had seen too much pain and sadness, but we had no choice. Mother and Daddy's little spare room that had been my nest for two years was much too small for the two of us—so, depressing as the situation was, we had to move in with Bob's parents.

We dropped our bags on the worn Persian rug. I looked around. The room was cheerless. Through the one small window a northern light painted the white walls a lifeless gray and while the window was open to the late summer breeze, it did little to chase the musty smell hanging onto everything. Two ancient iron beds held thin mattresses and the worn quilts, although beautifully handmade, were just as thin. I was glad it was summer time and not the dead of winter. A dark mahogany nightstand sat beneath a black and white print of Notre Dame. Across the room, a beautiful chest of drawers gleamed with the polish of many years. But there were no curtains, no frills of any kind. My shoulders sagged as I started to unpack.

Bob turned to me. "Well, Punchy, here we are. Don't know for how long but we'll make the best of it." I put my arms around him. "It's OK, really it is. We're lucky to have a place to sleep."

But that night, trying to sleep with Bob in one of the twin beds was a real challenge. After he was asleep, I gratefully crawled into the other one. I also knew there would be precious little lovemaking here in a room smack up against his parents' room.

The next morning, we paid our promised visit to Mother and Daddy and spent a couple of hours on the front porch, talking non-stop about our stay in Dixieland. It was our first shared adventure and still fresh in our minds so we didn't miss anything. They loved every word. Bob loved to talk and I gave him the stage while I sat back sipping coffee.

I was wrapped in old memories. It was that old familiar wicker settee that unsettled me. All I could think about was the day when war-beaten Bob, now my husband, came up these steps and walked back into my life—the day he christened me the all-forgiving-girl-next-door. Would I ever shake this? I wondered.

Our days settled into a routine of sorts, sleeping until noon and partying until midnight. I was itchy and irritable. And I was finding living with Bob's parents painful. Plunked down in a strange cold house with a family I hardly knew was a wet blanket to my usual ebullience. Somehow, I knew my bursts of joy would be frowned upon so I had to curb my spirits and behave according to what I thought was expected of me. Dr. and Mrs. Betts were well regarded in Easton and pillars of the church, as they say, and I was constantly on guard. Bob's father seemed to accept me into the family but I was never sure Bob's mother thought I was good enough for her son.

When we gathered in their plain living room after dinner, Dr. Betts would be sprawled in his chair reading "Laughter is the best medicine" in the Reader's digest, his belly shaking and wiggling as he chuckled to himself. He often dozed off and his snorts punctuating long pauses in the dull conversation made me want to giggle.

Somehow, I always got to sit on the old horsehair sofa. I hated that sofa.It bit me and pricked me unmercifully. But I sat there like a dutiful daughter-in-law, nodding and smiling, and stifling coughs from the cannel coal in the fireplace. Far from the sweet smell of apple wood, this was a heavy earthy smell like swamp mud. I sighed and let my mind drift to the soft evenings in the south I'd grown to love— where laughter sang through the house and magnolia trees dropped their petals silently, like snow, over the lawn. This room, unfortunately, brought back memories of my dark Depression years.

While Bob's mother was droning on, I was imagining Bob as a child, sitting in this long, Shaker inspired living room, reading by the smelly fire. I saw him exposed to all the harsh sounds and antiseptic odors of the hospital. I saw his father appear for dinner after performing surgery, still wearing his blood stained gown. He probably didn't give a second thought to his appearance until Mrs. Betts ordered him to change.

I was held captive those evenings, unable to move, waiting until Bob finally stood up and said, "We're off to meet the gang. See you later," and taking me by the hand, we would flee the boring apartment, hop in the car and drive up to Buck's, where we would meet our friends and other members of the 52-20 Club. This was a nickname for the emergency Veteran's bill passed by Congress, which guaranteed each veteran a twenty-dollar check every week for a year to keep them afloat until they found a job. It doesn't sound like a lot of money now, but in those days it bought many bags of groceries. I never knew what happened to that money. Maybe Bob gave some of it to his Mother.

As for me, I was embarrassed asking Bob for spending money. "What for," he would ask? "I need some stuff from the drug store" or "I need some underwear," I would answer, and he would open his wallet and hand me some bills. Oh, how I hated that. Even though he told me he was trying to put some of the money aside, I saw bills flying out of his wallet at Buck's but I kept quiet. I knew Bob and all the other guys from the war needed a cooling down period and I said nothing, but I remembered the days I was cashing my Ingersoll-Rand check and looking with pride at my healthy bankbook. Now, having to beg money from Bob made me half sick.

The monotony of living with the Betts was finally broken by the sudden appearance of Bob's brother Brooks, who was recently discharged from the Air Corp. Like us, he and his wife Helen had no place to live and like Bob, no job. I loved Brooks' booming laugh and his wonderful sense of humor that chased away the gloom in that dismal apartment. The four of us spent many evenings together mostly at Buck's, our favorite watering hole, where the name of the game was to get smashed and forget the war. .

One night Bob took on a dare. "Okay, Betts," a half crocked guy jeered. "I bet you can't drink a shot a minute with a beer chaser for seven minutes in a row."

"Oh, yeah? You're on," came my already tipsy husband's reply.

"Don't take the dare," I said urgently. "You'll get sick! Please, I beg of you. Don't do it!" He shoved me away.

By now, Bob, and his tormentor were sitting across from one another with a bottle of Four Roses and a pitcher of beer in the center of the table. Buck had come out from behind the bar with a worried look on his face. Several curious customers left their tables to watch what would happen. I stood with them, biting my knuckles.

The drinking began. How quickly a minute goes by! By the time the first shot and glass of beer had been downed the minute was up, and it was round two. The boys kept the minute-by-minute pace for at least four or five rounds. Suddenly, Bob slumped over, falling face down—his forehead crashing onto the wooden table with a loud bang. His drinking challenger didn't want the round to end and taunted antagonistically. "Hey, buddy, you still have two more rounds. C'mon, you said you could do it. Let's see you do it." He tried to pull Bob up by the collar.

At that Bob turned his head slightly, groaned and threw up all over the table. Good thing, too. It saved him from dying of alcoholic poisoning. Brooks and a couple of strong fellows, who were much more sober, stood Bob up and dragged him to the men's room, where he finished emptying his stomach. Afterward they managed to get his dead weight safely into the front seat of the Packard.

By this time, I was so hopping mad I could hardly see straight. My husband—the fool—nearly killed himself tonight. What kind of a man did I marry, anyhow? What was he trying to prove? The questions were bouncing around in my head making me wonder how this stupid behavior meshed with his decorations from his war experiences. I wanted to dump him and go home alone but it didn't happen. Instead, my wimpy side won. I was the caring wife, making sure my drunken husband got home safely.

This whole scene had my blood boiling but it did clear my head. Brooks and Helen were not in good shape and only too glad I was sober enough to drive everyone home. I turned the key in the ignition and the car responded. I headed for home.

By this time, Bob had come to life and decided to lean out the window, yelling things like: "Wheee! Look at us, Yahoo! Here we come. Watch out! Don't go so close to the line. Slower, little lady. You're goin' too fast!" He interjected every order with whistles and banging on the side of the car

"Gotta make shurr the little wifey knows the way home," he laughed, and then burst into song. "Oh, show me the way to go home, I'm tired and I wanna go to bed...oh I had a lil drink about l...." Brooks finally pulled him back and shut the window. We didn't need to stir up a police car.

It was very late when I pulled into the Betts driveway. I had no idea how we were going to get Bob out of the car, or into bed. My worries were further compounded when I saw Mrs. Betts standing on the porch. With a sinking heart, I turned off the engine. By this time she had come down the steps and was standing beside the car door. "Emmie," she said quietly, "Is he alright? They called me from Buck's and told me what happened. You know I worry so about his health and nights like these are a terrible drain on his strength."

I assured her he was okay and turned to Brooks who had come around and was lifting Bob out of the car. "Let's get him into bed," he said, and between the two of us, we lugged Bob up the six steps into the back hall. From there it was only a short distance to the bedroom, where he threw us off and straight-arrowed into bed like a dead duck. Mrs. Betts left the room and never brought up the subject of that night again.

I regretted quitting my job but Bob wouldn't hear of my going back to work. In those days, when you got married your whole life was focused on your husband. A job would be out of the question, but thinking about my days as a working girl brought a bittersweet pang that I had to put down as soon as it appeared.

The days loomed empty and senseless. Bob and I spent many afternoons stretched out on our beds listening to my modest stack of records that I had brought with me along with my record player. I remember the day I paid the last installment on that RCA record player. It was my first touch of ownership and it felt wonderful. In those hours Bob and I began to talk about ideas—not just the plans we had for a lifetime, but the things that excited us other than each other.

Bob told me how much he loved the printed word, especially poetry, and he introduced me to the beautiful words of John Donne and Robert Burns. Then I would turn on my record player to let the glorious sounds of Tchaikovsky's "Romeo and Juliet" fill the room while I explained how a composer, like an author, builds tension in his work by starting slowly then adding interest with more instruments and inserting richer harmonies into the score. I remember one afternoon in the fall when Bob rolled over onto one arm with his face intent on listening to what I was saying. "In music this is often accomplished by changing keys, modulating to the next higher one and then the next and so on, until the climax comes with a full orchestra in wild harmonic abandon, or so it seems, but these steps are well planned, just as they are when the writer drafts the action in his book."

Bob was fascinated with the comparison and asked to hear the music again and again. The memory of such afternoons lost in words and music are sweet ones indeed—two people who loved each other were reaching out to explore each other's minds.

Unfortunately all of the lessons learned in that tiny bedroom didn't help my outlook and time continued to hang heavily. We were drifting from day to day without a purpose and I was twitching from boredom. And I was very tired of trying to be what I thought Mrs. Betts wanted me to be. I wanted to get out of this room and the apartment as soon as possible.

On many occasions I would borrow the car and drive up to College Hill and surprise my parents. I guess I was hungry to relive some of the better parts of my old life and it made me feel good to see how relaxed and happy they were. They loved my visits and made me realize how lonely they were with all of their children gone.

We would sit in the old wicker porch furniture, drinking coffee and reminisce, recalling amusing events like the Sunday morning our preacher fell out of the pulpit flat on his face, still drunk from partying all night. Those times together, when our laughter floated on the Indian summer air, were precious and gave me much needed reinforcement.

One afternoon, while we were listening to music, Bob confessed that he was in a predicament and needed my advice. I was immediately on the alert. I couldn't take another confession from Bob. One was enough. However, I held myself in check and took a deep breath, waiting to hear what he had to say. Bob had never asked for my opinion before. He usually told me what he was doing and I went along with what he said.

"Emmie, I have to a find a job. But what kind of a job? I don't know what kind of a career I want or what kind of background I need. It's not like I have engineering or medical skills. What good is a liberal arts degree?"

His eyes were clouded with doubt and for an instant; he looked like a lost little boy by the fireplace. A voice inside me said here was an opportunity to do something important. Do it. I sat down next to him on the bed and felt a huge adrenaline rush flame my face but I plunged on

"You're forgetting something very important, Bob." I said as I moved closer and put my arm through his. "Even though you think you have no skills, just look at your college record. You graduated cum laude with a degree in English letters from Harvard. Doesn't this suggest anything to you?"

No response. Then, finally, he said with a gloomy voice, "Yeah, I know all that, but how's that going to get me a job? I don't know the first thing about business."

I could feel myself doing a two-step inside. Here was the obvious right in front of him, but he couldn't see it. "Why don't you put a call in to your old tutor and see if you can go to Cambridge and talk this out with him? You two had a wonderful relationship. I would call him and ask his help, if it were my problem," I offered.

I felt this was pretty cheeky of me. Who was I to advise Bob, a man with such an intellect, on how to proceed? Yet it was so clear to me that with Bob's love of books, the publishing business would be a natural fit.

A day or so later, Bob said, "I think I will give Ted Spencer a call. Maybe he'll have some ideas. I smiled and shook my head. This was an early indicator of how Bob would behave in the future—accept my suggestions, let them simmer in his mind, and then act on them.

Ted Spencer had several of his books of poetry published by Harcourt Brace and was only too happy to contact his editor about Bob. He was pretty sure he could get Bob an apprentice position with a quick advance to a junior editor's job.

"Hooray!" Bob shouted when he hung up the phone. "You did it, Punchy. You had the idea and it paid off. Let's get Brooks and Helen and go to Buck's for a steak!"

"Ok, but no more drinking contests. Promise? I never want to see you in that bad shape again."

On the way to Buck's, I sat next to a very happy Bob, who was bubbling with plans and ideas. Secretly, I was reveling in my own little coup, sensing what had happened today—it was just the beginning of the off stage but influential role I would be playing as Bob's wife. I slid into it with no harsh side effects and knew that with each opportunity, my role would become more effective.

In a few days, Ted called back to say he had arranged for an interview with one of the vice-presidents of the firm for the following Monday. That day I stood waving goodbye as Bob's train receded into a blur, thinking how vulnerable he must feel but knowing he would rather face the jungle of New York than be in a life-threatening situation in Europe. His nightmares still plagued him but hopefully, with the stability of a job and a home of our own, they would gradually fade away. As I walked back to the car, there wasn't a doubt in my mind that Bob would be offered a job at the prestigious publishing firm of Harcourt Brace and Company.

The late afternoon train pulled into Easton and had barely reached the platform when an exuberant Bob hopped down shouting, "I got the job!" I hoped my smile didn't show my smugness, for I knew he would come home with a job in his pocket. I also knew with his gregarious personality and keen intelligence, he would win at everything he tried.

"Oh, congratulations, darling! I'm so proud of you," I cried, throwing my arms around him. "No more 52-20 Club. You're employed. Now, let's go home and tell everyone."

CHAPTER 10

Kitchen In A Closet

IT was the fall of 1945, and just like thousands of other veterans, we were staying with our folks until we could find a place of our own. During the four years of the war, not a stick of lumber had gone into new home construction, and as a result, there was a shortage of living space for the returning servicemen.

However, now that Bob had a promising new job, we at least knew we had to be in or near New York City. Unfortunately, Harcourt Brace Publishing, like all publishing companies, didn't pay very much for junior positions. Bob's salary was twenty-seven dollars and fifty cents a week, barely enough to cover rent and food. But it was a start and he would be doing what he loved most—working with words and ideas. I could see his newfound happiness ironing out the care lines in his face.

We set out to find an apartment in New York City and with the name of a reliable real estate company carefully tucked into the glove compartment. Nervous? You bet! But we were filled with enthusiasm and the Betts' old Packard fairly flew down the highway toward the big city and a new adventure. When we emerged from the Holland tunnel and started up Park Avenue, we both gasped at the awe-inspiring forest of glass and steel in front of us. It transmitted a powerful message:

**Here is where you can make it—or not
Are you ready?**

Still full of determination, we opened the door of Midtown Realty to a daunting sight. The office was overflowing with people all looking for suitable housing in a high demand, low inventory market. We checked in with the receptionist who told us to have a seat. It wouldn't be too long, she said. I smiled and thanked her but the bleak feeling stealing over me was hard to shake

At last the call came. "Betts?" We hopped up and followed a perspiring man into his inner office. One look at the furrows lining his forehead and I knew he didn't have good news. "It's a helluva bad time for you vets. I don't have much to show you but you can check these out. Wish I could do more." He handed us a list of addresses."

We starting walking, checking out one address after another all over Manhattan but there was always something wrong. Either the price was way beyond our means, or the apartment was too small for two people or it was too big or in a neighborhood that gave us the willies. All day we trudged up and down the sidewalks ringing doorbells until someone would come to greet us, and in a rare instance, we talked to doormen, without any success, in the more elite buildings.

At the very last address on Riverside Drive, we found a vacancy in a charming New York apartment building. But the minute we stepped into the entrance the stench of cabbage and garlic mixed with clammy, stale air hit us like an old dishrag. The central lobby was filthy—hadn't been touched by soap and water or a paintbrush in years. We found the right apartment and rang the bell. Nobody answered. I was secretly relieved. The whole atmosphere reminded me of Miss Bliss' boarding house and my whole being shriveled at the thought of living in this dirty smelly place.

We dragged ourselves back to the car and headed home, weary and dejected. Clearly, what we needed was a small miracle. There was one tiny hope left. Bob's oldest brother James was the program director of the YMCA in New Rochelle. He too was involved in the overwhelming task of finding living space in the suburbs for returning servicemen. We called that night and asked if he knew of any apartments in his area.

"I'll look around and get back to you as soon as I know anything," he told us. "It's not going to be easy, but I know a few people I can contact. I'll try."

This tiny bit of personal attention was our warm blanket in what was turning out to be a rather cold world. We thought of going back to New York City to make one more try, but decided to wait and see what James could uncover.

The very next night James called with exciting news.

"Budd, I think I found you and Emmie a place to live. It's in the Presbyterian Church Manse here in New Rochelle and good friends of mine who live in the house are willing to rent you the third floor. Would you like to come up and see what it's like? I know it's not New York City but the commute is great—only a thirty minute train ride."

"Gee, thanks James. We'll be there tomorrow by noon. It sounds great!"

We were on the road by nine the next morning. Hope smiled at us all the way. I had a good feeling that we were about to see our very first home.

We found the modest three-story house with no trouble. With its nondescript gray shingle exterior it was far from the rose-covered cottage of my dreams, but as soon as we met Mrs. Dassler, the kindly friend of James, and smelled the scent of apple pie baking in the oven, I knew we had found a place of our own.

The first flight of stairs to the second floor was wide and easy, but the second flight to our rooms was steep and narrow. At the top of the staircase there was a tiny hall with a closet at one end, a big bathroom off to the right and to the left two small rooms with teeny-weeny playhouse-size windows in each room. The thought of living up here under the eves set my romantic heart aflutter and I was already placing furniture. Of course, we never thought how the summer sun would turn these rooms into an unbearable sauna.

We moved out of the Betts' apartment swiftly, temporarily stashing our few belongings at James and Ruth's house until we had a space for them. Just as quickly we started on furnishing our new apartment with a trip to a used furniture warehouse, which yielded a maroon pullout sofa, a gold tweed chair and an old drum we could use as a coffee table—not high design but serviceable. A couple of worn Orientals rugs, donated by Bob's mother covered the bare floors. We splurged on a new country style bedroom set—the first brand new twigs in our own nest. On the day the bedroom set arrived I felt as rich as J.P. Morgan.

The movers took one look at the narrow steps to the third floor and I could see they were not very happy. Huffing and cursing all the way, they struggled with the furniture step by step until everything but the refrigerator was in place. "You want this in the bathroom?" they questioned, looking at me as though I had lost my mind. "In the bathroom," I said. "It's the only place it will fit." A refrigerator in the bathroom! Now that was unique.

At last all was in place and I began setting up the housekeeping I'd dreamed about. While Bob was getting acclimated to his job and the grind of commuting, I was prowling through stores looking for bargains. We improvised a kitchen in the hall closet with a three burner electric plate on a shelf and another shelf below it for the cooking utensils. It's a wonder I didn't set the place on fire. The temperature inside that two-by-four space must have been over boiling point many times. With sweat cascading down my face, I somehow managed to turn out very respectable dinners, especially the fried chicken done to a turn in the indispensable black iron frying pan from home. The cook, however, needed a cold shower and a change of makeup before sitting down to her culinary effort..

When we had guests for dinner, I set the card table with the good silver my mother had picked out for me, and my grandmother's embroidered, white linen tea cloth with matching napkins. I kept the few crystal glasses that were wedding presents, along with four place settings of my mother's gold and white china, left over from our house of sunshine, in a box under our bed.

But I soon tired of making every tattered or dull element in the attic rooms look like Cinderella's gorgeous ball gown. Time started hanging like heavy draperies in my day, each day dragging more than the last. I don't know what I expected from marriage, what thrill I thought I would have playing house with no one to talk to, but I was bored making the beds and hanging up the clothes. I sorely needed something more to fire up my imagination. I tried my hand at some art projects but there was not enough space to set out my paints, and I gave up that plan. I felt useless, slogging through the days, waiting for a breakthrough.

We had been living in our attic three or four months when Bob bounded up the steps one night earlier than usual. He had a mischievous look on his face. "It was slow in the office," he said, looking very smug, "so I decided to give you the benefit of my company for an extra hour tonight. What do you say? Let's catch some lasagna down at Joe's. I have something great to tell you."

"What's the big surprise?" I said as we slid into a booth and ordered two beers. "I'm dying of curiosity."

Bob lifted his glass. "Here's to us, Punchy! You are looking at the new sales representative from Harcourt Brace. I'm going to visit bookstores from here to Florida, west to Texas and back through Oklahoma, Louisiana, Mississippi, Tennessee, and Ohio and on home to New York. And I am going to come home with large orders from all of them. We are going traveling, baby!" he exclaimed. "A sales representative," he repeated, starry eyed.

"We are what?" I said.

"You heard, Punchy. We are going on the road. I am going to be a traveling salesman!"

I was stunned.

"I was told today that they were assigning me to the southeast and we leave soon, in a couple of weeks. I have quite a territory—twenty-three bookstores to visit in as many cities. It'll take about six weeks of hard driving and hard selling before we can come home. Are you up for this or do you want to go back to Easton and wait until I get back? Or you could stay here in New Rochelle." He sat back, lit from within, waiting for my reaction.

I sipped my beer, mulling over this exciting bit of news. No, I was not going to stay home and miss this adventure. It sounded like the perfect way for me to change my dull days for more exciting ones.

Bob rushed on full of enthusiasm, giving me a chance to sit back and listen and think. "If I do well, and I know I will, it's a great step toward an editor's chair. Selling books is a great way to learn the ins and outs of the book business and I have a feeling I have a future at Harcourt Brace. Well, what do you say?"

By this time I'd started to imagine being on the road. "Oh, it sounds wonderful! I wouldn't miss this for anything." But what would I do while Bob was in the bookstores, I wondered? I didn't feature sitting in the car or wandering the streets.

Even as he spoke, an idea was forming in my mind. "But wait," I said, "if you are going to sell textbooks, why can't I make a deal with the Harvard Press and try to sell some of their music books? I have some sales training and enough musical knowledge to sell a few books. I have seen what the Harvard Press has published and they would not be hard to sell. They're beautiful. I have a feeling Harvard Press would welcome some representation." As usual I jumped in with both feet before thinking it through. My suggestion met with no comment and Bob's face was just as non-committal.

Just as Bob's plate arrived he said, "Sure, sounds like a good idea. We'll get on it." The energy in his voice had waned.

I watched him spread his napkin on his lap without looking up. "The lasagna's good," he said.

I pushed on. "If it's all right with you I'll try to reach Harvard Press tomorrow to see if they are interested.

"Okay."

But I already knew he was not crazy about this idea of my pitching books. Now I didn't even know if he really wanted me to go with him.

We finished our meal in silence, paid the check and left. All the way home, I got the cold shoulder from Bob. I felt I was put outside like an unwanted pet, and I did not like the view from there one bit.

When we were getting ready for bed, Bob brought up the proposed selling trip again, but this time in an entirely different way. "Why did you feel you had to do something on this trip?" he started. "Why couldn't you have been satisfied to go along and enjoy the different sights and people along the way? But no, that wasn't enough. Now you want to do your own thing. What is it with you, anyway?"

Ooh, I knew I had treaded on precious turf when I blurted out my idea. Now I was on the defensive and I felt the heat rising in my face. "Well," I said, "I thought it would fill all those hours when you were seeing bookstores. What was I supposed to do? Just sit in the car and wait and do the same thing the next day? That's not very appealing. If I had music stores to visit while you were attending to appointments, we would have something in common to share and maybe learn from each other. But if you want me to forget the whole thing or maybe stay home, just say so. I need to know."

His answer surprised me. He crossed the room to me and gave me a big kiss. "You little vixen," he said chuckling. "You always get your way somehow, but maybe that's why I love you so much."

The next day, I called the Harvard Press and was connected with the head of the book promotion department who said he would talk it over with his colleagues and let me know in a few days.

Several days passed before Mrs. Dassler yoo-hooed from the bottom of the steps to tell me I had a phone call waiting. After taking the stairs two at a time I heard a hearty, "Yes" to my idea. The Harvard Press was shipping me a sample case of books and a list of music stores to visit. I was hired! Just as I was about to go bonkers from wifely boredom I was going to become a representative of the prestigious Harvard University Press.

I was jumping with excitement. But I had to be careful, when I told Bob, not to sound as if I had just bested him in a contest. I was already learning how easily a man's ego can bruise.

But again, he surprised me. "How did it go?" he asked, as he undid his tie. "Did they buy the idea? I had time to think about it coming home on the train and I like the combination. There may even be some bookstores along the way that have music sections you could visit." He gave me a lovely hello kiss, then went into our white giant in the bathroom and pulled out two beers. Handing me one, he said, "OK, what gives with my little adventuresome wife?"

"Oh, they loved the idea and are sending a sample kit and all sorts of information. I can't tell you how excited I am about this trip—for you first of all and now that I can be useful and establish some contacts for Harvard Press, I feel on the top of the world—and you are just wonderful to go along with this." I said with a big grin. "I can't thank you enough. I love you very much for understanding." I kissed him right on his big smile.

That night we caused the temperature in our bed to rise to surprising heights –in contrast to the near freezing ones over dinner the night before.

The little blue Nash we had purchased when we moved from Easton was put through the works at the local gas station so we would be trouble free on our trip. But it was a bare bones model, straight off the assembly line in Detroit. The auto industry was still gearing up for full auto production after its war manufacturing efforts and these newly minted cars could have hidden glitches that could come upon us with no warning. The garage mechanic did tell us to keep a watch on the alternator wires. He tightened them but they did have a tendency to work loose, he said. Thinking we had everything under control, we packed up the little car and were all set to leave New Rochelle for points south.

We closed the little windows in our attic, adjusted the temperature gauge in the refrigerator and lugged our suitcases down the steps and into the car. The Dasslers were at the door, waving goodbye and wishing us a good trip. "See you in six weeks," we said as we drove off. "I bet they are glad we're out of their hair for a while," I murmured. I had the feeling lately that Mr. Dassler really wanted his house back. Mrs. Dassler was a love and often asked me to have lunch with her especially when she made lamb stew, which she knew I loved. Him? He was not a nice man. He dug a hole and buried a nest of baby blue jays once—said he hated blue jays. I never forgave him.

We spent the weekend saying goodbye to both sets of parents who were apprehensive about our leaving for parts unknown. But we were filled with purpose and when Monday came, we left early on the first leg of our trip. I would be the navigator until Bob's head began to droop and he'd say, "You drive. I need a nap."

I loved driving and I was always glad to spell him. I love to get behind the wheel. There is no mistaking the power that you feel when you have two tons of metal at your command. It certainly was not like reading maps and noting motels from the passenger side of the car. We made a good team deciding where to spend the night, where to stop for dinner and then, when we spotted a phone booth, calling ahead for reservations.

Baltimore. Our first stop and I was in a tizzy. Bob let me off in front of a tiny music store that was almost hidden in a block of row houses. He went on to his appointment saying he would pick me up in an hour. I was full of New York pizzazz as I stepped into this Lilliputian hideaway and asked for the owner. "Hello," said a pleasant elderly gentlemen who had eyebrows that looked like white wings, "May I help you?" I cleared my throat and began speaking. By the end of my rehearsed speech, he had ushered me into his office and I had his full attention. I left, glowing about the order he gave me.

That evening, Bob and I meandered around the old city enjoying the tiny shops, the sound of street venders hawking strawberries and the beautifully restored four-masted schooners tied up at the waterfront. In our wanderings, we came upon a little restaurant on a side street that served soft-shell crabs. Bob's eyes watered with delight as he dove into these. As a kid, eating soft shell crabs at his grandmother's house in Ocean View, Delaware, was better than birthdays any day.

The thrill of driving down Pennsylvania Avenue in Washington, DC, was hard to match. To be in our nation's capitol—to see first hand where this magnificent country of ours was governed was incomparable. I gazed in awe at all the beautiful buildings and monuments as we drove around searching for 1015 Fifteenth Street, Bob's next appointment. My list of music stores did not include Washington so when he disappeared into the front door of Hudson's bookstore, I was content to sit in the car and wait for him. It gave me a quiet hour to reflect on the history this beautiful city held in every piece of stone and marble. I had a lump as big as a grape in the back of my throat. I guess it was called patriotism.

Our itinerary from here on was daunting—Richmond, Norfolk, Raleigh, Winston-Salem, Charlotte—but we were young and full of the spirit of adventure. Bob was having pretty good luck with his sales and I was being received courteously in most of my appointed music stores and was fortunate enough to write up some impressive orders.

But the further south we went the hotter it became. There were times when, as we trudged from one bookstore and music store to another, I was close to tears. The hot sticky weather made me very cranky and short tempered and sometimes I had little tantrums. Heaven must have taken pity on me for Bob announced, over our Southern ham and beans dinner in Charlotte, that we were one day ahead of schedule. "Why don't we spend the extra time in Atlanta?" he asked.

It was a welcome break for both of us, especially for Bob. I watched him as he walked through the museums or stood gazing reverently at the many monuments to fallen war heroes. He was thirteen again—a star struck kid with a passion for the Civil War and all its heroes. It was wonderful to see him come to life in the presence of something he loved.

Two nights and days in Atlanta and we were renewed. Our minds were filled with the city's rich culture and our bodies thanked us for the extra rest. But soon it was time to leave and we turned the nose of the baby Nash southward to Jacksonville. The fierce late afternoon heat and oppressive humidity made us damp and crabby, and we longed for evening and the cool shelter of darkness.

Mercifully, the sun began to dip lower in the west bringing cool fragrant breezes through our windows. We had reached the orange groves and there is no perfume in the world more intoxicating than orange blossoms This unexpected delight washed over us like cool rain, and made us glad to be alive on that warm summer evening.

About three hours out of Jacksonville, according to our map, our stomachs began to protest so we pulled into a hamburger stand for something to eat. "Do you mind driving?" Bob asked me after we tidied up. "I'm beat."

"Sure, go ahead and catch a nap," I urged, and he climbed into the back seat where he burrowed in and made a bed among all the paraphernalia. The moon kept me company on the lonely road, it's pale light turning the orange trees into ghostly armies marching to nowhere in the darkness.

I was moving along at a nice clip and listening to a local radio station, lost in the amazing zeal of a preacher yelling across the airways, shouting about being saved, when I was suddenly jerked into the fight or flight mode. There were blinking lights behind me and the low threatening growl of a police siren inched closer to my ear. I quickly checked the speedometer—fifty miles an hour. I wasn't speeding. I slowed and pulled over to the shoulder. Why would the Highway Patrol stop me? I made a mental check of everything that could be wrong.

A big burly trooper pulled up behind me and got out of his car. He walked toward me. When he was abreast of my window, I could see a peculiar smirk on his face. He signaled for me to roll the window all the way down.

"Now, where would you be goin' this time of night, little lady? Don'tcha know it's comin' onto midnight, the witchin' hour?" He chuckled with a deeply malicious tone. "Little girls like you could get into an awful lot of trouble if you aren't careful." He put his hand on the window ledge and stuck his red face into the car. He smelled of orange liquor and witch hazel. I felt a wash of fear come over me. Memories of Mr. Adamson loomed like specters.

"Bob," I called out, "this trooper has pulled me over and I think you ought to talk with him. I'm not quite sure what I did? " I said wide eyed and more curious than scared.

Bob came out of the back seat like a jack-in-the-box and stood facing the trooper.

"Okay, officer," he demanded. "Just what is the charge here? What did my wife do? She never speeds. We're on a business trip and I need to catch forty winks before Jacksonville."

The officer stepped back for a minute, but not before he put both his hands on his hips, one hand resting squarely on his gun.

Bob didn't back down. He glanced at his watch. "I need for us to be moving along. I have an appointment in the morning with the book buyer at Burdines and we have reservations tonight at Doc and Bea's Seaside Motel. They're waiting up for us. Anything else you want to know? Any reason you want to detain us?"

The trooper was clearly nonplussed. Just how far he would go in harassing a young lady I will never know, but when he saw that Bob meant business, his brazen front vanished and he stood there looking like a kid caught with his hand in the cookie jar.

"Sorry, sir," he said, shoulders slumping. "We kind of like to check the roads at night to make sure nothing goes wrong. I apologize if I upset you and the lovely young lady." He walked back to his patrol car.

"Wow." I said. "What do you suppose that was all about?"

"You get in the passenger side. I'm driving."

When we reached Doc and Bea's Seaside Motel in Jacksonville everyone had gone to sleep. But a security guard helped us to find our beachfront room. It was way past midnight and never had a bed felt better.

The sun woke us early, giving us enough time to take a quick swim before breakfast. But we had appointments to keep and off we headed to the bookstores in Jacksonville. When we reached Bob's first stop, Burdines, he checked his map and pointed me to Bowman's Book and Music Store. "Meet me back here in front of the swinging doors at noon, okay?" he said.

"I'll be there with a big order in my pocket," I told him. I found Bowman's and from the gaslight and hand-lettered sign, it looked like it had been lifted from a picture postcard of Harley Street in London. It was indeed quaint. Inside there were comfortable chairs where customers could sit and read after browsing. There were old carved bookshelves complete with a rolling library ladder. I'd detected a delightful mix of smells, old leather bindings and sandalwood. In a far corner there was a collection of vintage violins and music stands. A very pretty white-haired lady stood behind the cash register.

"Yes," she said with a questioning look on her face. "May I help you?"

I introduced myself and launched into my spiel. When I finished, the lady came around the register and put her hand on my arm. "Sit here," she said offering me one of the chintz-covered chairs. "How old are you?" she asked me softly.

"Twenty-three."

"And how long have you been selling music books?"

I felt my face color. "To tell you the truth," I said, "this is my first trip. I am with my husband, who is on a bookselling trip for Harcourt Brace Publishing Company, and I came with him to test the market for Harvard Press music books."

"Well, I think you'll do very well, with a few little refinements. My name is Miss Bowman," she said. Her pale blue eyes were shining with kindness. "Would you like to hear some of my bits of wisdom?

I somehow knew she was about to give me something very important—something not taught in sales courses.

With her gentle eyes still holding my gaze, she said, "Never pressure a customer. They hate to be hurried or pushed and will walk out if they are not allowed to take their time. And always excite their interest in a book by telling them something about it. It's the intimate sharing of something you both love that brings them back to buy from you again."

Miss Bowman continued talking for quite awhile. She regaled me with tales of her father, who had owned the shop, and other stories of how she stayed in business. I was completely immersed in her tender teachings when suddenly I remembered to look at my watch. Oh, no! It was twelve thirty. I jumped up, and nearly up-ended my chair as I hurriedly stumbled toward the door, thanking Miss Bowman as I ran backwards waving goodbye.

While I knew Bob would be concerned I couldn't wait to tell him how energizing my time with Miss Bowman had been. Yes, I felt badly that he had been waiting for me for half an hour and I was prepared to apologize and promise to never let it happen again. As I caught sight of Bob, I saw that he looked angrier than a stuck bull. Before I could open my mouth, he grabbed my arm in a vise like grip and with his jaw set, he growled, "Let's go!" He started marching me down the street to the parking lot as if I were a recalcitrant five-year old.

I tried to jerk away. "Let me explain, please."

Bob unlocked the car door and threw his briefcase in the back seat. Then he clammed up tight, his jaw set as he arranged himself in front of the steering wheel just like one of those marble Civil War statues that he loved. I climbed in and slid beside him, feeling like a naughty child, but with a contradictory feeling bubbling up — a feeling from childhood that I had been wronged.

I was still quiet as Bob turned the key in the ignition. I would wait until we were on the road. By then he would've calmed down. I waited, but the car didn't start. Once. Twice, even after a fourth go around there was no ignition. It was dead. *Oh boy*, I thought. *Now what?*

"Damn! Damn! This stupid car," Bob yelled. He slammed his hands on the dashboard twice. It was not the first time we couldn't get the car going, and I had a feeling it wouldn't be the last. Three days ago, we had stopped in a gas station outside of Raleigh when the car suddenly sputtered and refused to go. Bob was disgusted and went across the street to a bar and had a beer, while I hung around watching as the mechanic fiddled with the engine. He had noticed Bob go across the street and turned to me with a wry smile and said, "Are you the one in the family with car smarts?"

"Well, my father and brother knew a lot about cars. We sure had plenty of old beat up ones when I was growing up so I do know the front end from the back." He laughed and wiped his hands on an oily rag. "Well, Miss, I can tell you this baby of yours isn't very reliable in the alternator department so be prepared. When it breaks down again, you impress the next mechanic with your auto knowledge and tell them you know what the trouble is." He wished us good luck as we drove off.

Now here we were again — stranded with a car that wouldn't start. Bob was really fuming. "What the hell is going to happen next? First you keep me waiting and waiting, making me look like some jerk from the sticks in front of my clients. And I'm hanging around waiting for my wife *who*," he said with exaggerated politeness, "*seems to have far more important things to do with her time than honor my time.*" He quieted for a second before he charged in with another loud bellow. "How could you stay on and on regardless of how it affected *my* schedule? I had to cancel a late afternoon meeting because I didn't know where the hell you were! Why were you so late? Answer me! And now, we have no wheels. Shit and double shit."

I had rarely heard Bob curse and I sat there unable to think of one thing to say, wanting to hide in a dark closet. Yet all the time he was ranting I was thinking that sometimes I had a valid reason for disappointing him and in some ways I was also responsible to Harvard Press for my business time, as much as he was to Harcourt Brace for his. But explanations wouldn't have mattered at this point because here we were; the two of us in a dead car, twelve hundred miles from home, and now we were having a humdinger of a fight to add to our adventure.

Eventually, Bob shut up and we both sat staring into space. It seemed like an hour of silence. I don't remember whose mouth started to twitch first, but in a small burst, we both started giggling and then at last we were laughing out loud.

"Well, this is a pretty kettle of fish," I said. "What are we going to do?"

Bob hopped out of the car. "I think a good start would be to alert the parking guy before he leaves for the day and we are stuck here for the night. You stay here and I'll see what I can do," and he ran to the attendant's booth.

Inside of ten minutes, a tow truck arrived quickly and took us to a Nash dealer. Before the car was put on the lift, I casually mentioned to the mechanic that it just might be alternator trouble. His eyebrows lifted and he had a funny look on his face but said nothing.

While Bob and the mechanic were laughing and trading stories, I sat in the waiting room, thinking about what had happened. I was wrong to be late, for certain, but was Bob's explosive reaction directed at my tardiness? It was so forceful that it seemed out of balance for my actions. Or did it go deeper? It seemed extreme and not at all what I had expected. I did not like being shouted at or treated like a backward child. I came into this marriage gladly, even though it meant giving up my role as a self-supporting single girl. I remembered how good I felt about myself just a few months ago, how pleased at the way I was handling my life. Cashing that weekly paycheck was ego building. But that sense of independence was gone and I missed it terribly. I sat there feeling insignificant and stupid. But then I remembered I hadn't felt that way in Miss Bowman's shop. Maybe the reason I wanted to hawk the music books was a hangover from those days where I felt like I was making a contribution to the world.

I turned my thoughts to Bob. I did not understand his behavior. .At times, he was almost like a stranger masquerading as Bob Betts. I was just seeing the tip of his complicated personality and it was daunting to realize I didn't really know the man I married. .

Back on the road with our little balky Nash outfitted with a new alternator, we drove to New Orleans without too many complications. Fortunately, we got a room in one of the famous old hotels in the French Quarter and from that moment on we were caught up in the magic of that City in all of its former glory. We showered and dressed in our finest and set out to explore Bourbon Street. I gaped at the old buildings with their delicate Spanish grillwork while my mind pictured delusional Southern belles - much like Blanche Dubois - in their filmy nightgowns, waving drunkenly from those beautiful balconies.

We wandered in and out of the cafes that lined Bourbon Street. We ordered one of the house specialties in Jean Lafitte's Absinthe House and mingled with the unique mix of Creole, Cajun and black customers listening to the blues sounds from saxophones, singing mournfully of life in New Orleans. And then we found Galatoire's. "Oh, Bob," I pleaded, "Let's have dinner here. This is one of New Orleans most famous restaurants. C'mon, let's splurge."

"You're on," he said. "After all the hamburger joints we've dined in so far, it's time we gave ourselves a taste of the grand." He took my arm and we went through the highly polished mahogany double doors into the bright white-tiled dining room.

We stood before the Maitre'd in his impeccable tuxedo "Oui?" he inquired politely. We fumbled with our request and finally pointed to our wedding rings.

"Ah, Mariee? Marry"? He graciously beckoned us to a secluded table for two behind a couple of potted palms. He was obviously delighted with us and fussed over us endlessly while he chattered away in French. We did a lot of nodding and smiling—though we didn't understand a word of what he was saying. He ordered the specialties of the house - two of everything including the shrimp Andouille, then a crisp lettuce wedge with a tangy Creole dressing, and for dessert, their famous cheesecake. The rich New Orleans coffee served in gold and white demitasse cups made our hair stand on end. This evening was a high point in our first book-selling trip and I know we over-tipped the waiter and the kindly Maitre'd, but it was worth it.

A low hung Southern moon followed us as we walked down the alleyways back to our hotel, where, lulled by the food and drinks, we made love steamily, New Orleans style, while a mournful saxophone outside our window softly played the blues.

Early next morning, we were packed and on our way west to Dallas, our taste buds still tingling from Cajun spices and memories of a very romantic night making me purr inside.

We had a full days trip ahead of us so we turned on the radio and settled in for another long haul. I was busy tracing our progress on the map when Bob suddenly poked my arm. "How would you like to go sailing on Galveston Bay?" he asked.

"Galveston Bay? Sailing? Who with?"

"Remember Willie Cleveland, my roommate from Harvard? I knew he lived in this part of the country and I gave him a call back at the hotel. He invited us to come and go sailing with him in his new boat. Is that okay with you?"

"You bet it is!"

Following Willie's instructions to Bob, we checked in at Motel-by-the Bay just about dinnertime. The nice lady directed us to a small restaurant down the road where we had deep fried catfish, standard menu fare in these parts we found out. I wrinkled my nose but after the first bite, I found the dish delicious and I happily dug in.

The next day dawned cloudless with an east wind. Willie was waiting for us by the bait shack and while the boys had a backslapping reunion, I stood by gulping in the fresh salty air mixed with the swampy smell from nearby tidal ponds When we boarded Willie's sailboat, I went aft and hunkered down on a pile of orange life jackets. Soon, the ballooning sails sent us skimming like terns over the little white caps. It was delightful. The hours flew by as fast as the gulls that kept pace with our thirty-foot boat. But too soon the setting sun told us the day was winding down and regretfully, Willie headed back to the marina where we glided silently into our slip at dockside.

The next morning Bob and I were back on the road—a long, long road. The state of Texas is a big fat mama, surrounded by other states—normal size children. Texas is so big you can drive eight hundred and fifty miles in any direction and not come to another state. I kept looking around for some sign or feeling of friendliness in Texas but found none. The unbelievable distances between towns were wearying. We had to stop often at ramshackle roadside stands just to recharge and feel grounded. The sense of isolation in such a large expanse was unsettling, especially with the sun—the ever-present sun—beating down on us day after day, with an intensity as huge as the land itself.

Bob and I played a game of carving the miles into small chunks so we could have sense of making some progress. Instead of saying it was four hundred miles to San Antonio, we cut it into eight little fifty-mile trips. But anyway we looked at it, we spent many days in the car in Texas, bleary-eyed from the vast rolling prairies, dotted with oilrigs and great herds of longhorn cattle. Miles and miles of this repetitious view made me think God didn't have much imagination when he planned Texas.

But at last, hot, dusty and very weary, we arrived in San Antonio. The sight of the beautiful Spanish architecture left to us by the Conquistadors was well worth the long hours in the car. It was a beautiful city but it struck me as being incongruous in this stark landscape. It almost seemed like it was plunked down on the prairie by mistake. We were lucky to find a vacancy in an attractive motel with its own little backyard restaurant. The barbeque pit was fired up and running. When resounding clangs from the dinner gong sounded, we filled up on baby back ribs and chicken until I felt like a pig fattened up for market.

The next morning, even before contacting our bookstores, we had to pay a visit to The Alamo. The minute Bob got out of the car I could see how the walls, with their colorful history, had grabbed his attention. He fairly bubbled with excitement telling me about the bloody siege long ago and once again, I was the attentive listener, self-conscious about my shallow education.

That old feeling of being left behind rushed over me again bringing with it the remembered bitterness against my sister for switching my high school curriculum. But that was long ago. Today, I could look with pride at my order book swelling with each city we visited. These were modest orders of one or two dozen books from each store but added together it was an impressive showing so far. Bob was on his second order book, which was welcome news to the office in New York. So, for neophytes in the bookselling business, we were doing nicely, thank you.

For the first time since leaving New Rochelle, we could now head eastward and leave Texas behind to the cowboys and the cattle. We both cheered loudly as we crossed the Sabine River. But our elation was short-lived when we realized we were crossing the Sabine River the second time— back toward Texas again.

"I cannot believe you did this!" Bob roared, pounding the steering wheel."

Reading the map was my job and I thought we were going in the right direction but when Bob started yelling at me like he did in Jacksonville, the same ball of fear rose inside of me. I cringed.

"What the hell are we doing going back over the river? We've already crossed it once. You're the navigator and you're supposed to make sure we're on the right road.." His jaw muscle was pulsating with anger. I shriveled under his attack. Once again hurt and miserable, I was left wondering how such a small thing could trigger so much anger.

"I must have misread the numbers somehow," I murmured, chagrinned at my glaring error but still confused as to why it was such a terrible thing to make a mistake.

"Let's pull over where I can take another look at the map. Don't be so cross. It's just a small mistake—not a major disaster." But I could sense he was in no mood to have me smooth his ruffled feathers.

After we looked at the map together we were at last on the on the right road and made it to Birmingham, Alabama, by dinnertime. As in every place we visited, we spent a while cruising the streets looking for a decent motel to spend the night. This time we were lucky to find one almost immediately. The VACANCY sign looked freshly painted and the garden around it was overloaded with flowering bushes. A jolly man with spiky red hair checked us in and directed us to a diner in the next block that specialized in Southern fried chicken and Southern pecan pie. All this good luck rubbed off on Bob and over a foaming glass of chilled beer, his wonderful smile came out of hiding and he said he was sorry about the little squabble about the river crossing. So we were friends once again, but weary ones, and after dinner had just enough energy left to get undressed and fall into bed like two stone pillars, romance forgotten.

In the middle of the night, I awoke shivering all over. At first I thought I was dreaming or that I might be getting sick, but when I cleared my head a bit I realized the room was as cold as an icebox. It wasn't the air conditioning, for sure. We didn't have any in there. During the night the temperature in Birmingham had taken an unusual nosedive. We put on sweaters and socks and tried to get warm under the covers but the rest of the night was restless and uncomfortable. Finally we gave in and decided to get started earlier than usual.

When we opened the door to start loading the car, we were astonished at the sparkling wonderland before us. There was ice everywhere—coating the trees and bushes, and power lines, many of which had collapsed under the weight of frozen rain. Tentatively, like new kittens, we crept to our car but the little Nash was sheathed in a transparent coating so thick we couldn't get the door open. I stood there for a second, waiting for Bob to explode. It wasn't my fault that we were stranded and Bob, though he looked as if he wanted to lash out at something or someone, had to swallow his impatience.

The owners of the motel invited us into their warm office for coffee and lots of talk about the monster storm and the dangerous road conditions. Around noon, we finally gathered courage and said goodbye to our generous hosts. With Bob driving, looking like a tightly wound robot, I tried to calm my fluttering stomach by humming a little prayerful song I'd learned from Rosie and Yanna years ago. It suddenly started singing inside my head, taking my attention from the dangers of the road and back to the warm kitchen of my childhood. With our prayers and a little bit of luck, Bob skillfully avoided skidding into lampposts or the few cars brave or foolish enough to be out on the treacherous streets.

We reached the highway safely. The road and our mood improved rapidly and soon we were humming toward Chattanooga. As frightening as the ice storm was, I had to admit the past twenty-four hours had filled my need for variety and was a welcome break from our monotonous plodding through the lone star state

Unfortunately Chattanooga didn't send shivers of delight through either Bob or me. It looked just like Birmingham —sleepy and stuck in a Civil War time warp. We both found the bookstores here lacking in spontaneity or forward thinking. Maybe Lexington would prove to be a bit more exciting, but to our dismay, we found that despite the picture-book countryside, the climate of the book lovers was dreary. There wasn't much of a market in Kentucky for the sophisticated reader.

We had been on the road for what seemed like months with days and nights a kaleidoscope of vistas, colors and smells. We saw miles of country new to us, from the perfumed orange groves in Georgia to the sandy beaches of Florida; the steamy mangrove regions in Louisiana; the arid earth of Texas and Oklahoma. We gaped at huge cotton fields and peanut farms, steamboats on the Mississippi, the glorious mansions of Natchez. We traveled over the Great Smokey Mountains of Tennessee with our radiator boiling over, and we saw rundown towns and lush Kentucky thoroughbred horse farms. We were getting to know our country as well as ourselves. Now when we heard a Southern drawl or a Texas twang, we remembered the land that spawned these accents and we felt we knew our countrymen a little better.

Each day handed us a different and exciting challenge and for a first time experience, we did pretty well. But there were strained moments like the day we crossed the Ohio River when I was behind the wheel and Bob was navigating. We crossed the Ohio River three times just as we had done on my watch over the Sabine River out of Texas. I never yelled at him but the little devil inside of me did throw him a couple of snide but good-natured remarks about river crossings.

We were now in Columbus with still over twelve-hundred miles and five cities to cover before reaching New Rochelle and more and more I found the prickles of home-sickness becoming my familiar bedfellows at night.

CHAPTER 11

Three Martini Lunches

WE pulled into our driveway in New Rochelle at eight-fifteen on a balmy spring night in May. It was wonderful to be back in our funny little garret again, and it didn't take us long to sink into our own bed. I think we slept until noon the next day

Bob was greeted in his office on Monday like a returning warrior, home with the spoils. The orders from the bookselling trip had far exceeded their expectations. As for my bookselling efforts, the sales manager at the Harvard Press was full of congratulations for a job well done and hinted at a second book trip in the future. I thanked him and said I would think about it, knowing full well that it would never happen. I had enough of bookselling. I had done it and for a raw recruit, I think I did fine. But a second time around did not appeal to me one bit. Besides, I had other things on my mind since seeing those wisteria covered Southern mansions. I had to find a better place to live than our third floor attic.

The way was opened quite by accident. When we arrived at a neighborhood party the next weekend, the room was filled with people, but from a far corner I heard loud laughter and someone saying "and the apartments I'm building." Like a homing pigeon I headed in his direction. He was a real estate developer in New Jersey and, as far as I was concerned, my guardian angel had sent him and I had to make myself known. I introduced myself and plunged right into the big question of the housing shortage and what was being done about it? It seemed the Government was lending some support, but, for the most part, it was up to private enterprise to start filling the gaps and he saw this as a great opportunity to expand his company. As a result, he was doing a land office business constructing what he described as garden type apartments—two-story buildings with green areas and parking, and playgrounds for children. I tucked one of his color brochures into my handbag.

First thing the next morning, I approached Bob with the idea of the garden apartments in Ridgefield in my mind. Bob balked. "New Jersey? I don't want to go to New Jersey. Why should we move? We are fine here."

"It won't hurt to take a look before they are all snapped up," I said. "You know we can't stay here forever. This was a way station until we found a decent place to live." I paused before starting to counter his argument with annoyance...

"You think it's been fine here? Well, just take a look around," I said and swept the room with my eyes. "I think it's time we talked seriously about getting out of here. I know you hate to be moving again just when you get to feel comfortable where you are but it is very cramped. You're gone all day. I guess you don't realize how and I have to wrestle with make-do appliances and not even a decent sink to wash dishes. Do you think it's even remotely fun to cook a meal in a closet, or to have to put the milk in the bathroom? What about our china closet under the bed? Is that where we are going to keep our good dishes forever? " While I began to feel like a hawking fishwife I kept going. "Besides, I think the Dasslers would be very happy to have their third floor back. It's been two years and it is time we moved on." I started pacing back and forth in our tiny living room.

Bob looked up from the newspaper. He was clearly annoyed. "Getting to New York from New Jersey is a pain and who wants to live across the river, anyhow?" he said, putting down the newspaper. "You don't have any idea what it's like to be locked into that commuting bit. Getting up at daybreak—the train, which is stifling hot in the summer and then cold enough to freeze your behind off in the winter. Well, let me tell you, Emmie, it's no fun. And it wouldn't be any better in New Jersey taking the bus—probably worse."

He continued venting his displeasure at the whole idea of moving to New Jersey. I sighed. Bob's stubbornness was starting to fuel my own. For each negative idea he expressed about Ridgefield, I had an equally positive reason for moving there.

A couple of days later, true to his fashion, Bob brought up the subject of the very same apartments. "I called Bob Shine today," he said, "and asked if any apartments were still available. There is one left. So if you are still set on this, we'll go take a look. He can show it to us on Sunday afternoon."

Just seeing the apartment complex from the car as we drove up pushed my nesting instinct into motion. I liked the way the colonial style buildings were set back from the street and nicely tucked into the surrounding woods. I had a mental picture of me unloading the groceries and putting them away in our kitchen. I had already moved in before we even saw at the apartment.

I was not disappointed. There was a generous living room with casement windows that opened wide enough to let in all of the outdoors, and the sun was shining in everywhere. The little galley kitchen, still bigger than my New Rochelle closet kitchen had a refrigerator in the same room and other brand-new appliances. No more would we have to wash dishes in the bathtub. There were two good-sized bedrooms and a modern bath. If we didn't take this place, we were just plain crazy.

In less than two weeks and with a feverish burst of energy we moved in. I loved everything about this transition, especially the opportunity to decorate a brand new space. I spent long hours at the sewing machine making slipcovers and draperies, pillows and bedspreads. I slaved at giving the featureless rooms warmth and adding charm with a bit of historical accuracy from colonial décor. While I was happily engrossed in sewing machines and fabrics and cooking elaborate meals in what I considered a state of the art kitchen, Bob began his commuting routine with nary a grumble.

In a couple of months, the apartment sparkled with new drapes and slipcovers—even a new spread for our bed. I was as house proud as a little peacock, wanting praise each night from Bob. But my euphoria didn't last long when all I got was "yeah, that's nice." So much for that. The day I found myself walking aimlessly around the apartment, I decided I had better find something creative to fill my days or I was going to explode. I heard about an oil painting class in a neighboring town and enrolled. For six weeks, I was a happy lady learning the basic rules of oil painting, which I had never studied formally. But then the class was over and my motivation went with it.

I didn't get it. How could a clean floor or a sparkling mirror be fulfilling? I tried to console myself with all sorts of excuses, and would finally go to bed at night relieved that the day was over. Every morning I bounced out of bed ready for an exciting day, only to find my positive attitude dissipating by ten o'clock, replaced with ennui. I finally admitted a depressing fact. My life was boring.

Bob was doing extremely well at Harcourt Brace. He had been assigned to a senior official who wanted Bob as his assistant. This was definitely the step up the ladder he'd been angling for. But this reassignment had a huge flaw—his boss was a roaring alcoholic and liked nothing better than lunches that went on all afternoon, accompanied by endless scotch and sodas.

Of course, Bob had to go along. Some days it was a miracle he made it home without falling down in the street. He would show up at our door in an alcoholic daze, unable to use his own keys in the lock or do anything except head to the bedroom and fall asleep. How I hated seeing my clear, confident husband reduced to a bleary-eyed, shambling lush.

I saw myself again as a child waiting for my besotted father to drag himself home. I was becoming more and more disillusioned with him and our marriage and I wondered if there was any truth to the old saying that you married someone who was just like your father. It began to creep into my consciousness that I might not want to live with Bob, the alcoholic. Sober, I loved him. Drunk, I couldn't abide him.

Very late one night, Bob came home so drunk that he barely made it up the stairs. He fell into the doorway, groped along the walls and never even said hello to me before stumbling into the bedroom and onto the bed, clothes and all. I felt jilted—like it was another woman or the end of a love affair, which maybe it was. I didn't disturb him. I went about my business packaging the food that had been waiting on the counter for Bob and then I sat alone and miserable at the dinner table, picking away at the cold meat and vegetables on my plate. Tears of anger and self-pity started rising, making me almost ill. How could he? Time after time he was tossing aside what we were trying to build in favor of a lonely alcoholic who would just as soon take anyone's company as Bob's. How could he bypass me for that guy? Was there something wrong with me?

The idea of climbing into bed next to a drunken husband was repugnant. There had been many nights that I found solace on the den couch, sleeping there until morning. Bob would leave with hardly a "so sorry about last night".

On this particular night, I was beginning to feel trapped in a morass and it frightened me. Somehow I had to get out of this mess while I still had the courage. Fortunately, I had some money stashed away —hopefully enough to pay for a railroad ticket, so I decided to take the night train to

Saranac Lake, where Dot and Uncle Dick were living while Uncle Dick recuperated from Tuberculosis. I yearned for a shoulder to cry on and someone to help me find my way out of the tangled forest of my life.

My hidden sugar bowl money yielded more than I thought so I could go ahead with my plan. I tiptoed into the bedroom where Bob was snoring loudly. He was out cold. I changed into a warm sweater and slacks, and packed a small bag with a couple of changes of clothing and a few essentials. He never stirred. I grabbed a coat from the hall closet and without leaving a note, I left the apartment with my heart thudding below my ribs, belying my calm determination. It was a long walk to the bus stop and I felt heartsick and utterly alone but I determined not to turn back because going home would not solve the problem. Luckily I didn't have long to wait before an express bus to New York's Penn station came and with no hesitation I climbed aboard.

An hour later I was shoving my money through the ticket seller's window saying, "One way to Saranac Lake, please." One way? Did I expect to stay there? I called Dot and Dick from a phone booth. The call wakened them. My voice was trembling. "Dot, I'm in Penn Station about to take the train to Saranac. It gets in around eight tomorrow morning. Can you meet me, please?"

"Are you okay?" Dot asked anxiously. Does Bob know you are coming? Do you have enough money for the trip?"

I assured her I did and that I would explain everything when I got there. I started crying as I hung up.

"Be careful traveling," Dot said. "I'll be waiting for you."

There were few passengers on the train that night, and I found a seat in the front of the car, where I could stretch my legs. I was happy that no one noticed a young woman traveling alone late at night. I was feeling very down in the dumps and would probably cry loudly if given half a chance and I didn't want an audience. After one of the longest nights in my life, the train arrived on time in Saranac Lake. My sister was standing on the platform, looking worried and tired. Gone were all the bitter feelings about being compared with her that I had harbored for so long. Now that I was married, I had some insight into her and how she was burdened with the worries of my future because my parents were so unsettled. Without those concerns she had relaxed and she and I were beginning to find a friendship that had been either undiscovered or buried for years.

"Are you hungry?" was her first question. "I have breakfast waiting at the cottage.—my special, waffles and bacon, fresh orange juice and lots of hot coffee. Dick can't wait to hear the tale of woe that sent you running off into the night. Neither can I," she added, as if this was a chapter in "True Romances.".

"Hi, kid!" Dick said when I came into the room. He was sitting up in bed and he looked better than he'd ever looked before. "You look like hell," he said, gruff but kind." Go wash your face and have some coffee. It'll make you feel better." A tiny bit of hope appeared in my heart. There might be a way to solve everything, I thought, as I dug hungrily into a hearty breakfast, surprised that I could eat. I finally pushed my chair back, stood up and announced in a firm voice, "I'm married to a drunk and I hate it!"

Dot sat up straight in her chair and adjusted her face to conceal her shock. Uncle Dick lowered his head and peered over his glasses "Oh ho! So that's why you ran away," he said. "Sounds like your old man all over again."

I flinched. Then, Dot put her arm around me and led me to the couch. "I'm so sorry to hear this. How long has this been going on?"

Now at last I could spill out the misery I had inside—how disillusioned I was with Bob and our marriage—how nothing seemed to be going right and, of course, I was blaming it all on his uncontrolled drinking. There were many problems, but his drinking was the worst.

Dick listened and instead of consoling me he said matter-of-factly, "Well, kid, Bob called around dawn looking for you. It's been a helluva night with you two ringing us up at all hours. He's on his way and probably will get here by early afternoon." He seemed amused by us and at the same time annoyed. "What are you going to do when he gets here? Are you going to have a teary and dramatic scene?" he said with a lopsided grin.

My resolve not to live with a drunk was a thin one when I heard this. He did care. He cared enough to follow me all the way up here. I swallowed hard. "Well, I guess we'll have to put everything on the table, Uncle Dick,"

I managed to spill out the feeling of emptiness in my life. I couldn't tell him that housework bored me—that chasing dust balls or admiring my streak-free windows just didn't have the power to thrill me because he wouldn't understand that. Dot loved housework. I couldn't tell him my desire to paint had been stifled. He had no interest in art or the creative world. I tried to tell him I was missing the joy of every moment that I remembered having years ago. Now my days were filled with apprehension about how Bob would behave when he came home. If only he could control his drinking life would be a lot brighter for me. I tried taking my problems to God but going to church didn't help. Besides, Bob frowned on anything that smacked of organized religion and I didn't want to argue with him about that too. Much as I hated to admit it, our honeymoon was long over and we were having big difficulties adjusting to the everyday side of married life. Bob's stimulating workday was the flip side of mine and I had nothing interesting to say to his inevitable question, "Well, what did you do today?" It was not a good situation. I rambled on an on to Dick.

By the time my sister cleared the lunch plates I had to beg off for a nap. I was sad and soul weary. Sleep came quickly. I don't know how long I was asleep when in the dimness of that state between sleep and consciousness, I became aware of far off voices, rising and falling—the bedroom door opening and closing—someone standing over me. I opened my eyes. "Hi," Bob said sheepishly, as he sat down on the side of the bed. He hadn't shaved and looked tired and disheveled like he "had been pulled through the eye of a needle," as my mother often said. "How about you and I go to a hotel and have a long, private talk. I've reserved a room and we can relax there. We shouldn't burden Dot and Dick."

Despite my anger, I found myself so glad to see him I was tongue-tied and could think of nothing else to say except, "Good idea. Give me a minute and I can pull myself together."

Bob left me to freshen up but when I reappeared in the living room and saw Dot and Dick staring at me, it was hard to act normal. My stomach was tossing like a stormy sea and attempts at small talk were awkward and dumb. Uncle Dick kept poking fun at us, which began to irritate me. Since he had been married for a long time, he may have thought this dilemma was something to laugh about, but to Bob and me it was just the opposite, testing deep concerns in both of us.

On the way to the hotel Bob and I hardly spoke. I was the little girl who had run away from home. All the words I thought of during the lonely eight-hour train trip were left behind with my self-assurance in that cold, dusty train coach. Here I was, mute and staring like a department store mannequin. Bob was silent too, until we stepped inside our room and he shut the door behind us. Abruptly, he took me in his arms and hugged me for a long time. Tears stung my eyes.

"I'm so sorry I caused this mess," he started. "I haven't been fair to you and I know it. Driving up here in the car gave me plenty of time to think about things. I've behaved in a rotten way and I want you to know I take full responsibility and give myself a failing mark at marriage." He crossed the room and lit a cigarette. "I don't know what we should do, Emmie, but maybe I should move to the Harvard Club until we figure out the future." He took a deep drag. I watched the smoke come out of his mouth. " It will give us time to think things through," he said.

Oh, my goodness! My whole body froze. This was terrifying and hardly what I expected to hear. Not having Bob in my life was unacceptable. In spite of everything I said to the contrary to Uncle Dick and my sister, Bob and I belonged together. We were building a close relationship and somehow I knew that it was harder than just saying I do. I did know at that very minute that I wanted to continue to try, but I also knew we needed to find out what marriage was all about. No one had really told us, and if they did, would we have listened?

"Is moving out the only solution you have? There are a few others that we could talk about. The only reason I came up here was to jolt you into some sort of action about controlling your drinking. You drink too much and you can't handle it and that's what started all of this. Once you admit to yourself that you have a problem with alcohol, we can work on it. But if you want to move out fine, but I don't think it's the answer."

I crossed over the room and moved closer to him "I am willing to do anything to help you, because I love you and want to spend my life with you, but not if booze sets the whole tone. Because if you let that happen, you are going to ruin your life, and our life together."

He looked straight at me. I saw regret and misery in his eyes as he said "I'm willing to do my damnedest to turn things around. I love you deeply and don't want to lose you, so if you're willing to take me back, I'm ready." His arms gathered me close once more and grateful tears swam in my eyes. I whispered the words that both of us wanted to hear, "Yes. Bob, let's go home."

For awhile, there were no more drunken homecomings. Our Saranac soap opera had come to the end of the first chapter. But a little voice inside of me cautioned against betting this was the "and they lived happily ever after" ending.

One night, Bob came home from work full of enthusiasm. I sensed he had a plan when he started the conversation with, "wouldn't it be nice to have a pet to play with and keep us company? He'd greet us with tail wagging like crazy when we walked through the door, wild with joy at our return. He would be a loving companion, right?"

Well, what a great sales presentation, I thought. I waited. He went on to say that there was a guy in the office who suggested we go look at a litter of Dalmatian puppies. "He knows the kennel owner and he raises champions," he said.

"A dog?" I said. My scalp tingled.. "No! I don't want a dog. Not now." You know who is going to have to take care of it, train it, baby sit it? Me. That's who. And it's the last thing I want to be doing."

"Oh, c'mon honey. You'll love having a dog once we get used to it and I promise I'll help." (Oooh, I'll remember those days until I die!)

Well, Bob was set on getting a dog, so early the next Saturday morning we set out to northern New Jersey and the kennel. For a while, I lost myself in the beauty of the landscape until we pulled up to a kennel and then to a pen full of black and white spots jumping all over each other, having a rollicking good morning tussle. There was no denying that these were beautiful animals, but I couldn't bring myself to any high pitch of enthusiasm. I strolled around the pen, my intuition screaming, "Don't do this! Don't let Bob get carried away, taking you with him!" But he had already picked out *his* dog.

"Look at this one, honey!" he exclaimed. "This little guy has more personality than all the others put together. See how he's jumping up and down, grabbing my finger like he's saying 'pick me, take me home with you'. This is the one, Emmie. Let's find the owner and tell him we want him."

I looked at the little bundle of energy and knew that Bob had picked the prize product of inbreeding for show only- the result being a puppy with the wired-up personality that Bob found so appealing. The dog had a highfalutin name—Huckleberry of Tomalin Hill. Bob promptly named him Hucky. .I sulked all the way home. My intuition told me this dog was bad news and would bring nothing but grief into my life.

It wasn't long before I had a dozen phone calls about Hucky from the neighbors, begging us to shut him up because he barked and howled non-stop when we were out. I made a huge scene and demanded Bob take him back to the breeder. Bob ignored me until the rental management office sent a nasty letter to us saying that if we couldn't control our pet, we would have to leave the premises. When I showed Bob this bit of news, he hit the ceiling.

"What did you expect?" I shouted. "This dog is a real pain and nothing but trouble. I tried to tell you that from the beginning,"

Bob left the room without responding, always a sure sign that he had washed his hands of the whole thing.

CHAPTER 12

The Reign Of Hucky, The Horrible

HUCKY won. We had to leave our charming apartment in Ridgefield.and the house hunting started all over again. I spent hours poring over the real estate section of the *New York Times.* Finally I found an ad for a house that fit our needs in Tarrytown, New York. Strangely enough, it was in another church manse—this time Episcopalian. As I dialed the number I fervently hoped for better accommodations than attic rooms. A friendly voice answered and introduced herself as Mrs. Walsh and immediately launched into a sales pitch about Tarrytown.

"It's full of fascinating history from the Revolutionary days and just up the road, is Sleepy Hollow, the inspiration for Washington Irving's 'Legend of Sleepy Hollow.' Oh, there is so much to tell you. Can you come up this weekend?"

She sounded like an agreeable lady who would put up with a dog. I crossed my fingers. "Before we go any further, I have to tell you we have a dog. Is this going to pose a problem?"

"Oh, that's fine dear, as along as he doesn't dig up my gardens," she said. "Flowers are my hobby and I would hate to have anything happen to them."

With a silent prayer, I assured her.

The next Saturday we drove to Tarrytown. We came upon a magnificent gray stone Episcopal Church with a lovely old Colonial house beside it. The grounds were well manicured, and I got a glimpse of a stunning flower garden. A little flag went up in my head. But I paid no attention.

The church's Reverend Walsh and Mrs. Walsh, his sweet wife, welcomed us and ushered us into a bright living room overlooking Mrs. Walsh's lovely garden. I fell in love with the way the sun chased every shadow from the dark corners; the Colonial fireplace, an architectural object of many yearnings—the big cheery eat-in kitchen and cozy attic bedroom. I nudged Bob. "Let's take it, it's perfect". He nodded and we signed the lease within an hour. The part Bob liked best was it was only three blocks to the railroad station. No more buses!

I forgot about the reason we had to move and we settled in happily, but it was not long before the cunning Hucky had somehow slipped into Mrs. Walsh's prize winning garden and had a field day, chomping the heads off her magnificent flowers. I had looked out the back window and seen him as he was halfway through his crazed rampage. I dragged him inside by the collar, while he whined and dug in his back legs. As we got inside he threw up all over our new rug. I was one mad housewife when Bob came in the door.

"You go talk to Mrs. Walsh." I demanded. "She's steaming! Those were her prize chrysanthemums!" But, as usual, Bob thought this whole caper was hilarious. He went next door to apologize to Mrs. Walsh and sweet-talked her into accepting the fact that Hucky had a few quirks. She was such a lovely lady with so much charity in her heart that she gave Bob a smile in return for his cross-my-heart promise it wouldn't happen again.

Now I was a warden, watching Huck constantly to make sure he stayed out of trouble. Bob was no help at all, sabotaging every effort I made to train this unruly animal. He thought Hucky was clever, cute and so what if he does misbehave? I would have some luck in making him stay when I gave him the order but then Bob would come along and destroy it all with "Hey, boy—how's my Hucky?" and of course, the dog would leap into Bob's arms. I finally gave up.

The winter months found us fantasizing about a trip, going through dozens of travel brochures that tempted us. We were hoping in April we could take the month off and bring our fantasies to life. We had a little nest egg that would allow us to do this, thanks to Bob. When the war ended, he was among the thousands of GI's coming home on the old Queen Mary and during the five day passage had won about five thousand dollars in poker– a tidy amount that would take us anywhere we wanted to go in fine style. Also, Bob had edited the American edition of an African safari tale, written by a white hunter from Scotland. In working together across the sea, Walter Bell and Bob became friends, and Walter had invited us to visit him and Katie in the Scottish highlands.

"Oh, how wonderful," I exclaimed. "How romantic! Imagine! The Scottish Highlands; the Hebrides; the Isle of Skye. Aren't we the lucky ones having this chance to stay in a hunting lodge with an African white hunter?" And, I wondered, what does one wear in Scotland? First thing on the list, though, was to make an appointment with the gynecologist for a check up. I wondered why my period was a week late and I wanted to be sure I was fit for the trip.

But our trip was still three months away and right now we had Christmas to think about and we were looking forward to celebrating with our friends and families. So, as soon as Bob's office closed, we gleefully packed up our little car with presents and were on our way to Easton for the three day holiday.

January came teasing me with its traditional thaw followed by bitter cold and snowy days where I curled up in our lumpy second-hand chair and daydreamed about all the sights awaiting us in Europe. It was on such an afternoon that the phone rang.

"Mrs. Betts?"

"Yes," I answered, wondering who was calling.

This is Dr. Braun's nurse. I have some good news for you. The test on the bunny was positive and you are six weeks into your pregnancy. Congratulations!"

The phone went dead in my hand. Me pregnant? I had let that thought come through my head once, and very quickly. Suddenly, with this real news I started wheeling and dancing around the room, beside myself with joy. I was going to have a baby!!! Me! I could hardly wait until Bob came home. As soon as I heard the door open and his familiar "Hi, honey, I'm home" I ran to him and threw my arms around him, laughing like a delighted child.

"Hey, whoa. What's going on? Did you win the lottery or something?"

I shook my head. "No, something much, much better. You, Mr. Betts, are going to be a daddy!"

Instantly, his smile disappeared, and he stiffened and stepped away from me. "Well, that's a fine state of affairs," he said curtly.

I was astonished. I thought he would be jubilant—not angry. Hadn't we made this baby together? What was wrong with him? I was hurt and angry, but worse, filled with disillusion. I felt my face crumpling with this kick in the teeth.

Bob turned cold eyes on me. "Just when you and I were planning a trip to Europe, you had to go and get pregnant. That was not a part of our plan." He stomped up the stairs.

Dinner that night was a silent affair. I was fuming. Where was Bob's tenderness—his joy at this incredulous news? Only the sound of knives and forks hitting the plates could be heard. By the end of the meal, my hurt had turned into real anger. I sat back in my chair and with a fury that would send people running in the other direction, I started firing my artillery.

I folded my arms across my chest. "Okay, Mr. Betts, will you please tell me what in the hell you meant by your cold reaction and nasty comments about my pregnancy? You may not know it, but you hurt me terribly. And you are forgetting that you did have quite a lot to do with this. This is what we both wanted so why are you so unhappy?" I took a big breath. Up until now I had only been bewildered when Bob turned against me. I knew sometimes I embarrassed him and he would react coldly but with this display of anger over my pregnancy, a real mean streak had surfaced in him. Like a spoiled child who couldn't have things his way, he had pouted and stomped off. God had touched us with this blessing and I should have been feeling full of grace but instead there was emptiness inside me, crying out for understanding.

Bob sat with a hangdog expression on his face. He said nothing for a while and then looked back at me with eyes that begged for forgiveness. He reached across the table for my hand. I hesitated for just a moment—still stinging from his behavior—then put my hand in his.

He cleared his throat. "I don't know why I said those things. I am sorry but your news was such a surprise I just wasn't prepared, that's all. Sometimes when I'm caught off guard I say things I don't mean. I was wrong. Please forgive me if I hurt you. I didn't mean to, honestly."

In the weeks before leaving for Europe, Bob calmed down about the baby and started accepting fatherhood. I had been hurt and shocked—the healing slowed by my remaining bitterness. My disillusion in him? Well, we were young and there was a lot of growing up ahead of us. Who could really know how each of us would mature?

The long flight to Paris, our first stop, left us weary but after eight hours in the hotel's heavenly featherbed, we were eager to explore the beautiful city of lights. We walked miles and miles every day and night, searching out the famous places and exploring little shops and museums until our legs gave out. We were charmed by off the beaten places, shaded by chestnut trees, and bordered by little shops selling baguettes and irresistible pastries. Fortunately, I did not suffer from morning sickness. I remember the first patisserie we discovered and how I started pointing at everything in the display case until we had the baker, still in his flour-covered apron, laughing and shaking his head at these eager young Americans.

After eighteen days we felt as if we belonged there, but it was time to move on. The channel boat to London pitched and tossed causing Bob to turn an unhappy shade of green. Fortunately, my stomach stayed steady. We checked in at the Brown Hotel, dropped our bags and soon we were out the door eager for all the sights in this great city. Next day, it was Eton and Canterbury then a few hours sleep and then the four a.m. train to Edinburgh and on to Inverness and the most exciting part of the whole trip—"Corriemoillie" and the Bells in Scotland.

It was easy to spot Walter our host. He was dressed in tweed knickers and woolen socks. He was a tall erect figure with the bearing of a Masai warrior and white-hair. His skin was weathered from years under the African sun.

"Hello, our American friends," he said in a rich Scottish brogue. His wife, Katie, stood by his side, holding out her hands. Her gray hair sprouted from both sides of her head, not sure which way to go, and her aging face held a glow that was captivating.

After much confusion stowing luggage and deciding who was to sit where in the old Bentley touring car, we settled ourselves for the trip to Garve, the little town where they lived. I stared out the window at the beauty of this wild land. I dimly heard Walter pointing out certain things along the way, but I was too busy drinking in the vast stretches of heather-covered moorland, gently rolling up to distant hills.

We drew up in front of a large century-old, three-storied stucco house. There were many gables jutting from the roof and two enormous chimneys, with many flues, which told me this house never knew central heating. I shivered just thinking of the frigid winter, when the wind swept through the house on an icy broom. Cathy and Alice, the village girls who helped in the house, stood waiting by the front door, giggling and blushing. They curtsied sweetly before taking our bags to our rooms. Katie told me how hard they worked to make the house shine for us—polishing and waxing and even grooming the cats. Now they had laid a tea in front of a crackling fire in the library. What a lovely way to welcome us, I thought.

Later, Bob and I stood in our bedroom gazing out of the old six-paned windows. The glow from the setting sun had caused the hills to shimmer with iridescent colors much like ripe Concord grapes and ancient gold coins.

"Beautiful, isn't it?" Bob said softly as he stood at my side. "No wonder Walter and Katie love this place. It's a piece out of the past. I would bet this part of Scotland hasn't changed since the days of Sir Walter Scott, and maybe he would come up here from Edinburgh for inspiration." He gathered me close and plucked a poem out of the air.

"Oh many a shaft at random sent/ Finds mark the archer little meant/ And many a word at random spoken/May soothe or wound a heart that's broken."

How touching, I thought-a literary gem at exactly the right moment. He kissed me tenderly. "I love you and I am happy—*very* happy about the baby.

Our first day in the Highlands ended on a beautiful note.

After a five-star breakfast, Walter took Bob by the arm and they disappeared. I was delighted when Katie asked me to come along while she fed the chickens. Together we laughed at all the fluttering and cackling from the little flock, as we tossed the seed on the ground. After we put away the bucket, we wandered down to the orchard for some crabapples for the deer. "They come very early in the morning," she said, "and they eat them right off the kitchen windowsill. It's a lovely sight." We walked slowly, talking about ourselves and our lives.

My admiration for these people grew steadily but the days were all too short. In the early morning, Cathy would slip quietly into our room, and place a breakfast tray of hot tea and scones on our bedside table. Such an endearing gesture—so unlike our rise and shine, get in the shower routine. One morning, as I was watching the deer have their breakfast of crabapples, Walter came into the kitchen, and asked if I would like to go shooting. Of course, I was thrilled that a legendary white hunter would ask me to accompany him on a shoot. "Can you handle a gun?" he asked with a kindly smile. "I've had a few lessons with a rifle," I told him, and "yes, I would love to come."

He steered me to the antique gun rack by the front door, and pulled out his favorite. Then he chose a delicately made shotgun for me, loaded his hunting jacket with shells, and we were ready. The two of us took off to chase the noisy crows, always making a ruckus, and disturbing the tranquility. We walked slowly, chatting like old chums, and finally reached the edge of the woods where the black birds tended to gather. Walter handed me my gun and loaded it for me and handed it back. "Are you ready?" he asked. I nodded and he fired off a shot to flush the birds. "Now," he commanded, and I aimed and fired along with him. A bunch of them came down. He turned to me with a big grin.

"Excellent shot, my dear," and patted me on the shoulder.

I don't think I hit one, but being the gentleman, he gave me the credit.

Walter and Katie never had children and a pregnant lady in their house was a rarity. They fluttered about like nursemaids, making sure of my comfort. This small exposure to parenthood impacted them so strongly that when they died they'd left a modest legacy for our child.

It was a wonderful month in Europe, but it was great to be back in our own country. We had the baby to look forward to—a boy for me or a girl for Bob, and a problem of where we were going to put a crib and other baby paraphernalia. One night, I stuck a newspaper ad for a house to rent in front of Bob, and started talking.

"You know," I began, "we are not very popular around here anymore."

"And just what is that supposed to mean?" Bob answered testily.

"You refuse to admit we have a problem with *your* dog. He's impossible to train and if you had to clean up his poop all day the way I do, maybe you would see things from my angle. I have to follow him constantly to make sure he doesn't surprise me with another disaster. Today, it was the phone books. When I came in from the store, it looked like a parade had gone through the living room. There was yellow and white ticker tape everywhere."

Bob howled with laughter at this, which started the steam rising in my head. I went on. "He demolished every one of them, and ate a lot of the paper, which, of course, he threw up all over the rug. And yesterday, he ate my angora gloves. Are you listening to this? "I shouted. " He had to stand on one of the chairs by the fireplace to get them. They were on the mantle! Last week, the phone rang and by the time I got back to the kitchen, he had gobbled up all the grease from the broiler pan, and there was all that gooey mess when he threw it up. Well, who do you think had to clean that up?" I paused, hoping I wouldn't start crying again. "Mrs. Walsh is deathly afraid of him. He snarls at her, if you can believe that of your precious dog. But most important of all is we are going to need more space for the baby.

Even if you are blind to your crazy dog the baby will need a crib and floor to put it on."

"So, get to the point. I know what it is—you have the moving bug again, don't you?"

I thought about that for a second. Just because we needed a bigger space didn't mean it was my problem.

"What is it with you? Can't you be satisfied with what you have?"

"Damn it, Bob! This time there are good reasons to move on. Until we find a house, every move is temporary. We both agreed to that. I can't let your dog off the leash, and he is getting bigger and stronger, and I'm pregnant and off balance. I'm afraid he'll pull me right down one of these times. What Hucky needs is a yard where he can run off all that energy or you'll have me in the loony bin. And then you won't have to move at all. "

As usual, Bob threw up his hands and walked away.

After dinner, I brought up the ad in the newspaper again. "Can't we just find out if it's still available," I pleaded. "It's probably taken by now, anyway."

"I can see I won't have any peace until we do, so go ahead. Make the call.

"Hello, who is this calling please?" asked a flowery voice on the other end of the line.

In a rush, I told her who I was, what I wanted, and was the house still available?

"Oh, yes, it is, but I have to know something about you," trilled the voice. "You see, we want only highly recommended tenants, and before we sign a lease, I would have to meet you, and make sure you are the kind of people we are looking for. Come up this weekend, and we can meet each other. From the sound of your voice, I think it will work out just fine."

I took a deep breath and said, " One more thing. We have a dog."

"Oh," she said, "I love dogs."

Hah! Wait until she meets this one, I said to myself.

By Saturday, Bob was in a better mood about our third move in five years. Frankly I was tired of the packing and unpacking and all the bickering that goes with moving. I silently prayed that the next house would work for us so we could at last settle down.

Our hopes were high as we searched out the address but when we parked beside the house, my heart fell. Was this it? This plain and non-descript box of a building? It was about as appealing as the stark and unforgiving house in Grant Wood's painting "American Gothic". No adornment softened the building's hard lines. A small front porch looked like an afterthought. There was no lawn, not even a green bush to grace the entrance. I looked at the hard-packed clay, rippled with rain-sculpted gullies, and asked about grass. "Grass? Oh, honey," laughed our realtor, who had lived up to her flowery voice, "We tried to grow grass, but that big tree makes it impossible for anything to grow under it. I sighed and scratched green lawn off my list. We walked up the cracked cement walk and up two wooden steps to the porch and front door. Inside, the rooms were small, square and stark, and I could see it would take a "heap o' livin'" to make this house a home. Don't be picky, cautioned the small voice inside of me.

The second floor held three small bedrooms and one bath, all looking like lost children longing for love. Compared to our charming little place in Tarrytown, this place was woebegone.

As our flowery realtor was flitting about, gushing about this and that, how convenient it was to the stores and the railroad station and how she knew we were the perfect couple for the house, I made an on-the-spot decision at the same time as Bob did. We would take it. It was not the enchanted country cottage I had visualized but we had a baby coming and we were in a time bind.

So our next home was in Bedford Hills, New York and as soon as we arranged the furniture and hung the freshly laundered curtains, the little "Grant Wood" house took on some warmth and the look of a home. We did some of the moving ourselves to save money and during the many times we loaded our car and made trips back and forth from Tarrytown, I thought of all the times my mother had to pack up and move. Sometimes it was because they couldn't afford the rent, but mostly they moved to chase job opportunities in other towns for my father. It was a matter of survival for us and certainly not the happy need facing us. Bob's words made me wonder. Did he have a point? Did I inherit a moving bug of sorts?

Everything we needed was just a short walk away, including the railroad station, which Bob considered a big plus. I began to make friends with the grocer, the butcher, the people who ran the cleaners and the owners of the drugstore that still had an up and running soda fountain where they treated me to a cherry Coke to celebrate my arrival in the village. For an obstetrician I was referred to the Mt. Kisco Medical Group. I felt all my doubts and fears dissolving as I gave myself over to Dr. Robertson, a kind and gentle person. We talked about things I should and should not do; what to expect at certain times; what to eat; how to dress, exercise, sex—everything. Then he asked if I had anything to say. When I told him that I hoped to have this baby by the Grantley Dick Reid method of natural childbirth, he jumped up, slapped the desk and shouted, "Hooray! At last I have a real girl! For months, I have been trying to coax these hilltop debs into Reid's method, but they all want to be knocked out and wake up with a baby in their arms. Now you come along and make my day!"

It wasn't long before Bob and I became "those people with the crazy dog." Fortunately that didn't stop the neighbors from asking us to join them for barbecues or church suppers. One night, at a VFW chicken dinner, we met Spud and Lucille, who made us feel like old friends from the very start. Spud and Bob became buddies and let down their hair whenever they could, stealing away many Saturday mornings to get in a round of golf. Of course, their favorite hole was the 19th hole, where the two of them loved to tarry and start the weekend with an alcoholic buzz.

The year was 1950. TV was in its infancy and one day we decided to break open our piggy bank, literally, and spring for a set. It was a great moment when the television arrived and was placed on the stand in the living room. Bob, not the greatest mechanic in the world, had asked Spud to help him put the antenna on the roof. This sounded like hold-your-breath time for me. I knew how things like this could turn into disasters where Bob was concerned. But bless ole' Spud. He appeared after work one evening, grinning like a Cheshire, good as his word and ready to tackle this operation.

We all trooped upstairs and I watched the two of them climb out the bedroom window to the porch roof. A chill went through me as I recalled the night my brother risked his life to restore our electricity. At any moment I expected a body to come hurtling down, landing with a thud on the porch roof. After what seemed a long time, I heard Spud yell, "Okay." He had the metal clamps in place around the chimney and the antenna was secured. Hooray! There it stood, ready to bring us the world. Flushed with their success, the boys decided to come down to get a fresh supply of beer and, while they were at it, they grabbed their five irons and a supply of practice balls.

"What are you crazy guys going to do?" I asked, suspecting mischief.

"Just a little practice round, honey," came the answer along with knee-slapping guffaws.

Like mischievous kids, up the ladder they went with their clubs and balls, and of course, their trusty six-pack. I could hear a lot of scrambling around while they got their footing, and then hooting and shouting, laughing far into the night each time they hit a golf shot over the neighbors' houses and into the beyond. More than once there was an unmistakable sound of tinkling glass or the clonk of something bouncing off metal, followed by hysterical laughter from the golfers on the roof. In the morning, an unsuspecting car owner would be scratching his head over a mysterious new dent. When there were no more balls, they stayed to finish off the beer, finally making their way shakily down the ladder.

August in 1950 was full of record highs, both in temperature and humidity. Our baby was due around the second week and everything was ready including my mother, who was coming to Bedford Hills to launch me into this awesome new world called motherhood. She was thrilled to do it. She had waited a long time for her first grandchild and being a part of everything was just what she wanted. It would be wonderful to have her there to take the edge off my nervousness and give me the support I needed.

The summer days and nights seemed endless. We sat on our little front porch in the evenings, drinking iced tea and trying to cool off, waiting, waiting, and waiting.,. feeling a little stir crazy. But on the morning of August 20th, I awakened with a different sense of myself and as I went through the morning rituals, everything seemed a little off center— disoriented—as if I were somewhere else. The feeling grew as the day progressed and then in the middle of the afternoon I became aware of a tiny contraction. It wasn't long before I was conscious of a certain rhythm in the tightening inside of me and, as the day wore on, the tightening became first-class cramps that built in strength and lasted longer each time. I was totally immersed in this miracle taking place in my body

Mt. Kisco Hospital was only about fifteen minutes away, but Bob drove like he was on the Indianapolis Speedway. "Please," I begged, "slow down. I don't want to arrive in the emergency ward instead of maternity!" My plea did little good, and minutes later we flew into the hospital grounds, screeching to a stop in front of the admitting door. I expected to see smoking tires, but my imagination was doing overtime. Every cell in my body was shouting, "I'm having a baby!!"

The smiling nurse brought a wheelchair to the car. "Regulations," she told us. "Bye, honey," I said, as I gave Bob a kiss. "The next time we meet, we'll be three." My voice croaked. None of this seemed real.

They put me to bed in the labor room and proceeded with the pre-birth prep. By now I was in a steady two-minute rhythm that was leaving me breathless and putting cartoon stars in my eyes. Dr. Robertson came in to check on me regularly, winking and smiling with pleasure at my progress. As I was one of his first natural childbirth patients, he was as anxious for this baby to arrive as I was and could hardly wait to document all that went on. I settled in. Wave after wave came, shaking and squeezing me, kneading me like dough. My body glistened with sweat as I worked with this wondrous power that had taken hold of me. I was in its spell, riding the crests and valleys, awestruck by its strength. People were coming and going, but I was only dimly aware of the movement around me. The world that I inhabited now was a private one and I meant to explore every inch of it.

"Well, hello, it looks like your big moment isn't too far away," Dr. Robertson said, patting my hand after they wheeled me into the delivery room. I managed a nod and a quick smile before being engulfed in another relentless spasm. The delivery room nurses went to work. All hands were now at the ready and they were on each side of me, wiping my face, speaking softly, encouraging me with each push. Miraculously, there was no pain! I was somewhere outside of myself, but conscious of a tremendous pressure in my belly that rose and fell like all the winds of the universe blowing through me. How long I rode through this strange new land I can't say, but, all at once, I felt a wet, squirming, wiggling mass pass out of me and, instantly, all was quiet and I was at peace.

"You have a beautiful baby girl and you get a gold star for your splendid achievement." The doctor leaned over and gave me a hug, wet face to wet face. And then he placed my first child on my deflated tummy and, in that moment, I became the brightest star in the heavens—shimmering and glowing with creation. In the act of childbirth came a fulfillment I had never experienced and with it a wisdom that told me I had accomplished what nature and God intended for me. When I looked down into that tiny face for the first time and felt the warmth of her little body, heaven itself opened its doors and gave me a precious part of the universe.

Five days of bliss followed—five days to be waited on, to recuperate and get to know my new daughter Brooks. It was a wonderful gift. Each afternoon, after the baby had her five o'clock feeding, Bob would knock softly on the door and pay us a visit. I remember how wan and tired he looked. After a kiss for us both he sank into the chair next to my bed and in minutes fell fast asleep. Fatherhood is really wearing him down, I thought. I didn't know it was physical exhaustion from pounding the pavements, interviewing for a job. He never told me he had been fired until we were settled back home and had a chance to talk, and then it all came out.

It was not a pretty story. When Bob was hired as a junior editor the management took in another young aspirant at the same time. The name of this man was Bill Jovanovich who went on to become the third name associated with Harcourt Brace. Knowing how talented Bob was, Jovanovich, who aspired to run the Company someday, knew he had to get rid of this Bob Betts who endangered his ambitions. So he played office politics and Bob was the victim.

The fall of 1950 was an anxious time with a new baby and no job in sight. As the fruitless months dragged on I could see Bob's self-confidence slipping away. He was having trouble sleeping and had one cold after another—a sure sign his system was down. Each morning he took the train to the city hopeful of finding a job to support us but each night he came home looking tired and beat. I remembered that same look on my father's face years ago—that look of desperation and defeat.

"How did it go today? Any luck?"

He would shake his head, as he went straight to the fridge for a beer. He spent the evenings slouched in the spring-sprung chair in front of our little black and white TV, his big dog Hucky sprawled all over him. It was a depressing sight and it tore at my heart but there wasn't much I could do.

One evening Bob burst in shouting, "Guess what, honey? I went to see Julian Bryan today and he wants to hire me as a writer. He's doing a new documentary on Robert Flaherty—you know, the legendary film producer of "Nanook of the North" —and he wants me to start first thing on Monday morning."

"Oh, how wonderful. You made it. I knew you would. It was just a matter of time and connecting with the right person." I went on congratulating him, fueling his excitement. I hadn't a clue as to who Julian Bryan was or what he did, but I thanked my angels for sending him.

Julian Bryan's job did not pay well. Documentary filmmakers starve most of the time. However, we managed to get along on the meager salary. Bob loved what he was doing and that is what counted, so we didn't mind pinching pennies and doing without certain luxuries. We were thankful for our health, a place to live, and for our beautiful baby Brooks.

So life in the small town of Bedford Hills settled down in a quiet way with the exception of Hucky, still our problem dog that lit up Bob's life but made me miserable.

One evening we were sitting on the steps of our porch, having an after dinner cigarette. Hucky was nowhere to be seen, probably doing mischief at a neighbor's place when Bob startled me by saying "You hate that dog, don't you? Why? Why can't you relax and have fun with him, the way I do."

I almost choked on a mouthful of smoke. What could I say to this totally obtuse statement? Anger rose in my chest and I started speaking softly, trying to tell Bob that since the dog came into our lives, the happiness went out of it for me.

"Oh, come on, honey," he said, talking to me like a child. "He's just a dog with a lot of spirit. Can't you see that? Why are you getting so upset? You're just mad because he knows how to outsmart you."

That did it. My nails dug into my palms and I started shouting and screaming about what a total mess Hucky was making of my life until Bob got up and said, "Well, you'd better grow up," and he stomped into the house. I sat there weeping, wondering if indeed I was going a little crazy— wondering how I was ever going to go on with this horrible dog.

We hardly spoke to each other for days—one more victory for Hucky.

For me, the days that followed brought back the familiar emptiness that I first experienced while housekeeping, but now I had more work to do with diapers and caring for a baby, and I was tired. Each night, it was difficult for me to match Bob's zip from his adrenaline surges coupled with his intellectual stimulation taking place all day. Documentary film making was a creative give-and-take shared by a dozen people or more. Housework and caring for a little child was another story. It was a dead end job with few grown up rewards.

There was no way that I could match his mood and mind. I knew it and keenly felt I was out of my league in trying to talk with him about my day. Even sharing time with Brooks was awkward. By the time Bob arrived home, it was always too late to see his baby as she was already in bed for the night. A few times he woke her for some playtime and then it would be hours before I could get her to fall asleep again. So we quit that. Our conversation at the dinner table most nights was a monologue centered on what had happened on location that day, it was certainly not how Brooks liked her creamed spinach or who we saw on our trips to the village in the baby buggy. I had nothing to contribute so I found myself an audience of one.

And then a new wrinkle appeared in Bob's daily accounting. A girl. Over dinner on one particular night, as I was listening with half an ear to his panorama of events, I suddenly realized he had been sprinkling the conversation with stories about somebody's brilliant young niece.

"Who?" I asked innocently. I *think* it was innocent.

"Oh, she's the niece of Aldous Huxley. You know, the English novelist and critic who wrote "Brave New World. " And is she ever bright! She astounds me with her intelligence. Julian is giving her a temporary job. She's gathering research materials for her doctorate at Harvard."

(Score a big one for her, I thought. Two peas in a pod, both graduates of Harvard—how very chummy). Despite his casual mentioning of her temporary position, I could tell he was impressed with this bright young member of the intellectual Huxley clan. It was like the attraction of a planet to a star. He was in his element—heady with the mind games he could play. I knew that Bob was happiest swimming around in an intellectually elite pond and now the sparkling waters of a new attraction beckoned. The more Bob raved about this girl, the more the distance between us grew. I knew I couldn't compete with this—never felt I could compete with Bob's Harvard classmates, and now with *his* baby and *his* home to care for, the gap became even wider. There was no mistaking his message. There was no room in their rarified universe for an ordinary housewife whose only conversation that day had been with the driver of the Diaper Service truck.

I felt powerless. I seethed. I sulked! My green eyes flashed warning signals saying, be careful what you say. You are dealing with one very angry lady.

But he didn't seem to get my message. Each night when he started his hallelujah chorus about what's-her-name, I stood up, cleared the table and left him alone to finish his dinner. I couldn't stand his insufferable intellectual snobbery. At times, he derived a sort of fiendish joy from putting me down or just joking around as he called it. I didn't sense that it was nice or that it was funny. Part of me was certain this star-struck crush would pass but while it was going on, he was as insensitive as a blob of clay as to how much he was hurting me. But fortunately, after a while, she just disappeared from Bob's conversation. He never mentioned her again. I hope she got her sought-after doctorate, married a huge, pedantic bore and had a lot of little eggheads tied to her apron strings. And then maybe, someday she may get to feel as I did when she appeared in my life scattering pieces of my broken ego all over my dinner plate every night.

CHAPTER 13

Wounded Cherub

LITTLE by little, after the Huxley siren turned to dust, our life in Bedford Hills resumed its comfortable hum. I was thrilled to find out I was pregnant again. And this time, when I broke the news to Bob, he grabbed me and gave me a big kiss. "Wonderful news, honey," he said. "Now this time what's it gonna be? A sister for Brooks or maybe a brother to show her what a guy is like." I think this time he was happy to hear the news. But of course the old problem of outgrowing our living space reared up and started its familiar song that told me to begin another campaign.

On a steamy summer evening, I heard the screen door's clunk and Bob's familiar greeting. I came into the living room and took his suit jacket from his arm, reached up and touched his perspiring face. "You look like you've been through the wringer. I'll get us a beer." I had been waiting for his arrival for hours and hoped I could steer the conversation that evening in my direction. When I saw how beat up he looked, I hesitated. Maybe this sultry night was not the ideal time to bring up the subject of moving. Just mentioning the word to Bob was like unlocking the cougar's cage.

"Wouldn't you know," he said, as he yanked at his tie, "it's the hottest day of the summer, and the damn air conditioning on the train was broken."

"Let's sit on the front porch and cool off." I offered. "I have your favorites tonight; corn on the cob, cold fried chicken and fried green tomatoes– but it can wait. You need some relaxing time."

He smiled. "Thanks, honey. That sounds great."

I handed Bob a frosty glass and we pulled up rockers and draped our feet on the porch railing. We chatted about the miserable train ride, the forecast of more high temperatures, and wondered was it ever going to rain? Then we fell silent, listening to the steady singing of the cicadas, announcing more hot weather. Finally, Bob turned to me, "Now, come on, Emmie. What's with all this special treatment? You have something cooking in that curly head of yours—I know it."

I felt a flush go through me. I took a sip of beer. "Okay, so you can see right through me, but that doesn't make what I am about to say any less important. Please, hear me out. "

Bob shrugged and I saw a wary look on his face. "Go ahead. What is it this time? I never know what to expect from you." His face relaxed and he gave me a wry smile. I smiled in return, relieved.

"Okay, with baby number two on the way, our family is growing, right? And it makes me crazy to see hundreds of dollars going out every month for this sorry little place, when we could be paying on a mortgage for our own house. Face it. We are going to need more space." We went back to rocking in silence. Finally, he turned to me with a knowing look. "Yeah," he said, "You're right. It makes a lot of sense. Let's do it. "

The very next day I began scouring the real estate ads, and whenever I could get a baby sitter I went house hunting by myself. After lots of legwork and in less than a month's time I found the perfect house in the perfect neighborhood for the perfect price and just five miles south of Bedford Hills, in the old town of Mt. Kisco. Bob liked it as much as I did. We put in an offer and soon, along with the bank, we were proud owners of an historic Hudson Valley house called the Moger House which had served as a hospital for wounded officers during the American Revolution. It was the oldest house in Mt. Kisco, the conveyance deed listing the year 1910 when the house had been moved to our hillside orchard from near the railroad tracks. When we stripped off the wallpaper in the front hall, we discovered scribbled messages on the crumbling plaster walls. Tracing our fingers over those loving words written so long ago by the solders to their families was a humbling experience. We felt the breath of life still in them, and it gave us a strong connection with our country's beginnings.

Aside from being large enough for our growing family, the house had a separate apartment, which we were able to rent to friends. Those were the days before credit cards, days when I had charge accounts at the grocery store, the hardware store and the druggist. Some months my household allowance was stretched to the limit, and this little cushion of rental money got me out of many a hole.

There was a bay window, which framed a prized sugar maple tree in front. In the fall the tree turned from deep green to flaming orange, flooding the whole second floor with a golden glow that lit up our souls as well as the small bedrooms. The hand-hewn floors were two-hundred-year-old pine. Unfortunately, thick layers of paint hardened to a flint-like finish hid their beauty and Bob and I wanted to bring them back to their original splendor. We rented an industrial sized sander from the hardware store for what we thought would be a weekend job. I was terrified when I first took hold of the machine. I could hardly hold on as it went thrashing around like a caged tiger on wheels. God only knows how the tiny baby growing inside of me managed to weather this tornado of activity. The job took weeks but it was the first hands-on, dirty and backbreaking task that Bob and I had ever tackled together, and over those laborious days and nights, when we were cursing and sweating and even laughing together, our relationship blossomed in a new way. We discovered how meaningful working together toward a common goal can be.

One day while straightening up in the den, I stopped suddenly and studied the west wall. It just didn't seem right somehow. It stretched a good thirty feet wall to wall —a solid mass of plaster. Something is missing I thought. I pictured living in this big house in 1908 and tried to imagine how my days would evolve. I could see the mother of the house sitting down to her knitting by a kerosene lamp after the family was tucked in bed, or the father reading by the recently installed electric lamps. But how did they heat these big rooms? No way could a family in the early 1900's exist without a wood burning stove or a fireplace. Where had it been? For all practical purposes, it should have been in this room. Curious, I ran out to the front yard to look at the roof. There were two chimneys, one for the oil burner, but why the other chimney?

The next morning, after I dropped Brooks at nursery school, I went to the old Hardware Store—one of my favorite places. I loved looking in the many bins and drawers and I liked the smell of paint and turpentine. But instead of poking around, this time I walked directly to the back of the store where the old-timers were gathered around a pot- bellied stove reminiscing. I lingered in the background until there was a break in the conversation.

"Good morning," I said. "I don't want to disturb you, but I have a question—maybe one of you can answer?" Several men in worn flannel shirts and suspenders looked up at me, politely, but bemused.

"Does anyone here remember when the old Moger house was moved from downtown to Grove Street?" I asked.

As I watched their faces I knew I had opened up some dusty trunks of memories. "Yes, Miss. I sure do," one of them finally said. "I was a young thing. Maybe eight or nine. Me and my dad joined lots of folks to watch that move. It wasn't every day a big house like that gets moved and it was kinda like the circus come to town. Blocked off Main Street, they did. Most of the town turned out to see it."

I watched as the older men leaned in to hear more and the storyteller warmed up his tale for his audience. "They had four teams of horses, I recall, and it took almost all day for them to pull that monster through town and up the hill. They had miles of rope and winches and all kinds of pulleys, and them horses, whoa! They was foamin' at the mouth, pullin' for all they was worth. It was quite a sight, let me tell you"

I nervously waited as he fell silent for a minute. The rest of the men were quiet too, clearly picturing this daring feat. At last I interrupted the silence by asking him if he remembered a fireplace in one of the downstairs rooms?

"Well, now, can't say that I do, but I remember a woodstove. It was in the parlor, on the back wall," he answered.

Bingo! "Well," I said, "if there was a wood stove in that room, surely there had to be a flue behind it, right?" I now had the onlookers involved, and they all nodded in agreement. I smiled. "Does anyone here know of a good fireplace/chimney man who can come look at this wall?"

Cecil Bellows, the man they recommended was at my door a little after nine the next morning. I followed him around as he went tapping every inch of that wall, listening with finely tuned ears to the sounds. He climbed the roof to inspect the chimney. When he was satisfied that he had checked everything, he told me what I had hoped to hear. Yes, there was definitely a hollow space in the middle of the den wall.

"Almost certain, it had a flue. Maybe an old fireplace bed as well," he said, as I strained to understand his Cockney speech. Desperate to have that hearth I'd always dreamed about, I let Cecil go to work ripping out the wall. Every day I would check on him, between trips to the washing machine. "Anything yet, Cecil?" I'd ask eagerly. But nothing until one day Cecil popped into the kitchen while I was putting the dishes away. He was covered with plaster dust and century old grime and wearing the biggest English grin I had ever seen.

"She's there, as nice a fire bed as ever was built," he said. "You were dead right, and you are going to have your fireplace for sure,"

I felt like kissing him but instead grabbed his filthy hand and shook it for all I was worth. "Oh, Cecil, thank you so much. You've made me a very happy woman." Underneath the plaster dust, I saw him blush.

Within weeks he'd installed a black slate hearth and added a white Colonial mantle just like the beautiful one in my fantasy. Bob came home early and we carefully laid a fire in our brand new fireplace. We were as excited as Brooks was when she clapped her little hands asking for toasted marshmallows as soon as she saw the logs. As the fire grew bigger and brighter smoke began to billow out from the opening. Oh, my God, it didn't work, I thought as smoke filled the room. Bob and I grabbed Brooks, and we ran coughing and choking outside to see if smoke was coming out of the chimney. None. In seconds, Cecil was scrambling on the roof like a monkey. "Found the trouble," he yelled. "Forgot the cap was still on her." Moments later the chimney spewed smoke like the stack of the Queen Mary at full speed. We popped the cork on the champagne we had saved for a special occasion, and christened our new hearth. Bob gave me a squeeze. "Hat's off to you, Punchy. You did it!"

Anne was born on January 26th, 1953. Bob and I rejoiced once again for a healthy baby. And a little girl! I especially reveled in the fantasy of watching our two girls so close in age grow up together, but at the same time I became aware of how my sister Dot and I never had the closeness that Anne and Brooks would share. And now here I was experiencing the joy of motherhood that would never be hers. She wanted so much to share my pregnancies that the moment she knew there was a baby on the way, she started knitting. The boxes that came to our house months later were filled with exquisite little sweaters and hats and booties and blankets and many other lovely baby thing that spoke of her unfulfilled yearning to be knitting for her own. As I opened these boxes, I was humbled by her show of love.

In my vision, I planned on making Brooks and Anne sister dresses—saw them dressed alike at the beach, out to dinner, to family gatherings. I saw Bob and me smiling proudly when people would remark about our darling children. Never mind all the screaming fights with tears and slamming of doors they might have when they were older. That didn't seem possible as I held this tiny miracle in the warmth of my arm. I studied her with tears in my eyes, aware of her little puffs of breath and the incomparable sweet perfume of her new being. She was exquisite. Her eyes, scrunched tightly against the light, were rimmed with impossibly long, lush eyelashes and her translucent skin, with its warm peach undertones, reminded me of a delicate Botticelli painting—so beautiful I couldn't quite believe this was my baby. I wondered about the genes this baby was given. I hoped and prayed she would have a long and happy life.

As the baskets and flowers filled the hospital room and I lay there loving all the attention, I heard high-pitched screams coming from the nursery. They splintered the maternity ward's serenity night after night. My heart began to ache for the mother of this baby. How would she keep her sanity through all that screaming? I asked the nurse that question one day as she took a sleeping Anne from my arms after a feeding. She turned to me with a knowing look, "Somehow, they all turn out okay." She said. "Nothing is wrong with that baby."

Four days later we were home, fussing and cooing over Anne, and settling in with Miss Hope, a grandmotherly soul and long-time baby nurse that Bob's parent's had thoughtfully provided. At last we settled down and Miss Hope took Anne upstairs to the little room we had set aside as her nursery. Bob and I sat down and put up our feet up on the hassock, gratefully sipping our cocktails.

"Well, Mrs. Betts, you did it again," Bob said. "How do you manage to have such beautiful babies, and stay so beautiful yourself?" He leaned over and gave me a kiss. I put my head against the back of the love seat and thought about this latest hurdle we had successfully cleared. The road trips, the nomadic life, the chaos—it was all behind us. Now, we had a new baby, and though I was perfectly aware that we would have challenges, Bob and I agreed we were very lucky to have come this far unscathed. I had learned to never mention Hucky—our ongoing point of disagreement. For tonight, Bob had shut him up in the garage. For once, he was not going to take over our lives.

Just as cocktails were soothing our frazzled spirits, my head came up. What was that? Did I hear a high wailed screaming? I waited. Yes, there it was again—and it was coming from upstairs. With a sinking heart, I realized why the baby nurse in the hospital had evaded answering my question directly. It was *our* baby making all that noise and she kept it up for three long miserable months. She was colicky and as colic goes, she was fine during the day but her relentless screaming was nightly torture.

And so she ushered in the lowest time in my life—ensnared by the non-stop care of two little people and one big one, Bob, and *his* unruly dog. I cooked and cleaned and shopped and washed and ironed. I cleaned up poop from both babies and an animal. All this on three hours or less sleep, deprived by Anne's nocturnal screaming, hampered by little money and after Miss Hope left, no household help. My despair was a twenty-four hour sentence.

On top of this, Bob was unhappy in his job with Julian Bryan. He was making a pitifully small salary and knew he was not providing for his family the way he wanted to. I think he began to realize this when he asked me to put together drinks and a little supper for a few friends. When he walked into the dining room and saw my pathetic display of cold cuts, sliced bread and cheese he turned to me saying "Is this what you are planning to serve tonight? Don't you have some other dish more inviting?   I thought we were going to have a little supper not a picnic!   I told them it was casual but not this casual."   I knew he was upset with me.

His words stung. "Sorry," I snapped. " I stretched my budget as far as I could". I turned on my heel and left to answer the door.

I was mad with the universe for giving me so much to do with so little help. And on top of this, Bob kept coming down with strep throat regularly. Nights of tortured ravings from his fevered mind combined with the extra care needed for someone sick had me worn to a frazzle. I cried a lot in those days and I didn't receive sympathy from anyone—not even my doctor. But I had learned from the past that the bad times would eventually turn around and of course they did.

After three very lean years in the documentary film business, Bob came home one night looking light years younger. The minute I saw him, and he gave me an extra tight hug, I could tell something wonderful had happened. I could hardly wait to hear what it was. But first, Brooks had to show her Daddy her latest drawing and tell him all about her day at nursery school. While they were having their time together, I went into the kitchen and made cold drinks, all the time having a fit keeping my patience. Brooks finally toddled upstairs to her room.

I handed Bob his drink. "OK, dear," What's happened? Did you get a raise? Or did Julian win an Oscar?" We sat down at the kitchen table.

"Better than that," Bob said with an incredulous look on his face. "I really can't believe this but I have been offered a high paying job as a copywriter at Kudner—a prestigious advertising company in New York. They want me to start as soon as possible."

"Oh, it sounds wonderful," I cried. "Are you going to take it?

"I'll have to think about it," was all he said.

Days passed and nothing more was said about it. I started to worry that the job offer would go away, but when I asked him about it, he looked peculiar and quickly changed the subject. I was puzzled.

We were finishing dinner the following Sunday and I asked if he wanted to share any doubts he had about taking this job. I was getting impatient as this sounded like a marvelous opportunity. "I can't understand why you're so hesitant?" I said. "I'd think you'd be jumping for joy."

I can still see the worried look on his face as he got up from the table and went to get another beer. He popped the cap, tilted his head back and drank thirstily. Then he started pacing up and down in our long narrow kitchen. I sat still watching him. Whatever was on his mind was serious and meant a great deal to him but I was perplexed and getting annoyed. I wished he didn't have such a hard time communicating with me. It went on for more minutes than I could stand. I sighed and finally said, "For Pete's sake, Bob. Let's have it. What is bothering you so much that you can't find the words to tell me? I hate the way you can keep me in the dark." He turned a little boy face to me but didn't say anything. That was it. I folded my napkin slowly, carefully placed it on the table, took my dishes to the sink and started for upstairs. When I was halfway across the kitchen, I heard him say,

"I don't know. I can't help but feel if I took this job and started working in an advertising firm—getting paid a huge salary to write stuff that sells things to people who don't really want them, or who can't even afford them—I would be prostituting my talents. To me, it sounds immoral. And in a way, I think it is."

So this was it—this spiritual tug of war that was eating him. I must have looked at him as if he had grown another head. Immoral? Prostituting his talents? Really! How egotistical and pure can one be, was my first angry thought. I was dumbfounded. "I think I'll put the kids to bed now," was all I could say and I left him standing, looking at the floor.

I went upstairs where Brooks had been waiting for me to read her a story before Anne would wake and start her nightly screaming for attention. As I went about the nightly routines, my mind kept dancing with Bob's words. I went over them again and again and slowly I began to see my husband in a new light. I began to understand. He was St. George fighting the dragon. This was his lonely battle and I couldn't help him. In minutes, Bob had revealed a code by which he lived and in many ways, echoed what my mother had preached to me for many years. "To thine own self be true". I could hear her saying this as I gave Brooks a kiss and turned on her night light. Bob's standards were high ones and he was trying to live up to them. I should have known this was the reason for his dilemma.

And with this understanding, my anger dispersed like mist before the sunshine.

When the house had quieted down for the night, I went downstairs and into the den where Bob was paying bills. I came up behind him and put my arms around him.

"Thanks, darling, for sharing your innermost thoughts. I really couldn't understand why you were taking so long to make up your mind. Now I can. I know you will do what you feel is right and I will be with you all the way."

Bob took the job.

If Life Magazine wanted to do a story on the typical fifties suburban family, ours would have qualified—father, mother, two kids. Our little girls were chubby, adorable, three-and-five-year- old hellions. We had a lovely old Hudson River 1748 Dutch Colonial, which had blossomed with our sweat and tears. Father commuted to New York City and his advertising job. We had a crazy dog, three cats, a canary, two cars in the garage and a desk full of bills. It was a happy time, yet there remained a missing piece. That piece was a boy—a son for my husband to take fishing and play catch with on long summer evenings. Bob and I talked about this a lot and finally got serious. We made lots of love and I prayed hard. Way out in the deep dark of space, beyond where stars are born, someone, something heard us and before long I was expecting. We were exultant! The tests for determining sex had not been invented but my gut feeling said BOY!

It was in the early months of my pregnancy and I was cleaning up the lunch dishes when I heard the unmistakable sound of a dogfight somewhere down the street. I knew before I ran to the window that it had to be Hucky and the neighbor's Border collie who were snarling enemies from the first day they eyed each other. As the growling and howling escalated I dropped my dishtowel and ran, grabbed a broom from the garage and flew out to the street. There I saw the ugliest dog fight I had ever witnessed. Both dogs were both going for the kill, slashing and tearing at each other's flesh.

There would be no winner—just two badly mangled animals. The sight of all that fury sickened my stomach and I thought my head was going to fly apart from the rush of adrenaline. I slapped and hit them over and over with the broom handle, screaming loudly for help.

Finally, someone came with a bucket of water and threw it over the dogs. It gave me a minute to put my hand through Hucky's collar and pull him off the other dog. By then I was dizzy. My head was pounding and I could hardly see but I made it to our garage, lurching and tugging the bloody animal behind me. I slammed the door shut and locked it and collapsed on the back steps, my heart going at high speed. I thought I was going to faint so I put my head between my knees and finally, after many minutes, my dizziness faded and I began to breath normally.

A few weeks later a very angry neighbor appeared at my door. Her eyes were shooting sparks. "You've got to do something about your crazy dog," she yelled. "He is terrifying everyone and this morning was the last straw! He attacked Peter, my six-year-old, and bit him so badly I had to rush him to the emergency room. She started to cry. . I was tongue-tied and pulled apart by my emotions and tried to tell her I would do what I could. God help me get rid of this frightening animal, I prayed. I was just about out of my mind with this dog. That evening, when two-year-old Anne walked by Hucky's bed, he bared his teeth and growled menacingly. I was terrified and snatched her out of his way. This was it. I had made up my mind.

The minute Bob walked through the door I was onto him like a mother tiger. I screamed and shouted out the whole story ending with "If you don't get rid of your dog first thing in the morning, I am leaving and taking the kids with me." He never said a word but turned and went upstairs.

The next morning I was feeding Anne in her high chair when Bob appeared in the kitchen. He took the dog leash off the hook and snapped it on Hucky's collar. Without saying a word, Bob went out the back door with him and I never saw that damned dog again.

We waited impatiently through the long winter months. I bought everything blue for the nursery—even a blue Rhino from the Met. The curtains had "Little Boy Blue" on them and the roses in the soft knitted crib sheets were blue ones. The girls could hardly wait to see their baby brother sleeping in his crib. It was a beautiful, quiet time for all of us.

The last day of March that year was leaving like a lion in great pain, howling his discomfort and throwing tons of snow in his path. Wouldn't you know around suppertime, when we were snug in our house listening to the song of the wind, I began to feel funny in the tummy?

"Bob," I finally said in a strained voice. "I don't like telling you this, but it kinda looks like we're going to have an April Fool's baby.

"Are you putting me on?" he asked nervously.

"No. I'm going upstairs to change and you can call the sitter."

The labor was short and the delivery easy. "Congratulations, Emmie", my dear doctor said. "You have the son you wanted." With tears streaming down my face, I asked to see my baby, but the nurses pushed my head down saying, "not now." Lying there, I remembered my girls being placed on my jiggly belly right after delivery. Why wasn't this happening with my baby boy?

In the recovery room, I again asked to see him but again I was refused. "We'll bring him to you when you are in your room," they told me. Back in the quiet of the maternity ward, Bob sat on my bed, holding my hand, and we congratulated each other, thanking the powers that be for the gift of a son. There was a soft knock on the door and my dear doctor walked in. Instead of his customary smile, however, his face was haggard and drawn. I felt my scalp tighten. Something was not right. He took my hand and cleared his throat and I saw tears welling up in his eyes. Oh, my God, something is wrong. I know it! I felt it in the delivery room, again in the recovery room and now the black cloud of fear was smothering me. My head started pounding as the adrenaline rushed through me.

"Emmie and Bob," he began. "I'm afraid I have some disturbing news about your son." He paused and the silence screamed in my ears. Regaining his composure, he continued. "You see, instead of five fingers on his left hand, he only has three—long pause—and instead of a forearm, his hand starts at his elbow and is bent backwards like a bird's wing."

We sat, silent, motionless as if turned to stone. I was conscious of the hand on the clock jumping from second to second, in tiny jerking motions. I felt Bob's squeezing my hand hard.

Dr. Robertson could hardly talk. "This has touched me deeply," he said softly. I have been delivering babies for twenty-five years and nothing ever went wrong. Now to have this happen to you and Bob has upset me terribly. I can't begin to tell you how sorry I am, but I promise you I will put you in touch with the finest specialists and we will do everything possible to help you. I think this son of yours is lucky to have you as parents as I am sure you will give him the love and attention he will need." He gave me a hug and shook Bob's hand." May God bless you all," he said. And then he turned and walked silently from the room.

The walls in the room were moving back and forth, pulsating blackness was coming at me from every direction. I pushed down the panic that threatened to tear me apart and clung to Bob, letting a torrent of tears flood my being—heaving sobs that washed through me again and again until I was weak and simpering. I was clinging desperately to Bob, conscious of his strong arms around me, calming me with a quiet strength.

Another knock at the door and this time, it was the nurse with Budd, our baby boy. She placed him in my waiting arms. He was a living, breathing pink and white cherub, with a beautiful head covered in pale gold down and as I held him, softly telling him how beautiful he was, he opened his eyes. They were big, deep violet pools and looked straight into mine. The bonding was immediate and, from that moment, I loved him completely and unconditionally.

In between feeding times, I lay in my bed, wondering, wondering. What had gone wrong? Why did this happen to my darling baby boy? Dear Dr. Robertson had made it a point to say it was not our fault—and not to blame ourselves. As our knowledge grew about these abnormalities, so did our faith in ourselves. As he had told us, Budd was lucky to have us as parents.

A knock on the door the next day and a kindly looking man came in and introduced himself. He was one of the specialists that Dr. Robertson had requested. Eagerly, I started bombarding him with questions. He was an intelligent communicator and I learned much about this new world we were going to explore. He advised me that when Budd was about two or three, we should introduce him to a prosthesis and of course, I got all the pertinent names and addresses. But the most illuminating information he gave me was that Budd's deformity was due to an interruption in the oxygen supply to the fetus. At nine weeks, the baby was developing arms and legs and any stoppage in the flow of oxygen would cause permanent damage to his limbs. After he left, I lay there, thinking. Today was April 3, 1956. I started counting the months back to the time when the little pea inside of me was nine weeks old. I came to August 1955. I remembered how hot it was—and then I remembered the horrible day of the dogfight— Oh, my God! My heart started a wild dance. I had to do this again. So I carefully counted back from today to when Budd would be nine weeks old. There it was. The answer was the same—painfully clear. I turned my face to the pillow and cried and cried and cried.

Budd joined our little family with no trouble. It was as if an angel had come to live with us. He never cried and was peaceful and content wherever he was. He grew into a real live Rubenesque cherub, fat and happy. Everyone loved him, especially Anne who took him under her very feisty wing and adopted him as her own.

I remember so well a sunny afternoon in our dining room. Bob's mother, who was staying in our little guest apartment, was sitting on the window seat sewing. Budd had just awakened from a nap and lay there gurgling his feeling of well-being. I changed him and started playing with him, burying my face in his fat cheeks. He loved being tossed up in the air and had no fear, trusting me to catch him and laughing with delight. We were having a splendid time when all of a sudden, the sunlight disappeared with the voice of Bob's mother.

"Oh, don't do that, Emmie! He's enough of a cripple already." My heart stopped. I was shocked. How could she say that? Is this how she pictured Budd –a cripple? How dare she think that, let alone say it. Her backwoods attitude made me furious. I went right on with our game but through clenched teeth I hissed "He'll be a cripple only if we make him one."

CHAPTER 14

The Cocktail Hour

WE had been living in Mt. Kisco for seven years when I began to notice certain evasiveness in the kids who came to the door asking for Brooks. Why couldn't they look me in the eye? They seemed shifty and street smart and really too old for Brooks who was only seven at the time. And the unsavory gangs hanging around the Sweet Shop gave me the willies. My uneasiness finally turned into a desire to move to a less worrisome environment.

Over the hill from Mt. Kisco lay a small town with young families and an unparalleled school system. Chappaqua. The name sang a sweet song inside of me. We had a group of stimulating friends in this town through Bob's business connections, and whenever we were invited to parties at their homes, Bob was always accepted eagerly. He knew he could talk the language of advertising or publishing with the guys and have a good time.

Although he had been content with our two-hundred-year-old Colonial, he hated it when it needed another twenty-six gallons of paint. It was backbreaking, sweaty work for him, not to mention the bee stings and cuss words that came along with it. But now that the house glowed like Times Square, that little voice inside of me said it was the perfect time for turning it over to a new owner.

I began dropping hints about the advantages of living in Chappaqua. Over cocktails one night he said, "You know, I hear from the guys Chappaqua has a terrific school system. I think our kids would really benefit from this. Find me a house I don't have to paint and let's do it." I nearly fell over with relief. He had finally gotten the message.

On a chilly day in November 1959, we moved into our new home on Ludlow Drive in Chappaqua, New York. It was a gracious Georgian style house shaded by lush specimen trees within a generous back yard that in warm months was filled with noisy kids playing ball, or on winter's freezing days brought them to our flooded badminton court to play ice hockey. Even the adults loved to come and showed up often with skates and, of course, a supply of hot toddies.

I soon got into the routine. Every morning, I drove Bob to the train station, waving to friends along the way, who were doing the exact same thing—wives driving with car coats slung hastily over their nightgowns—freshly dressed and cleanly shaven husbands riding in the passenger seat—the morning commuting ritual. When I returned home the kids were up and dressed for school and waiting for breakfast. Then came the mad dash for the bus stop, piles of books and brown lunch bags clutched under their arms.

Adapting to the role of the Chappaqua homemaker was easy. Bob took me into town one day to buy me what all the other gals wore—a corduroy car coat and coordinating slacks. This was a first for Bob. I guess he was noticing what the other wives wore and wanted me to look just like them. It was the final touch that made me feel I had been accepted into the inner circle at last and it was exhilarating to realize this was exactly where we should be.

For so many years, I was the little girl with her nose pressed against the outside of the candy store window. Now I had the key to the store. Now I could breathe the same air as those people who in the past I thought were far above me. This beautiful house gave me a security I had longed for in all those dark impoverished days when I was so young. Now that my mother and father were nicely established in a cheerful apartment and my brothers were married with steady jobs, I no longer fretted about my family and began to enjoy living in the lovely village of Chappaqua.

In the long days of summer, the local field club was the gathering spot. It didn't pretend to compete with the swishier clubs in the area and it's relaxed atmosphere appealed to us.. There was no modern turquoise tiled pool. Instead, the kids splashed happily in the damned up creek and there were plenty of trees for old-fashioned rope swings. We ate our tuna fish sandwiches under the century old trees instead of dining in an air-conditioned clubhouse, and sat around catching up on the local "did you hear?," while the dad's sweated away the week's frustrations on the scruffy tennis courts. Just like many small towns across America, the fourth of July was the time to celebrate and everyone turned out for the parade on Main Street. We waved our little flags and cheered loudly when our kids marched by in their Boy or Girl Scout uniforms. Of course, everyone had to have a hot dog and a soda before going on to a day of games at our field club. Hours later, with memories of the tennis and swim tournaments happily bouncing around in our heads, the sinking sun signaled the start of the cocktail hour, with dinner to follow. Card tables were set up for the bar and blankets were spread on the ground for the fried chicken and potato salad dinners. Somebody would have a portable radio going.   As dusk came we could see the men, weaving from too many cocktails, setting up the fireworks display. It always started a tingle of excitement inside of me, coupled with a gnawing worry. Would the martini happy husbands know which end of the firecracker was up? But all went well and after we were dazzled by the final display of fireworks splitting in the sky into thousands of sparkling hues, we gathered our kids and blankets and headed for our homes, feeling just great.

Budd was a little guy when we held our first cocktail-dinner-on-a-tray patio party on a warm June evening. There was just enough of a breeze to set the Japanese lanterns dancing from light post to light post. I was filled with a festive feeling and a bit nervous. But these were friendly folks and this was far from being a formal affair. "Don't dress," I had told everyone.

I began to relax. I had connected my old record player to an outside socket and had a pile of the latest dance records nearby — no fancy hi-fi sound system—Bob and I were barely meeting the mortgage payments on the house. After dinner, I'd planned to start the music and get everyone in the mood to kick up their heels. That is, except Bob who made every excuse in the world not to get out on a dance floor.   The guests began to arrive and with the first guests came the drinking. Once that began, it went on and on. This was the ritual in Chappaqua and in many bedroom communities during the late Fifties and Sixties. Dinner was always served very late and by that time nobody really knew what they were eating or cared. Though I had worked hard all day, faithfully following recipes from the latest home magazines, I just might as well have served TV dinners.

After dessert and coffee, I put on the first record and this was Bob's cue to having another drink. First one couple got up to dance and then several were on the patio swaying to their favorite melodies as the sounds of the *Beach Boys*, the *Mamas and the Papas*, and Frank Sinatra floated through all the backyards. It was what I had hoped would happen. The music touched my friend Bruno, a big Italian Romeo and flirt, who bowed in front of me and asked, "May I have this dance?" Getting into the spirit, I replied, "Ooh, but of course," and we began wheeling around the patio, having a great time. Unbeknownst to me, my little three-year-old was hanging out his window. When he saw Bruno dancing with me, he ran headlong down the stairs and out to the patio. Standing there in front of us, in his seersucker PJ'S with the circus clowns printed all over them, he yelled, "What are you doing holding my mother?"

Bruno was taken aback and answered, "Well, we're dancing."

To which Budd replied, "Well, I don't like it."

I took Budd's hand and we excused ourselves to go back upstairs. On the way, I tried to explain to him that this was called "social dancing" and was perfectly acceptable, but he was not convinced and he was still very upset. After that he continued his vigil at every gathering we had, always making sure that everything was being conducted according to his storybook world. It was very touching and I loved him for his show of protectiveness.

Social life in Chappaqua was practiced like a religion and every weekend, rather than attending services, somebody had a party. We rotated houses. We found ourselves part of the crowd who worked for Time and Life magazines and it was a wild one. The phone line was busy with invitations.

One Saturday night at our house, however, leaves me with a painful memory that time has not dimmed. We had invited some neighbors for drinks and dinner and as usual, the cocktail hour had gone way beyond the reasonable time. We must have been on our third round of drinks with Bob recalling a story he had told many times, when Brooks suddenly appeared. She was red faced and very agitated. She tried to talk to us, but wasn't allowed to interrupt until her father finished his story. A couple of minutes passed—a long time for a little girl.

When the laughter had died down, Bob finally turned to her and said, "Now Brooks, what is it that you want?"

She could hardly get the words out and was babbling incoherently about playing hide and seek in the cellar, "and ...and. we locked Budd in a suitcase and we can't open it. We got afraid. Please come downstairs and help." Her tears were spilling down her cheeks.

At first, we were all stupefied, then leapt to our feet and raced for the cellar, taking the stairs two at a time. There we found Anne crying beside a very small suitcase. We were frantic, wildly searching around for something to pry apart the lock on the front. Bob finally found a crowbar, wedged it behind the lock and quickly popped it out. There was Budd, curled in a fetal position, sweating and purple faced but still breathing. He was okay, with apparently no ill effects from his imprisonment. Once we saw there was no danger, the white lightening adrenaline stopped coursing through our bodies and we calmed down. All of us, except Bob, who was shaking with anger.

He grabbed Brooks by the shoulder. "Get upstairs," he snarled. "You're going to pay for this carelessness young lady." Full of uncontrollable anger, he marched her up to her room where he proceeded to whale the daylights out of her—a totally irrational reaction. When he came back downstairs, he had another drink. I cowered before him, a shaking ghost of my usual confident self. I managed to pull him aside for a moment and begged him to calm down but he shook me off. "I'll show her just how careless she has been. She needs to be taught a good lesson." His face was ugly—pulled apart by rage. He was breathing hard and repeating, "she needs a good lesson."

As he made for her room again, I grabbed his arm, "Please, leave her alone," I begged but he gave me a vicious shove that knocked me against the wall. "You stay out of this," he shouted. The screams and sobs from my darling Brooks tore me apart but I stood cemented to the floor by my fear and the red wall of Bob's blazing anger —unable to make my feet go up those stairs and do something to stop this. Oh, God, please help me, I breathed over and over.

When this terrible night finally ended, I went up to Brooks and tried to comfort her but she turned her back and told me to go away.

The next morning, no one spoke. I was a cold robot dishing out breakfast—consumed by a chilling insight about the man I married—that he could be mean and ferocious. My sleepless night had been filled with prayers that this kind of behavior would never surface again. But where did this out-of-control anger come from? Was it born in childhood—part of his nature—or was it bred in the horror of the War and set loose by alcohol? Brooks has never understood or forgiven her father for what he did to her and sadly, neither have I.

When Budd was about to turn four, we made an appointment at the Kessler Rehabilitation Institute in New Jersey. It was the hospital for veterans who had lost limbs in World War II, fitting them with prostheses and offering help and support in all areas. I will always remember our first visit. We were seated in a small auditorium with a few dozen others, all there for an orientation to the world of artificial legs and arms. On stage were two men and a teenage boy who was seated in a wheelchair. He had neither arms nor legs. Budd never took his eyes off this boy. The doctor in charge explained how prosthesis worked as he strapped the artificial legs on this boy and then his artificial arms. By this time, I was distraught— shaking with emotion and holding back the tears. But when everything was in place and the boy started walking back and forth on the stage, explaining how he held a book—a knife and fork—a pencil to write with.— my great sadness turned to awe and gratitude. There was no doubt Budd was in the right place.

We started on a series of visits to familiarize Budd with wearing his prosthesis. This would be just another challenge for Budd as he was a soldier every inch of the way. For years he had adjusted to people staring at him and especially the kids, who were curious and cruel, too. I can remember a story he told us about one of his playmates who made fun of his little arm. Budd's answer was "Come here and I can show you how funny it is when I poke you in the eye with it"

We spent two weeks of a very hot July with James and Ruth, Bob's brother and his wife, who lived in Summit, New Jersey. We traveled back and forth daily to the institute not far away for his lessons. It was a long day for a little boy and by the time we left each afternoon, his eyes were drooping and it was only a matter of minutes before he fell asleep on the back seat of the car. As I drove to Summit and the warm welcome we always found there, my whole being gave thanks and was flooded with love and admiration for this little man snoozing in the back of car. His courage rang like an angel chorus.

He wore his new arm, as he called it, dutifully for about two and a half years. Every six months we went to New York City to the Hanger Company, to have a fitting on a new prosthesis to accommodate his growth. He soon went to the heart of all the people who worked there and they treated him like a little prince. After all, it wasn't everyday they had a cute little boy to brighten their day.

I will always remember the hot day in June when he came home from school, stomped upstairs, opened his closet door and threw the prosthesis on the floor. "No more, Mom," he said. "I don't need it. I can do more without the arm." And he grabbed his baseball mitt and dashed down the stairs and outside to his waiting buddies for their usual game in the backyard.

That was the end of the prosthesis. We had exposed him to it and when it came time for him to decide, the choice was his and his alone.

CHAPTER 15

Cowboys

THE Convair 580 met the tarmac with a no-nonsense thump as we bumped down the runway to the minuscule terminal in Jackson Hole, Wyoming. A dream born in Daddy's movie theater when I was just a romantic seven-year-old was coming true. That little girl had fallen completely in love with cowboys and vowed someday that she would ride horses, eat chuck wagon dinners and sleep under the big sky just as they did in the movies. Now as a grown-up mom, it had not been easy persuading Bob that it was time for us to venture outside of our tidy lives and experience life beyond the Mississippi. But finally he got tired of my hounding him and agreed.

The pilot taxied to the front of the terminal. We took seven steps down to high-desert that is Wyoming, to an exciting change in our lives. In front of us was the magnificent Teton mountain range, green and lush up to the snow line, then rising to soaring white peaks. It was hard to realize that only ten hours ago we had been in a finely manicured suburb of New York City

Brooks, mesmerized by the grandeur in front of her, wasn't moving a muscle, but Anne had her eyes out for a cowboy. When she spotted one wearing his hat, she let out a hoot loud enough to turn heads, and made sure she stood next to him at the car rental counter, adoration written all over her face. Budd? Well, it was love at first sight. His mouth hung open as he stared at those majestic mountains. We had to pull him away from the view to get him in the car. As he often says, "Mom, when we went to Jackson Hole that first summer, I loved everything about it and I will be eternally grateful you pushed us into going."

We headed north to the Turner family ranch, the Triangle X. Hal, the oldest of the three Turner boys, saw us drive through the gate looking for a place to park. He waved and came over to the car. "Howdy, folks," he said in a booming voice. "You must be the Betts family, right? Welcome to our ranch. You can park your car right up the road by your cabin—third one up. We're saddlin'up, gettin' ready to go down to the river for supper, so if you change quick like, I'll get you all horses and you can come along."

"Yippee—I—Ooooo," yelled Budd, as he made a mad dash for the cabin, slamming the screen door behind him. We all were right behind him and, in record time, had changed our city clothes for jeans and cowboy boots. We hurried down to the corral, where Hal picked out horses for us and helped us mount. (I laugh to this day when I remember old Flare— the horse that Budd rode. She was twenty-eight years old and wouldn't move beyond a fast walk if a hive full of bees landed on her. But Budd loved every inch of his trusty mountain horse. It was a kick riding behind him, seeing his little legs sticking straight out on each side. Flare's bushy, brown back was as wide as she was tall. No way could Budd's short legs bend around her. But never mind. He loved that horse and when we went back to Chappaqua, he had me send carrots through the mail for her. The following winter she died and, when we told Budd, he was heartbroken. He looked at us with tears in his eyes and asked, "Do you think I rode her too fast?" We had to suppress a smile and assure him that he couldn't have caused her death. "She was very old for a horse, and it was her time," we told him.

After an exhilarating twenty-minute ride, Hal led us to a stand of trees by the river, where we dismounted and tied up our horses. I looked to the western sky and saw how the sun hung low against a shaken-out blanket of clouds, promising a golden sunset. We headed for the bar table, where the older guests were gathered, while the kids dashed down to the river to skip stones in the sparkling water. They had already found their groups and were having their own games of "getting to know you".

We piled our dinner plates high with chuck wagon chow, found a log to sit on by the blazing camp fire and dug hungrily into our hearty ranch dinner of pork chops with beans and fresh salad. It all tasted wonderful. Over the crackling of the logs and the happy shouts of kids, the soft strumming of a guitar caught my attention. John, the middle Turner son, was running his hand lovingly over his guitar strings, warming up for some cowboy songs. He began singing those sad Western ballads about my

Daddy's in jail, the dog died, my house burned down and my gal left me at the altar.

The evening gradually wound down and after joining hands and singing, "Good Night Ladies," we stumbled through the underbrush to find our horses. They whinnied with pleasure, knowing they were going back to their corral. The slow ride home under a chalky moon was a quiet one. Everyone felt the stillness of this night, broken only by the horses making their muffled animal noises. The Turner family had given us a never-to-be-forgotten piece of their world and a perfect contrast to our Chappaqua lifestyle.

Our little three-room cabin was one of the original buildings and had a unique personality. Even though the front porch sagged and the roof tilted in odd directions, the appeal of being in the West was in every weather-beaten piece of wood. At the end of the two weeks, we had fallen in love with the Western ranch life and signed up for the same time the following year.

Our love for Jackson Hole grew with each succeeding year. We often laughed about having split personalities with one foot in Wyoming and the other in New York—a long way from Easton, Pa where we started our journey.

It was July of 1969, near the end of the turbulent sixties. We were enjoying another great time at the ranch, as usual, and didn't want to think of going back home. Hal stopped by the cabin one night to chat and told us a friend of his was developing twelve hundred acres on a hillside across the valley for home sites. This was what I was waiting for. Wonder of wonders, Bob expressed an interest. We made an appointment for the next morning and, as I drifted into sleep that night, I knew we were going to have a little piece of this paradise to call our own.

Ten months later, Bob and I stood on the deck of our little mountain hideaway, hardly able to believe our good fortune. The house was wonderful—just what we had envisioned. In less than fourteen hundred square feet our wonderful architect Bob Koedt had found space for a large living/dining area with open kitchen plus two bedrooms and two baths. Up a winding staircase was an open deck with a little bedroom and bath tucked under the eaves. The wide deck wrapped the house on two sides. The thrill of seeing a dream materialize is one of life's greatest joys. I gave Bob a big hug and told him how much I loved him for making this possible.

"You deserve it, Punchy," he said softly. Punchy. He hadn't called me by that name in a long, long time.

Jackson hole opened our lives and minds and our little mountain cabin opened its door to many, giving them a bit of the magic we had found. Bob was inspired to write two books about the west. In his first book, entitled "Along the Ramparts of the Tetons" his dedication says it all:

"For my wife, Emmie.

>Except for her, I would never have gone to Jackson Hole to visit.
>Except for her, I would never have had so many kids
>To take to Jackson Hole.
>Except for her, I would never have put down some roots
>In Jackson Hole and become fascinated with its past."
>Robert B. Betts

CHAPTER 16

Buttercup Dies

THE decade of the Sixties was a wild time-a frightening yet exciting experience for us as well as our kids. They were yesterday's children bordering on young adulthood, trying to understand strange new urges and changes going on inside of them, trying to make sense of what the health teachers and parents were talking about. Hormones? This was something new in their lives. All of a sudden, this change was to blame for their doing crazy things they had not even thought about a year ago. For us parents, this decade coincided with our time in life—our mid-life. Was it a time for sobering evaluation? Perhaps. Who were we? What were we doing with our lives now that we had reached the halfway mark? We weren't sure but in the meantime, we were having a mad frolic.

I was skipping through the days as carefree as a child, scatterbrained and mindless of most responsibilities. All I cared about it seemed, was having fun all my waking hours—and sometimes way into the night. Ego-enhancing affairs were happening all around us from mild flirtations to marriage breakups, adding a titillating edge to our encounters. We were tumbleweeds in time's desert.

And then came the Cuban missile crisis and we began to know fear. Was it possible that bombs could come raining down on us? Where could we hide? Some of our neighbors installed bomb shelters in their yards and when Bob and I didn't rush out to do this, our kids were really upset. "Don't you love us" they cried? No sooner had we calmed those fears when first, our President John Kennedy was assassinated and then Martin Luther King and Robert Kennedy.

But, there was more. Before we knew it, we were involved in a war that very few understood or supported. There were massive demonstrations protesting this involvement but the government just wasn't listening. Instead, the war was escalating. Then the horrible shooting of students at Kent University in Ohio, who were demonstrating for peace, shocked the nation.

Drugs ruled now, taking minds and lives by the score. Boys grew ponytails down to the seat of their pants. Hippies were born out of distaste and distrust of their parents' lifestyles. The so-called nuclear family came apart at the seams, spilling out kids who became flower children and lived together in communes. They hated what we stood for and lashed out in every way they could. We knew we had to bend and try to understand what was happening to all of us. And that is how we began questioning everything— our beliefs, our lifestyle, and our standards. Were we just products of another generation? Did we blindly accept the morals given to us by our parents? Yes, we questioned. But we also didn't want to miss out on any of the fun if the world was going to end tomorrow. If our parents' morals were wrong, we would certainly find out as we went bouncing from one crisis to another.

It was a constant round of parties on the weekends. During the week we gathered at one of our favorite watering holes until the wee hours. In this frenzied pursuit of the good life many chores of daily living were postponed or forgotten. I was run ragged by too little sleep—cleaning, laundry, shopping, running a home as well as a business, trying to do it all just like the super moms the magazines featured. It was hectic and insane. The kids got TV dinners until they rebelled and shamed me into cooking a decent meal. I would promise to pick them up after school and completely forget, leaving them standing there as the afternoon's sun faded into dusk, waiting and waiting for me to show. One time, I remembered too late, jumped into the car and made a mad dash to the school. There was Anne, steam coming out of her ears. When she saw me pull up, she started giving me her version of hell, screaming at me in a voice that could be heard for blocks. I tried to laugh it off but inside I hated myself for treating her in such a tawdry fashion.

After too many broken promises, all of my kids gave up and stopped asking me for rides home. If it hadn't been for our faithful maid Susie to help me, the house would have looked as tired and worn as I did, but she kept it shining and kept the laundry going and everyone in clean clothes. Some of the time the animals' food and water dishes were left empty overnight and my sweet little canary Buttercup's cage was without clean paper or water. These important everyday things were overlooked too often in my crazy running after the good life and I went merrily on, ignoring the pets, the house... all of my responsibilities.

Looking back I can see how our kids' respect for us must have suffered with each questionable act they witnessed—and there were many! The drinking was heavier—the parties were later with flirtations that often led to blatant affairs. We became like kids ourselves, without boundaries, tossing aside many of the no-nos and plunging into this new "devil-may-care" world. It suddenly became an accepted thing—pairing off with someone else's mate at parties— just good friends? Not always. Sometimes it was serious enough to become a threat to all that we held dear. This change in mid-life morality picked us up, shook us and tossed us around like a playful dog's toy. I have to believe our hormones were kicking up, just like our kids were, and we were having just as much trouble dealing with them as they were. We forgot we were supposed to be the steady oaks in a forest of falling trees.

It started innocently enough. Barbara and Bruno lived just two doors away and we soon found ourselves together whenever possible. Bob thought Barbara was lovely and would manage to be next to her as much as he could, freshening her drinks or lighting her cigarette, and she wallowed in his attention. This, of course, threw Bruno and me together, which was fun and quite wonderful.

We both loved music and on many nights we listened to his collection of recordings for hours, talking about a thousand things, drinking and dancing until much too late. Our friendships deepened and the four of us started traveling together with our children—to Bermuda,,—to Myrtle Beach—and then sometimes we left the kids with a sitter and headed for the city to a new restaurant and a hit show. We were having the time of our lives and we threw ourselves into this new experience with abandon. There was unspoken acceptance of our relationships with one another, along with reckless disregard for the consequences. Immature? Naïve? You bet! But the hormones were raging in all of us, pushing us into dark corners for expression.

Bob was in an advertising world of words — Bruno was producing shows on TV—Both were pressure cooker careers that left their brains worn out by Friday What better way to release this stress than to play on the weekend starting with Bloody Marys on Saturday after tennis or golf and graduating to Scotch or gin as the day wore on. Then home to feed the kids, dress, pick up the sitter and gaily run to another party.

We tried every alcoholic combination that was known and made up a few of our own, but we were not into drugs. In those days of "anything goes," the tobacco companies made millions from us, for everyone smoked—heavily! The stale stench of the living room the morning after we had a party always upset my stomach. There would be dozens of ashtrays overflowing with cigarette butts, dirty glasses and dishes with hardened, half-eaten food left on tables and underneath furniture. It was a daunting cleanup for anyone, especially for one with a throbbing hangover. One morning I even found one of our guests asleep under the dining room table. Crazy things were happening but we took them in stride, picking ourselves up with Bloody Marys and going off again to catch the weekend merry-go-round.

There were times when the memory gets hazy—times when, late at night and too full of booze, a crazy need in some of us turned affection to passion, and the brief paring left us feeling hollow, asking why. Where does the blame lie if there is blame? The muddled Sixties confused my generation and knocked us off balance..

The beginning of my important turnaround came one New Year's Eve when Bob and I arrived home very late and very full of partying. We tried not to awaken the kids but, unfortunately, before I could turn on a light, I tripped and fell over Sherry, our Golden Retriever, who was lying smack in front of the door. She yelped when I landed on her and woke Brooks, who came down the stairs to see me lying splay-legged across the poor dog. I knew I had hurt Sherry but, loyal sweet animal, all she did was thump her tail in greeting. I was ashamed and embarrassed and I tried to make light of what happened. I hastily said goodnight, and conscious of Brooks' judgmental stare as she went back up to her room, I went into the dining room to cover Buttercup's cage. I had forgotten—again. As I approached the cage, I saw my little yellow canary in the bottom, on his back, his feet pointing upward.

I was shocked and covered with guilt. How could I forget to feed and water him, to clean his cage or cover him at night? My eyes filled with tears and, as I climbed the steps to bed, I felt more than a tinge of disgust and self-loathing for the way we had been living. There was no excuse to cause suffering on those entrusted to your care no matter how much the world's craziness affected you.

The next morning, the kids and I fashioned a little coffin for Buttercup and buried him in the back yard under the lilac bushes. I turned and went back into the kitchen where Bob was having his late morning coffee. I wrapped my arms around his shoulders. "Honey," I said, with difficulty, "I think we need to talk about all this nutty social life we are having. I am about done in and would like a weekend just to ourselves. What do you say?" He looked at me with surprise but said "Sure, fine with me."

We took the kids out to dinner and then a movie. By ten o'clock we were all sound asleep.

It was time to come back to earth. But now we were two different people—older, sadder and wiser, the consuming flame that had threatened us had burned out – it had turned to a flickering ash. The tarnish that had darkened our once silver-bright union would take a lot of work to remove but we were hungering to restore the glow. We were tired and disgusted with "makin' whoopee." It had lost its sparkle and all we had now was the bitter aftertaste. We missed the beautiful life we had treated so carelessly. We both knew what had to be done and, without saying much about it, we started the painful job of putting a marriage back together again. But the hormone insurrection in my body was far from over, still seething, waiting for one more chance to challenge us and the strength of our relationship.

December 1969. On my Christmas card I wrote, "Life has been purring along and all of us are doing great. The kids are excelling in school. Bob is being showered with praise as a natural in his field, and I am finding creative outlet in my fabric shop. Yes, this has been a real down-to-earth, "Father Knows Best" year."

But under the rosy picture was a different story, tucked out of sight in a corner of my mind.

"One morning, as you come awake, you are conscious of a change—a slight refocus on the way you see things. You can't put a label on this feeling, but it is there and making itself known—curious, this uneasiness. Going through the rituals of an ordinary get-ready-for-school-and-work-day, the feeling persists, nagging behind the bustle of morning departures. When the house is at last quiet, a second cup of coffee is taken out to the patio and absent-mindedly sipped, all the while you are aware of a strange new sensation—searching for an explanation. A long time goes by. The coffee is stone cold by now—no matter. As you ponder this new side of you, a tantalizing flicker begins to cast a dim light.

You are back at the party last Saturday night when a friend and neighbor corners you. He is obviously in a merry mood inspired by too many cocktails. He is also in an amorous mood, beginning with joking and teasing, which soon turns serious. The eye contact leading to a soft kiss starts the heart pounding and the chemistry flowing. Shaken, you break apart—an unspoken agreement to quit it separates you, and back to the party you go. But that encounter impacted both of you deeply. Now, as you sit there in the cool quiet of an early morning in May, you face the truth of what has been bothering you."

The allure of an affair was now in the forefront of my mind. If thoughts are like lions relentlessly stalking their prey, then sooner or later, the thoughts would eat me alive. Each time it resurfaced, the possibility turned into probability. My nights were tormented hours, when I tossed and turned while Bob slept peacefully, unaware of what was going on inside of me. I diligently examined every crack and crevice in my past, hoping to uncover a reason why I was so sorely tempted to stray. If only I could talk this over with him but we were never able to communicate intimately—never really knew what each other was thinking or feeling. We had an unspoken agreement. We managed our days very well but at night, we were strangers in so many ways, afraid of confrontation.

This underlying, disturbing part of our life's fabric bothered me constantly. What happens when a marriage withers? Was there a chance it could revive in a more nurturing climate and start growing again? Is that what was needed? Or, maybe a good shake up?

I started to make sense out of this change in me. Dark memories of hurtful things began to appear. The putdowns in front of people—the jokes on me were supposed to be funny but hurt me deeply and wounded my ego.

"Oh, c'mon, honey. Can't you take a joke?" Bob would say. I remembered the night he humiliated me at a party, making unkind remarks in a joking fashion about how I looked. I went back even further to the shameless affection he displayed for the Huxley niece with whom he worked, raving on about how smart she was, what a stunning personality she had and on and on—and she dressed beautifully, too. This made me seethe.. What did Bob expect from me? I was running a house and raising our first child. We had no help and very little money, certainly not much left over for pretty clothes, so I took to the sewing machine for my meager wardrobe. But I didn't pass the test. I didn't measure up to what Bob wanted, whatever that was.

The floodgates were open now, the tumbling stream of memories reaching for daylight and recognition—unhappy memories shoved too long in dark places. One time, when we came home after a dinner party with Bob's business friends, his fierce anger resulted in a resounding slap across my face.

"You hit me again and I walk out of the door for good," I spat out. It was enough to sober him for once. But I think deep inside I was afraid that one of these nights I wouldn't be able to fend off his rage. Too much to drink at a party would set him off the minute we got home and he would accuse me of saying things that I had never uttered—wild, crazy ideas that his booze-confused mind had invented. I even apologized for something he thought I had said, which was a crazy twist in his mind.. I hated being such a doormat, but I had no recourse. There was a part of me that hungered for someone who would look at me with desire in his eyes saying, "I want you."

The estrogen raging through my body was changing me from day to day. Now I was conscious of a libido so strong I was sure it had to be broadcasting my desires to the world. Maybe it did for it was only a short time before I realized I was being pursued by someone who was well thought of in the area. The thrill of it caught me by surprise.   Long ago I had put aside any thoughts of being a temptress and to find myself in this role was a shock. I would look at my frazzled six a.m face in the bathroom mirror and wasn't sure who I was or what I was doing. I knew I could make that phone call anytime and start a trip into dark and dangerous waters. But I didn't make that call. He did. I think he knew the time was ripe to make his move. He also knew I wouldn't turn him away..

So, the charade started.

The days now took on radiance with a zing so intoxicating that even the smallest chore was a pleasure. At first, I didn't allow myself to acknowledge the deep feeling of guilt under the dazzle. I knew I should end this insanity. Instead, I was floating a mile high, on a make-believe cloud, dizzily lost.

Where had the respectable suburban wife, mother and businesswoman gone? In more rational moments, when I still felt connected to the real world, I was conscious of uneasy feelings creeping into my waking hours and keeping me awake at night. I hated myself and was deeply ashamed, but I was the fly in the spider web, trapped in a sticky mess, spellbound and bewitched by emotions as strong as the tides at sea.

By now, we were meeting in places off the beaten path—far away from Chappaqua—even in New Jersey. He was careful, making sure we would not cause suspicions. I went along like a well trained puppy. All the while the little voice inside of me was crying out for the return of sanity.

I began to have physical manifestations telling me something was really going wrong. I found myself going in and out of the present—I couldn't concentrate—I didn't hear when someone spoke to me. What was going on?

Driving to the supermarket one day, I felt as though the inside of the car was closing in on me and I couldn't breathe. My heart rate shot up and hit the bell—the top—it couldn't go beyond. How I stayed steady enough to make it to the Medical Center I don't remember. But when I burst in, wild-eyed and panting, Miss Lauren took one look at me, came around the counter and steered me right into an empty examining room. My pupils must have been huge for she said almost immediately, "You are having a panic attack, but just stay calm. We'll fix you up in a hurry. I'll be right back."

It wasn't a minute before my dear doctor was on the spot. "Well, what's been happening in your life lately? You look pretty shook up," he remarked in a kind voice.

"Too many parties—You know about the fast life we lead in Chappaqua," I laughed with false brightness. I gratefully accepted his prescription for Valium and promised him I would get more sleep. On the way home, I was as nervous and edgy as an antelope sensing lions in the tall grass, waiting for their chance to strike, expecting this dark beast in my mind to surface at any moment and take me away. I was plain scared it would happen again.

Bob was concerned. "What did the doctor say exactly? What causes these attacks?" he asked.

"Oh, he put it down to stress and lack of sleep and he gave me a prescription for Valium to calm me down and he said not to worry—that it probably had something to do with hormonal changes, too." This explanation satisfied him.

The neighbors had a dinner party one Saturday night that lasted until the wee hours. I went to bed exhausted. But suddenly, in the midst of a deep sleep, I awakened to find myself shaking uncontrollably. Every part of my body from my teeth to my legs was convulsing and, again, I couldn't breathe. My frenzied thrashing woke up Bob who was on the alert immediately, putting a call in to our doctor. "Have her take a Valium and you'd better bring her into the emergency room," he instructed. "We'll look her over and maybe take a few tests to see that everything is OK."

It was a weird scene, getting dressed at three in the morning, driving to the hospital in the dark with nobody around. The tests were all normal, of course. It was then that I knew I needed spiritual help if I was going to come out of this whole. I began praying and meditating. Never before had I been so desperate for help. Never before in my whole life had I felt so in need of my faith.

One afternoon during a quiet moment, I relived some of the sad moments in my life regarding my father. It was painful dredging up the feelings of shame and disappointment, when I would stand in the shadows, witnessing yet another scene—my mother screaming at my father, who was reeling drunk in front of her, weaving back and forth, slobbering "I'm sorry, Lil, I'm so sorry." until I had to turn my thoughts away.   Did my father's behavior pave the way for my callousness? Did I build up an Everest-size resentment of men because I had been let down, disillusioned so many times as a child? In digging into the past for some explanation, I began to make some sense out of the loony tune I was going through. Small comfort. I had come out of the clouds long enough to realize I was making a mess of my life. I knew I loved my husband—there were parts of him, though, that I didn't love and they hurt me deeply.

Summer was upon us and that meant another two weeks on the ranch in Wyoming. It was a reprieve—a chance to break away and breathe the clean air that would hopefully clear my befuddled mind and put my troubled soul to rest for a while.

Of course, the two weeks went by like the blink of an eye and there we were on the plane headed back to Chappaqua. My heart was a lead ball, knowing that I was going back into an impossible situation. I hardly said a word during the flight. I was praying so hard, asking God to help me find a way to get out of all this nasty business without hurting anybody. This was a lot to ask for, but I asked with all my heart and soul. I think I even came to making a bargain with God. I believe it went something like this: If you send me the answer, dear God, I promise with my whole being to honor each and every stipulation connected with it for as long as it takes.

The plane touched down in good time and forty minutes later we were back in our house, unpacking, and settling in for the rest of the summer. A week later the answer came with an event we couldn't have imagined in our wildest dreams and sent us careening down a path that would change all of our lives.

The afternoon was winding down bringing the cool breezes of early evening. It had been one of those sultry August days and Bob and I were on the patio relaxing with our feet up on chairs and our hands around our icy glasses. I closed my eyes and put my head back, enjoying the cicada's songs, rising and falling like an orchestrated chorus—a suspended moment in time when everything felt good and in its rightful place. Suddenly, like a gunshot, the ring of the telephone shattered my reverie into little pin points in my eyes. I groaned, pulled myself out of the chair and went into the kitchen to answer the call.

At first, the voice was muffled and indistinct until finally she identified herself. It was Kathy, my niece from Boston, sobbing and incoherent.

"What's wrong? Why are you crying?" I asked, on the alert.

"Oh, Aunt Emmie," the words spilled out, garbled by tears, "My father is dead. He dropped dead on the tennis court. He played the club champion. It was too hot. We begged him not to go. I'm so scared. I don't know what to do"

I could picture Kathy sitting by the phone, terrified, tears streaming down her face. A tight band around my chest took my breath away making me dizzy and weak. Oh, no, I thought. This can't be—only four months after the death of Cecelia, her mom. I felt my legs giving way and I leaned on the table to steady myself. I broke in on her sobbing story and tried to soothe her as best I could.

"Oh, Kathy dear, I know you're scared but we are here and we'll help you. Please try not to worry. I'm putting Uncle Budd on the phone right now and listen carefully to what he has to tell you. He will know what you should do. Just hang on."

I put the phone down and walked out to the patio, slowly, my head spinning, grabbing what I could for support. There was no easy way to break the news to Bob that his brother had suffered a fatal heart attack.

"Who was on the phone?" he asked, idly twirling the ice in his glass. "It's Kathy," I answered, and took a deep breath. "John dropped dead on the tennis court tonight. You'd better talk to her. She's in shock and half-hysterical."

"Oh, my God," he cried, jumping up, his glass shattering as it landed on the flagstones. He dashed into the kitchen to the phone, his face distorted by disbelief.

I sat down on the patio wall in a trance, only half aware of the crickets chirruping in the hedge or the darkening sky above me. I could hear Bob talking. In that moment of instant intuitive understanding, I knew we were going to take John and Cecilia's five kids into our home and raise them as our own family. The magnitude of taking on such a responsibility job was daunting, but I have always believed that we are given only that which we can handle, so I was not afraid. We would manage. I know we would manage. With the clarity of second sight, I also knew this unbelievable turn of events held the answer I was desperately seeking—how to end the affair that threatened everything I held dear. I had prayed that no one would be hurt, but my supplication went unheeded. Others were left bruised, suffering from an unspeakable loss and selfish little me was going to get off scot-free but instinctively I knew I had been given a big job. I vowed I would be a mother and a wife with all of my heart.

It was a long time until Bob finally came out to join me. He was visibly shaken, but calm.

"I talked with Kathy's oldest brother Dick—told him I was driving up to Boston tonight. He didn't want me to do it—wants to do everything himself, because John made him guardian of the kids after Cecilia died, but I persuaded him I could be of some help. Poor guy, he has a big load on his shoulders—twenty-two years old and going for a Harvard doctorate—and now with a family to take care of." He sighed and turned to me. "How about making a sandwich and some coffee I can take with me while I go change and pack?" His lackluster face and drooping shoulders showed his pain. I put my arms around him "You know you can count on me for whatever you and those kids need," I said. He gave me a loving squeeze and went back into the house.

I fixed myself a tall cool drink and tried to compose myself while I put together a couple of sandwiches. My emotions were rocking me crazily. I felt caught in an undertow—sweeping me far away from the shore—away from my comfortable and familiar life. Would I be able to cushion the shock of telling our children of this tragedy? How would they react to this monumental change in their lives—their status in the family? I knew their first reactions would be positive ones, echoing Bob's and mine. But how would they really feel in their hearts about what we were doing? It took a long time before those true feelings were revealed but at the time I remember Budd saying, "I always wanted a brother and now I have four!"

Inside of half an hour, Bob had showered and packed and was on his way. My heart was heavy as I kissed him goodbye and told him again he could count on me.

After he had gone I sat alone on the dark patio, thinking back over the years leading to tonight. I mused how sometimes life gives you a whopping big problem and expects you to handle it. And here was one that had no equal. I remember when Cecilia was diagnosed with cancer. Twelve-year-old Kathy stepped in more and more to assume the household chores and be a surrogate mom to her very small brother, Johnny. It was impossible for Kathy to have any life of her own and I could understand her utter hopelessness, surveying the never-ending disarray when she came home from school. Her father John was a well-respected history professor at Boston College but helpless around the house. It was a deplorable situation, a nightmare of disorganization that only worsened as Cecilia's health went downhill. I thought of Dick trying to run the house and write his thesis at the same time. I knew it wouldn't work.

The days following John's death were filled with confusion. There was much to be done for the funeral. Bob stayed and got things going but he had to return to his job so the phone calls back and forth between Boston and Chappaqua were constant. But there was a phone call I dreaded –the call that would end the affair—and it wasn't long before he called. .

I summoned up the courage to meet him. There was no mistaking my tone when I told him some place legitimate. Grudgingly, he suggested his office.

"You sounded cool on the phone," he said as I walked in. "Aren't you happy to see me?" He came toward me. I backed away, feeling my face flush.

"Please sit down," I said firmly. "I have something to tell you." I swallowed hard and tried to control my shaking. Finally I said, "Something totally out of the blue has happened and it's going to change everything." I took a deep breath. "I came to tell you that whatever you think we had between us is over. I'm not going to see you anymore."

The lines in his face hardened and I distinctly felt a malevolent reaction. As I told him about John's death and the five children coming to live with us, I could see his face change and take on a darkness that was almost hostile. A shiver went through me.

"I take it I don't matter anymore, right?" he said, almost hissing through tight lips. His eyes were full of accusation and this sudden change in him startled me. I didn't expect him to react this way but it spoke volumes. How odd that it took a crisis like this to strip his facade and show me his true colors? Now I realized he was used to demanding, and getting his way. I was dumbfounded at his lack of compassion for what I was facing—there was no expression of sympathy for the five orphaned children. Nothing. Only icy silence. He knew he couldn't control me anymore and it unleashed his ugly anger. As I turned to leave, he said, "I hope you're feeling proud of yourself, Miss Nightingale." His bitter words followed me as I closed the door quietly.

The tumultuous time in my life that threatened to destroy me was finished. I was free. No more would I steal around corners—no more would I carelessly forget to pick up my kids or feed the dogs and cats —no more would I act like an irresponsible child. Tears of gratitude made the drive home tricky but I made it—just as I had made it safely through, with the help of my God and my guardian angels, one of the most precarious periods in my lifetime.

Many caring friends and weeping relatives came to John's funeral service. Two of Cecilia's sisters stayed on to take care of the house and lend support, giving Bob and me time to spend long hours counseling Kathy and her brothers ranging in age from Dick, twenty-two years old to seven-year-old John They were a pathetic group, hanging on to each other for fear one of them might disappear, too. When we left for Chappaqua, we promised to return as soon as we could. We were grateful for Cecelia's sisters, who were going to try to make order out of a sink full of days of unwashed dishes and laundry piled to the ceiling on the washing machine. Clearly, the house had been neglected for a long time.

The Boston tragedy dominated our conversation day and night. It was obvious no one was offering to step forward to take the children and perform the multitudinous tasks required to keep a family going. "Honey," Bob said, when we had a chance to sit down and talk seriously. "We are the only ones in either family that can offer a home for these kids. Fortunately, we have the money and can make the space. Are you with me on this?" He ran his hands through his hair. "Oh, God, what a horror this has been," he said.

I looked at his anguished face and my heart turned over. For reasons we will never know, we were handed a huge job and the minute I heard the news, I knew we would take the children.

"I'll be with you every step of the way. We'll be fine, I know it," I whispered, almost like a prayer.

Bob put his head in his hands and he muffled hoarsely, "You are one helluva woman, Punchy. I couldn't do this without your."

The only way we could fit five more people in our house was to convert our garage into a bunk room for the four boys. Now that Anne was in college, her little bedroom and bath above the garage, would be perfect for Kathy. On holidays, they would just have to share. It was now late July and we would have to hire someone to do this before school started in September. Luckily, we found a contractor who started work immediately and within six weeks, the former garage was a cozy room for the boys.

"Let's take everybody to Bermuda for a week before school starts," Bob announced one night, "We can rent a couple of cottages at Cambridge Beaches and the kids can have free run. There's a quiet beach and a marina with sailboats and motorboats and I remember some tennis courts—and it's near the ferry to Hamilton. All of us could use some time off after what we've been through and this will give everyone a chance to get to know each other, now that we are one big family. Are you game?" he asked me.

Of course, the idea was met with loud cheers from all eight kids. I can remember assembling in the airport—ten of us in different shades of expectancy. Some were wary, while others laughed and joked about it. I could see curious glances at each other, wondering.

Seven days is not a long time but the trip to Bermuda served to break the ice. It was puzzling sorting out all the different likes and dislikes, the habits of each kid, who was closest to whom—the many facets of each one's personality But at the end of the week, we felt the fragile ties between all of us gaining strength.

When the bunkroom was finally finished and ready for the new family, Dick and his four younger siblings, drove into our driveway in a rented van loaded with boxes and suitcases. I stood on the patio feeling small and helpless and scared stiff. What had we done? Woodenly, I led the way into the house as they trooped in, their belongings seeming to fill every square foot of space. Everywhere I turned, there was another child, waiting for me to help him get settled. It was mad confusion, and it resulted in a pounding headache and further feelings of inadequacy. I started mouthing little prayers as I went about shepherding this new flock to their proper places. They set to work unpacking, and I was relieved to see how happy

Kathy was to share Anne's room   I closed the door behind them. "I need a good stiff drink," I said to Bob. He took me in his arms, patting me gently.

"Thank you from the bottom of my heart for doing this. I'll never forget it."

It wasn't as easy as we all made it look. I was dismayed to see there was very little these five children had in common with one another and the discord was uncomfortable as they disagreed on practically everything. . .

Dick and Jim were both in college in Boston but Kathy, Chris and John had to adjust to the Chappaqua School. In a short time, we could see Kathy and Chris were both excellent students and they fit in with hardly a problem. But seven-year-old Johnny was another story.

He had nightmares; he would eat only hamburgers and orange juice; he constantly tussled with his schoolmates—couldn't make friends and he was failing in school. Even though he tested high he was unable to perform. There were constant phone calls from his school about his sullen, uncooperative behavior and many conferences with the staff to see how we could help this sad, little boy. Bob and I met with the school counselor and arranged to have Johnny meet with him several times a week but soon we gave up on that. Johnny just clammed up and would not talk. I tried helping him with his home work—he just sat at the kitchen table drawing doodles. It didn't take a psychiatrist's education to see he was the child who was hurt the most by losing his parents. I felt like screaming and shouting at him but had to bite my tongue. I had a constant headache.

Chris was four years older, and bigger and stronger. Johnny was underdeveloped for his age. It was obvious he adored Chris and I imagined Johnny wished he could be on the football team, bring home A's from school and have a host of friends like Chris. But it never happened. And there wasn't much we could do about it.

Budd and Kathy were the same age and had a few sparing sessions when she tried "mothering" him but they patched things up and Budd went his merry way. Everyday was another interesting lesson, calling on my store of kid-raising knowledge. It seemed as if there was always a situation presenting itself in one of three ways—mild hysteria, simmering anger or full-blown crisis. The high-pitch living started from the moment consciousness took over at 6:00 a.m.

After years of relative calm, 6:30 a.m. now found me in the kitchen making bag lunches complete with bananas, 7:30 a.m. saw me monitoring the school kids at the bus stop, 7:32 the kids would look in their brown bags, see the bananas and toss them high into the trees or into the bushes. All this went on behind our backs, of course, as I was chatting with my fellow monitors. But we went right on putting bananas in their lunch bags! Back home to dress and open the shop by 9:30. To jump from one gear to the other demanded I have a body with a well-oiled transmission system, but, at times, this sturdy, dependable me began to shudder and shake and threatened to break down. I lost weight as well as the shine in my hair and I was dead tired all the time. It took all I had in me to move this tribe peacefully through the days and put in my share of time at Threadneedle House, and then some nights I faced a second dose of something I did not like—the PTA! By bedtime I was done in, falling into a dreamless sleep, grateful for the chance to recharge.

Weekends hit the highest decibel point. The house seemed to rock and roll. Dick and Jim would arrive in Chappaqua from college to spend the two days with their brothers and sister. When these five Boston kids got together, usually at the kitchen table, they were in a word—LOUD! They all wanted the floor at the same time and were always interrupting each other to make a point. Holidays strained the space. Picture the ten of us in a modest-sized house, sitting around a small kitchen table, bumping into each other on constant trips to the fridge for Cokes, or to the cookie jar, everyone jumping up and down and shouting to be heard. There were times when I exploded.

I remember one incident in particular. My head had been pounding for hours and when I left the shouting in the dining room and carried the dishes to the kitchen, I deliberately hurled each one into the sink where it landed with a loud crash. The shouting in the dining room ceased.as all five faces stared at me. I slowly took off my apron, put on my jacket, opened the back door and left, car tires squealing as I sped up the driveway. I felt like a balloon set free.

The Croton Reservoir a few miles away offered a quiet refuge for my troubled soul. I sat in the car, watching the soft gray dusk slowly blanketing the water. And then the tears came, shaking my whole body with the release of pent up frustrations. I began praying for the help I so desperately needed.

Thanksgiving that year was the first time all ten of us were together since the time we spent in Bermuda. Brooks, home from Boston University, was relegated to the playroom couch now that Kathy had the other bed in Anne's room. Being thrown out of her former share with Anne did not set well with Brooks. Maybe, in my zeal to make things work, I was asking too much from my sensitive first-born daughter. She was not happy so she went back to Boston the day after Thanksgiving.

But Anne had arrived with three huge pieces of luggage. Of course, we were all jammed in the kitchen, everyone talking at once, the clamor rising and bouncing off the walls. "Enough," I shouted finally and shooed the crowd into the playroom so I could get dinner on. Anne disappeared with Kathy upstairs to their room. As I was going about my dinner preparations suddenly Anne screamed from the top of the stairs.

"Mom! Where the hell am I supposed to put my clothes? Kathy's got every drawer filled with her stuff and is sitting here saying she's not going to move any of it. And the closet is so packed with her clothes I haven't got anyplace to put mine. You've got to make her give me half of the drawers and the closet—NOW!"

I had been dreading a confrontation like this, putting the possibility out of my mind while knowing it was inevitable. With hot flashes going through me, I went upstairs to hopefully make peace between the cousins. It took time and compromises on both sides but, finally, lines were drawn between what was Kathy's side and what was Anne's. And much was carted to storage bags in the basement. The air had cooled and settled down—at least on the surface. But there were other times when I pointed my finger at them asking "How can we expect to get along with the Russians if we constantly fight like this at home?" Anne went back to school in a couple of days and life was calmer.

Still John continued to be a worry for all of us.

Budd was burning up the track at Greeley High School and would probably graduate in his junior year. He was still a happy cherub, with a wonderful mix of friends, always bringing light into the house. Anne, in her second year at the University of New Mexico, was talking about transferring to Rochester Institute of Technology and Brooks was looking forward to graduation from Boston University.. Dick and Jim showed up faithfully every weekend. Here at home, sports were on top of the list. Football jerseys of all colors now met my eye everywhere—hanging on a line in the basement, in the washing machine, draped over the playroom furniture or decorating the boys' room. These "things" seemed to have lives of their own. With my business to run as well as a household of people to care for, I thanked the powers that be for my cleaning angel, Susie. Twice a week, she appeared and kept the house from falling down around us.,

The months turned into years. Brooks and Anne had graduated and Kathy and Budd were now in college. Anne was taking a year off to "find herself" and Brooks had an excellent job at BBD&O—a top advertising agency in New York. Dick earned his doctorate at Harvard and was snapped up by Brookings Institute. How proud his parents would've been. Jim was finishing his senior years at Boston College and planning to marry. And now Chris had left for his first year at Stanford University in California. The house was gradually emptying—no longer the central place for so many lives but it continued to vibrate on weekends and holidays when all ten of us were there. I was reminded of the children's counting song "Ten little Indians, Nine little Indians.........and then there was one"—Johnny.

For Johnny, there was no more Chris to hang out with. He was alone. Each day he shut himself up in his room, playing his stereo at the highest level. We felt his loneliness and wanted so to help him but he had shunned the school psychiatrist and clammed up around us, too. It must have been so frightening for him to see the people he loved just go away.

One night, we took him to the movies. Over pizza afterwards, we asked him how he would like changing schools? Wouldn't it be more fun living with kids his own age instead of coming home to an empty house that held no interest for a thirteen year old boy? We could visit some nearby prep schools. "How about it?" we asked. He just shrugged his shoulders and turned away. End of discussion.

But a couple of nights later, he appeared on the patio with a questioning look on his face.

"Hey, Johnny, pull up a chair," Bob said. "What's up? You got something on your mind?"

"Yeah, I do." He sat down, stretching his arms above his head –a habit he had when he was nervous. "I've been thinking about what you said about schools and maybe we should go look at a couple next week."

Bob and I exchanged looks. "Right on, Johnny," we said.

Finding a school for Johnny was a little like Goldilocks selecting the right bed, the right chair and the right bowl. One school was too small, the next too big and another had girls—Heaven forbid! Still another had goals far beyond Johnny's ability. Finally, Johnny found the right match— Brooks School in North Andover, MA, where Johnny joined the freshman class in the fall of 1979. Although we had a tinge of uneasiness, we did feel we had done our best for Johnny.

At last the decade with our Boston kids, which had demanded every ounce of our wit and energy, was nearing the finish line.

CHAPTER 17

The Newspaper Clipping

SINCE I was a little girl, New York City's magic had gotten under my skin. I wanted with all my heart to be a part of that wonderful place. And somehow, someday, I knew my wish would come true. In the meantime, I never let a chance go by without dropping big hints to Bob. Now that Johnny was settled in prep school, I felt that the time had come. I was itching to branch out and make a new start. But was Bob?

It had been another hot and humid August day. Bob came in the door, weary and damp from the stifling train ride, and headed straight upstairs and into the shower. As he was dressing, he shouted downstairs, "Get dressed, honey, let's go out to dinner. It's too hot to cook."

A table on the shady porch of a new restaurant in town beckoned and we sank into the cushioned chairs, grateful for the refreshing evening breezes stirring the giant maples. When the drinks arrived, we settled back in our quiet corner to have a catch-up time with each other. "Cheers," we said, as we lifted our glasses. After a long pause, Bob said, "Emmie, I have a great idea. I see no reason to have a big house anymore. What do you say we sell the house and move to the city?"

I was dumbfounded. How amazing the mind is. I thought—how it stores knowledge until the time it is needed and brings it forth like turning the page of a book. All my little hints and nudges had paid off and never mind that the idea came from me long ago. Here was Bob handing me the chance to realize one of my fondest dreams. I wondered if he realized the gift he had given me.

Monday morning, at the stroke of nine, I called the office of the Corcoran Group Real Estate in New York and made an appointment for the next day with Ms. Barbara Corcoran herself. I caught an early commuter train and was in her office before she arrived. When we met, I laid out my prerequisites and I could see her eyes widen as I went down the list.

First, it had to be in a desirable location, preferably within walking distance of Bob's office. Second, it had to be no higher than the second floor because my husband had a fear of heights and fire. Third, I would like a view other than that of a brick building across the street. Fourth, it had to be a rental as we were trying out city living and didn't want to commit to buying until we were sure we wanted to stay.

She looked at me with a look that said this woman is crazy. "You're never going to find all that in one place," she told me. "In New York, you have to be prepared to compromise. Everybody comprises!"

Just then her phone rang and she turned to answer it. I asked if I could read her copy of the *New York Times* in the meantime, and she nodded as she picked up the receiver. I had looked at the "Times" in Chappaqua, but apparently it wasn't the same edition, for when I looked at the apartments for rent section I saw something new that made me come to attention. At the bottom of the column was a small, inch-high advertisement starting with "Beekman Place. Trees". Well, that's a bonus, I thought. Trees? That means a low floor! Rental for a year—wonderful. Just what we were looking for! I called the number in the ad. A man answered. He could meet me there in half an hour. I was so excited I could hardly talk.

"Thank you very much for your time, Barbara," I said breathlessly, "but I think I have found something in the paper that sounds very promising. I'm on my way to see it."

I can still see her, her hand holding a pencil in the air, her mouth open and a very surprised look on her face.

We said goodbye to Ludlow Drive with no regrets. We couldn't have asked for a better place to raise our family and support Bob's career. Now that we were moving to New York, I could no longer stay a partner in Threadneedle House and quickly found an eager buyer of my share. It was a tender moment when I turned over my key but after twelve years of watching my little business grow, it was time for me to bow out. So the last connection with Chappaqua had been severed.

On moving day, as I did the required broom cleaning, I indulged myself in a bit of nostalgia. Each room held such powerful memories. The kitchen, the heart of the home, was full of pictures of thousands of meals, complete with volumes of talk; the living and dining rooms echoed with the sound of many parties, sane family gatherings as well as insane drunken free-for-alls. I could hear myself reading bedtime stories to small children, talking to Brooks while she was putting on her wedding dress, saying hello and goodbye many times as one person after the other went through our kitchen door. The tender moments, the angry, tearful ones, and the happy celebrations—they were all there keeping me company on my last walk through the house. My last look at the backyard was tear-misted as I recalled our kids' games—the games that taught them the importance of getting along with others.

With a final clunk, we shut the car doors and started up the driveway. Slowly we passed the patio, bare now, except for the ghosts of friends and family who had gathered there so often for fun and companionship all these years. We paused at the top of the driveway in front of our mailbox — number twenty-four Ludlow Drive.

"Goodbye," I whispered, as we left the house behind us. "I will never forget you."

Beekman Place is a two-block hideaway, lined with elegant apartment houses, charming town houses and a few postwar, sterile concrete apartment buildings that seemed out-of-place next to turn-of-the-century architecture. Our apartment was in one of these newer buildings. It seemed ideal at first—on the second floor with trees outside our living room window. True, in my heart, I longed for the graciousness of a rambling prewar building, complete with high ceilings, big rooms and a fireplace. But I also knew it was unrealistic price-wise, so I had to forego the dream.

I was thrilled just to be in Manhattan. It was enough to have a twenty-seven foot living room with a bank of windows wrapping the corner, giving us a generous slice of river view and the endless delight of watching the steady stream of river traffic. The kitchen was small but well planned and I enjoyed the convenience of having everything within an arm's length.

I took to city living with high enthusiasm with the exception of the cockroaches. Here I was, at age 57, feeling like a kid again. There was so much to see and do that I would wake in the morning zinging with impatience to get out there and explore. How could one not respond to the vitality of New York City? Six million hearts can generate a powerful beat—a rhythm I felt as I joined countless others on the busy streets. This was such a welcome change from a sleepy village in the "burbs." I remember some people asking how could I stand all that noise and dirt, to say nothing of the crime. But others would look at me wistfully. "Oh," they would say, "how lucky you are. I would love to live in New York City." Yes, I did consider myself lucky.

I joined the museums, found art classes at Marymount College and exercise classes at the YWCA, and explored the Madison Avenue shops 'til my legs and my checkbook begged for mercy. Bob seemed happy and content with our latest move. He loved the accessibility of everything from restaurants and movies. And of course, taking a fifteen-minute walk from his office instead of an uncomfortable hour on the train was like receiving a gift every day.

I discovered the bus system. You could see the city for very little money and there seemed to be a bus going anywhere you wanted to go. I never went near the subways. Going into the deep of the earth never appealed to me.

One day I was late for an art class and rushed down to the corner for the bus only to see it pull away, which made me curse at myself for being late. But right behind it was another bus and this one stopped. It was totally empty. I got on, out of breath, and in my hurry threw my seventy-five cents in the slot but forgot I had my door key still in my hand. "Oh, no, look what I did," I wailed to the bus driver. "Can you open the box and get my key back?"

"No way, lady," he replied with a laugh. "These boxes get emptied once a week and I couldn't get to the change if I wanted to."

I took a seat, mad at myself for being so dumb. In the very next block, the driver stopped the bus and turned to me. "You mind if I duck in here?" he asked. "I'll be right back." He was out of the door in a flash and disappeared into one of those little news stores that sell cigarettes, magazines and lottery tickets.

In less than a minute, he jumped back into his seat, started the bus and pulled out to stop for a red light. Turning to me he said, with a wink, "If you don't tell anyone about the lottery ticket, I won't tell anyone about your lost key." We had a good chuckle and on we went uptown.

Fall turned to winter and our first Christmas in the city was upon us. We loved every bit of it. I remember selecting a tree from the dozens standing at a corner vender and lugging it up the elevator and into our living room, where its twinkling lights sang in our happy hearts. Like wide-eyed kids we took in all the wondrous delights of the season from the skaters and the tree in Rockefeller Center to performances of the famous Rockettes and the "Nutcracker" and the fantastic Christmas scenes in Fifth Avenue store windows. I can still hear the bells of the Salvation Army lads and lassies ringing on every street corner. But, too soon, it was over and we faced the post holiday doldrums. But one evening, we heard from Chappaqua friends who had recently purchased a home in Florida. "Come on down for a few days," Dick was saying. "You guys need to get out into the sunshine for some golf. I guarantee you will fall in love with this place." It didn't take much urging and in a few days we were on our way.

Well, he was right. It was a beautiful area and, in a word, seductive. The people were very friendly, the weather couldn't be better and, if there was a bit too much emphasis on party life, we tended to brush it off.

I think it was on our third visit, while Bob was playing golf with Dick, when Lolly and I went house hunting. There were four houses for sale. The first three were just so-so and didn't appeal to me at all, but the fourth stood there waiting for me—a one-story Georgian Colonial. Built just two years before, it stood on the shores of a man-made lake and just minutes to the beach. How wonderful it would be to fall asleep listening to the sound of crashing breakers, I thought. I took one look and said to the realtor, "Yes! I love this house! Can you secure it until my husband sees it?" With a broad smile she assured me there would be no problem. I felt joy running through me like an electric charge. "Promise you'll let me spring this on Bob," I pleaded with Lolly, who giggled and put her hand over her heart.

Late in the afternoon, when we gathered at poolside for cocktails with the boys we listened patiently to their golf stories and then, during a pause, the talk shifted to what Lolly and I had done with our time. "And what kind of mischief did you get into?" Bob asked me in a teasing way.

"Oh," I answered nonchalantly, "I bought a house." Dead silence.

"You are putting me on," he said, incredulous.

"Not a bit. I saw the most beautiful house in Lost Tree and you are going to love it. Instead of staying at hotels or with friends like Lolly and Dick, we'll have our own place for the kids and our friends to visit, as well as your business friends. It will be our winter vacation house and now that we have more time to relax and enjoy life, it will be perfect. You'll see," I ended breathlessly. The look on his face reflected his feelings—who is this nutty gal I'm married to?

Bob and I moved to two different rhythms. I've watched him laboriously research, ponder and weigh everything in making decisions. It worked just the opposite for me. My action was almost always instantaneous, which sometimes caused us to spit at each other for days. But once he got over the shock of actually owning a piece of this beautiful area, he settled down and learned to love it. We added a pool and patio on the back of the house, an inspired addition that saved our sanity many times. When we would arrive from New York, tired and dusty, the first thing we always did was change into our suits and dive into the cool, refreshing water. It was a wonderful treat and proved to be great therapy in the troubled days that lay ahead.

I never tired of the beach. It was a source of life and inspiration. It spoke to me on overcast days, when the stiff breeze dressed the gray waves in lace caps and the air was alive with shrieking gulls. On walks we passed people who could have been criminals on the run or heads of state. The beach held no judgment. Time stopped here with infinity's message written in each crunching step; written in the roll and crash of the water, written in the frowning clouds above us. Here I felt at home.

The beach held other wonders—sea turtles. Every spring they return to their birthplace to lay their eggs. I was fortunate one moonlit night to witness this miracle of nature. Coming from the sea were the unmistakable tank-like tracks, leading to a seven hundred pound leatherback. Sitting quietly by, my heart was beating in rhythm with hers as she dug out her nest. At last, satisfied with her efforts, she settled down. The process of birth began and, as she produced her eggs, I saw crystalline tears the size of robin's eggs sliding down her wrinkled face. The chord she touched deep inside of me sang with joy. By dawn, she was gone.

Over the years, we found we could only take Florida in small bites; a couple of weeks at a time, but then the inevitable restlessness would appear and tell us it was time to go back to the hustle and bustle. It was nearing one of those times when Bob announced at the breakfast table, "I've had enough golf to last me a lifetime. Let's do something different today. Let's take a long walk down to Riviera Beach and have lunch in the hotel. Wanna go?" It didn't take me long to don a long sleeve shirt and grab the sunscreen and protective hat and set off on our adventure. Well! much to our surprise and Bob's dismay it turned out that the beach next to ours was a town beach and open to anyone. It seemed that this beach didn't have any restrictions and as we walked its length, we were aware that no one had any clothes on. It was a gay, nude beach, for God's sake, and here we were, innocents, trudging past these naked people who stared at us as hard as we tried to avoid staring at them. When we came upon a lovemaking couple, Bob was beet red from embarrassment. I have to giggle when I remember how he positioned himself between the beach and me, hurrying me along telling me, "You don't want to look there, don't look there."

It was only a day or so after this when we drove up to John's Island, a sister Barrier- Island to our north, to check out a driveway we were thinking of for our house. The area was beautiful and lush with towering Southern pines holding hands over the quiet streets. The homes were expensive but sedate. We parked the car and, as we were walking, we noticed many people looking up, standing like statues frozen in time, shock written all over their faces. It was then we looked up and saw debris raining down from the heavens. At first we couldn't comprehend the enormity of what our eyes were telling us but we soon realized what had happened. It was the day the Challenger blew up. As I stood there transfixed by the tragedy, all I could remember was the news shot of the seven astronauts walking toward the shuttle and Christie McAuliffe eating an apple, giving us a big grin and a thumbs up. Bob and I looked at each other, our eyes tearful and full of disbelief at what we had seen. "Oh, God, Bob, why did this happen? What could have gone wrong? I was cold, shaking with emotion. Bob put his arm around me and gently led me back to the car. I kept saying, "Oh, why, why, why?"

The plane trips back and forth took on a familiar pattern and we were now old hands at this commuting business. It was easy to slide out of one lifestyle and into another and the days and weeks went by with hardly a ripple. But Bob kept close touch with the office and one day was called back to New York to attend an important client meeting. We took an afternoon flight and arrived in New York, as it was turning dark. "Let's call Brooks," I said, "and see if she can meet us at Billy's for a steak and then we can stop at the deli on the way home and get some breakfast stuff."

"Good idea," Bob said eagerly.

Dinner with Brooks was a lovely two hours of reconnection. As our family was scattered all over the lower forty-eight, there were long lean stretches of time without seeing them and we often found ourselves hungry for their company. An evening like this started our hearts humming once again.

As we were walking home down Fiftieth Street toward Beekman Place, we were happily chatting, recounting a funny story from Lost Tree. We were in a silly mood and when we reached the corner by our building, Brooks dared me to try to climb the old fashioned lamp post. ""OK, here I go," I said laughing like a little kid. I was grabbing the post when out of the black space between two cars stepped a small, dark man.

"Mom," Brooks hissed, "he's got a gun." I felt fear choking me. "Give me your wallet," he demanded of Bob, in an indiscernible dialect. We froze. "I said give me your wallet," he repeated in a low menacing voice. We suddenly came to life. In an instant when brains seem to transmit one thought to another, Brooks and I shouted almost together "Throw the wallet on the pavement." This spurred Bob to action. He threw the wallet onto the pavement. The little man scooped out the money and was gone. All in the space of ten seconds!—gone into the same black night where he had been hiding.

We all said our prayers of thanks. This little drama happened right in front of our apartment building but just outside the line of vision of the doorman. Who knows what impact the doorman's appearance would have had on the mugger? In record time, two policemen arrived and asked us dozens of questions; what did he look like? Did he have an accomplice? What kind of gun? Where did it happen? What time? etc. One of the patrolmen took Bob aside and asked him if he needed any money. He explained that the New York City Police had a slush fund for emergencies like this and if Bob needed cash for groceries, they would be glad to put in a request.

After that shaky experience, whenever we ventured out after dark, we were always conscious of a third dimension to our supposedly safe street.

Bob was now CEO of William Esty. When he moved into that coveted corner office on the fourteenth floor, he must have felt good about everything—his career, his family, and his friends. He was also more in demand with the clients who wanted his presence at special functions. And it so happened that we were in Washington, D.C attending the Ford Theater gala as guests of one of R.J.Reynolds Tobacco Co. Vice-presidents, when the ruthless takeover of Nabisco was announced. Bob's face turned a pale shade of gray when his client and supposed friend burst into our suite at the Hays-Adams Hotel shouting, "We did it! We are all going to be rich as sin!!" I saw Bob flinch and his jaw set. It was the moment of truth for him –the moment when he realized what greed could do to a fine century-old company like Nabisco. I could tell he was disillusioned. Bob was an honorable and moral human being and the dirty dealings associated with this industry-shaking takeover must have ripped the heart out of the advertising world for him.

But our house in Lost Tree in Florida salved much of the wound. He was happy there. It was a perfect mix of climate, friends and carefree existence and it was easy to keep clients happy by inviting them to come and spend time with us in Florida. They eagerly chose to do business on the golf course and over cocktails and dinner instead of a stuffy New York office. So it was with this new found zest and freedom from structure that he readily accepted an invitation to join old Harvard friends on a get-away-vacation in the Bahamas. It promised to be a welcome break from Lost Tree, which could be a bit confining at times.

The minute we stepped off the launch, magic dust rained down on us. We each had a comfy island cottage nestled in the lush green foliage, just a short walk from the beach. Bahamian cuisine, featuring the island standby, conch, prepared in a dozen delicious ways awaited us each night on the outdoor terrace. In the morning, a soft-spoken Bahamian girl brought us a basket of fresh fruit, hot rolls and island brewed coffee. It was bliss to shed our New York clothes, as well as our mainland and east coast attitude. This tiny spit of land surrounded by sparkling turquoise water made overcrowded Florida look plastic and manmade and we surrendered happily to the enchantment we found here at Pink Sands. We loved padding around in our bathing suits until dinnertime, when the boys put on their seersuckers and the girls slipped on a cool, nothing-of-a-dress. Satiny breezes, tinged with the scent of bougainvillea, played around us on the terrace. Add to this the sound of steel drums from across the water, the low singsong of the kitchen help, broken now and then by their infectious laughter, plus tantalizing smells of cooking and, of course, the glow from the special island fruit punch and you have the ingredients for star-studded evenings. And so the days went by in a perfumed haze.

One afternoon, we were having our usual afternoon siesta, enjoying the distant hum around us, when Bob suddenly got up, pulled something from his coat pocket and handed it to me.

"I think you ought to read this," he said quietly. "I tore this out of the paper the morning we left. I think it's going to be important to us." He turned toward the window and stood watching the kids on the beach play volleyball. He handed me an article from the Science section of the New York Times. It was about prostate cancer. Suddenly, the warm breeze took on a slight chill and a shadow dimmed the sunshine. Little tendrils of alertness brushed up and down my back. As I read on, my alertness turned to worry. I had noticed Bob getting up a lot at night to go to the bathroom, but never paid it much mind.

"Are you worried?" I asked. "Should you have seen a doctor before now?"

"Yeah, I guess so, he said, his forehead full of furrows. He drew heavily on his cigarette. "But you know how we tend to put things off. We're all guilty of procrastinating about unpleasant things. Right?"

A sense of foreboding came at me like a tidal wave. I said as brightly as I could, "It may not be anything, darling. The article points that out."

"True," he continued, "But I will get to this the minute we're home, I promise." We dropped the discussion. Neither of us wanted to think about it when our friends were waiting to start up the party once again.

The last night at Pink Sands was one of celebration and we lost ourselves in a rousing farewell evening, so much so that the next morning was a big, foggy blur. Somehow, we got ourselves together to catch the launch back to the mainland and the airport.

Back in New York, Bob lost no time in contacting his doctor. Several phone calls later, he had an appointment with a top urologist for the next day who scheduled him immediately for a biopsy at Lenox Hill Hospital. We grabbed a taxi to the hospital. We filled out the necessary papers and were given directions on where to go. Bob disappeared with a nurse and I sank down into the slippery leather couch in the waiting room, feeling like a windup toy that wasn't working quite right.

It was dark outside when I was finally allowed to see Bob. I walked into his room. He looked pale and shaken as I took his hand and bent down to kiss his cheek. A stringent smell of anesthesia rose from his skin. His lips were cracked and dry. "Hi, honey," he said in a hoarse voice. "Did you talk to the doctor? When will we know the results?"

"No, I haven't seen the doctor and I didn't get a chance to ask any questions. I imagine it will take time before the results come back," I replied.

Bob asked for some water. I gave him a straw and held the water carafe for him while he drank thirstily. "Thanks, I needed that." Then he whispered, "Emmie, there's a chart hanging at the foot of the bed. Bring it to me, please. I want to see what the doctor wrote on it."

I handed it to him. After a long pause he looked up. "What does carcinoma mean?" I was shocked at his question. Lights danced before my eyes. Oh, God, I cried silently. Tell me it isn't so. I can't tell Bob, I can't! I swallowed hard. "It must be a medical term," I lied.

Five words —inoperable cancer of the prostate—changed everything in our lives. The doctor said there was every chance that Bob had a long time—five, ten years—even beyond but my instincts told me he was just being kind, hoping the disease would creep and not gallop. The doctor ordered radiation treatments for Bob immediately.

After the diagnosis, the most important things in our lives were family, friends and learning to live in the moment. No longer did we desire to travel to exotic places or own the latest car and clothes. We lived day-by-day, pretending all was fine and after the radiation therapy, we ran away to Florida where the sun chased away our dark thoughts.

We spent lazy days by the pool reading or playing with our many visitors. We walked the beach, soaking up the sun and salt air. Each day we arose determined to lick our shared demon, depression. We bought bicycles and started an invigorating routine of early morning rides in the cool of the day. We went restaurant hopping with friends. We went shopping for the kids. We took exploratory vacations to the Keys and Sanibel and Captiva islands.—We imported friends for weekends.—We sought out funny movies. Although the radiation was slowing the progress of the cancer, it had not been kind to our love life. But we were discovering the joy of companionship in many new ways and we found solace in this closeness. But the fear and specter of the future was always lurking around the corner, threatening our resolve, creating a never-ending battle that forced us to cling desperately to friends and family and each other.

All eight kids kept in touch faithfully Brooks took time off from her job in New York to fly down and spend weekends with us and Anne, working for Northern Telecom and now married to Jim, was a faithful correspondent. Budd, working hard establishing his guest ranch business in Dubois, Wyoming, called us regularly. Our five new children were all in the Boston area, working or finishing school and the only time we could all come together was the Thanksgiving.holiday in New York. Crowding ten people around the harvest board was a little difficult in our small apartment and although at times it got slightly hysterical, having all of us there was the best medicine we could give Bob.

The bright spot in our lives came with the birth of our first grandchild, Christine. Within two days of her arrival, we flew to Denver where they lived, for a look at this precious bundle. This was a great pick-me-up for both of us and when Bob held that tiny girl his eyes glistened with joy and the grin never left his face. We fed her; we cuddled her; we sang her lullabies and ultimately, we discovered the real joy of being grandparents.

In October, our blessings were doubled by the birth of Lindsay to Budd and Emi. We flew out to Wyoming to welcome another twig on the family tree. We toasted this newest cherub many times during that long weekend and came home with thankful hearts for two beautiful little grandchildren

Before we closed up the Florida house, in the late spring of 1987, Anne and Jim came to visit with Christie, who was now a bouncing one year-old. Luckily, Brooks had some free time so she flew down from New York to be with all of us. When they arrived, Bob's spirits went from dark to light and when the house was filled with those he loved they recharged his energy better than the many naps he was taking. This joy could only come from our kids and Bob was not ashamed to admit he needed them to fill the silence with happy talk and laughter.

While the boys were playing golf one afternoon, Brooks, Anne and I put Christie in her stroller and wheeled her around the compound, showing her off to all the neighbors, ending up eventually at the beach. When Christie saw all that water and heard the ocean's roar, she was wide-eyed, squirming with delight and squealing happily when the waves broke and came up around her feet. We ambled back to the house, full of good spirits, and joined the boys in the kitchen for cold drinks. During a lull in the hubbub, Brooks said, "Anne, what's that funny brown spider mark on your jaw? That's new, isn't it?"

"Oh, that," she answered. "I went to my skin man in Dallas and he said it was nothing to worry about. He froze it."

Today, the scene itself is frozen in time. Nobody said anything. The only sound came from Christie, who was making happy noises over some chicken bits on her highchair tray. We all looked at each other, fear mirrored in our eyes. Finally, Bob spoke up. "How long have you had this mark?"

"I don't remember but I have noticed the mark getting bigger and darker."

"Promise me you'll see a dermatologist the minute you get home," Bob pleaded. "Don't waste any time."

The happy upbeat laughter of the visit was gone. In its place came a heavy foreboding impossible to shake.

The usual chores of shutting down the house for the summer occupied us for the rest of the week so Anne's spider mark was forgotten, for the time being.

We were home for just a few days when the phone rang one night. Bob took the call. It was Anne, sobbing so hard he could hardly hear what she was saying but he knew it was bad news. He handed me the phone. "You talk to her. I can't," he said collapsing into a chair.

"Oh, Mom," Anne cried, choking on her tears. "The biopsy was malignant—Clark IV —the worst kind of melanoma. What am I gonna do? I'm so scared. I need you. Can you come?"

"Oh, Anne," I whispered to my terrified little girl, who was longing for me to tell her the diagnosis wasn't so. I was dizzy. My head was spinning in a mad circle. I was trying to keep my balance and at the same time trying to hold myself together for Bob. His cancer had taken all his defenses and I can still see him now, pale and frail, sitting at the dining room table, tears spilling over, saying, "She's going to die. I know it. It's all over."

I took a big breath to steady myself. "Anne, darling, we will try to figure out the next step. This has knocked us for a loop just like you and it will take some hard thinking about the next step so hang in there. You know we will turn the world upside down to help you. We'll be in touch as soon as we have a plan. Hug that darling baby of yours and Jim, too. Love you so much." And I hung up the phone very carefully.

Bob was a shambles.

It took all my acting ability to comfort him and appear positive. What I wanted to do was to scream and kick and shout to the universe, "Why, are you doing this to us?" I sat next to him and gently took his hands. My voice was threatening to break down any moment. I started talking. "Bob, we can help Anne. We can get her the finest medical attention possible and you can do it—I know you can. You can call your doctors and ask for their help. I know they will do anything they can for her and for us."

He raised his head and his beaten down look gradually changed to one of determination. "Of course," he said. "I'll get right on it."

He started the ball rolling. He would call on the President of the United States if he knew it would help his family. He got through to the top medical men at New York Presbyterian Hospital and in less than a week, Anne had an appointment with their top cancer specialist at Mayo Clinic in Rochester, MN. How I longed to be with her but Bob could not face this and of course, I stayed home with him. We stayed by the phone, waiting and waiting for some news. When it came, it was not encouraging. The doctor was not optimistic. Too much time had elapsed since the frozen procedure in Dallas, but he would do all that he could. An emergency operation was scheduled for the next day.

Sleep was impossible and I was up at dawn roaming the apartment, praying that the news from Rochester would be good news. The phone call came at around ten o'clock. Jim's tired voice told me the doctor had performed a T section which meant he removed the lymph glands in her lower jaw and neck. He feared it was too late to search out every hidden killer cell but he did his very best.

Anne returned to Denver to face chemotherapy and radiation. It stopped the spread of the cancer. We all breathed our grateful thanks to God for this remission, which would allow her life to go on. We prayed hard that we were seeing a miracle in action.

CHAPTER 18

Elf On Call

THE fabric of our lives was starting to wear thin. But our New York apartment was like chicken soup—warm and comforting. Our days settled into a quiet routine where we each had our places to go and little chores to do. Since Bob loved going out at night, we usually ended our day with dinner at one of our many favorite restaurants, where the light-hearted atmosphere did wonders for his troubled soul. Toward the end of the day, when the sun had deserted us, our apartment could get very quiet and depression was apt to steal in from the dark corners.   I was only too glad to go restaurant hopping with him.

When July came we packed up and flew to our little mountain cabin in Wyoming, knowing this much needed change would be wonderful therapy for Bob. The mountain air gave him deep sleep at night and the sun warmed his face to a golden tan during the day. But this was not for long. In August, a call came from the doctor saying Bob's latest tests showed an increase in cancer cells, which meant we had to return to New York for more radiation.

Before locking the door on our little cabin, we walked out on the deck. Our hearts were saddened by the grayed sun trying to shine through the valley's fouled air. It was the summer of the Yellowstone fires north of Jackson Hole and the air was thick with soot and ash floating down from the north, piling up on the deck, on the car, like so much dirty snow. How ironic it all was.   Beautiful Jackson Hole was under siege. Our lives were under siege. We both knew this was probably Bob's final goodbye to Wyoming.

The day after we arrived in New York Bob started a six-week radiation schedule. My heart ached as I watched him bravely set out twice a week for his treatments, looking like he didn't have a friend in the world. A couple of hours later, when I heard the key turning in the door lock, I knew he was home. Smiling weakly, he always headed for the bedroom and a long nap. I told him what a brave man he was but his reply was, "Well, so what? Bravery can't lick cancer." I think by this time, his spirits and body were beaten down to the point of surrender.

It took tremendous effort each morning for us to shake off the feelings of doom that came with awakening. Bob started asking for his breakfast in bed. Never before, in all the years we lived together, did he ever enjoy this indulgence but suddenly, he was not embarrassed to admit that he liked it. It became a ritual every day. Bob clicked on the TV news channel at 6:30 a.m. and while he watched and eased himself into the day, I prepared his breakfast. I tried to surprise him with something that I knew he liked; pancakes with spicy sage sausages or Pennsylvania Dutch bacon, fried tomatoes and English muffins, or eggs Benedict and Hollandaise sauce, to name a few. The menu kept him guessing and took his mind off less enjoyable things. The steroids gave him an appetite he never had as a well man and his eyes lit up when I appeared with his breakfast. Forget about the calories or fat content. This was a time when taste was the ultimate goal. For Bob, this simple pleasure of the breakfast hour to himself, watching the news and pretending not to hear the striking of the time clock in his brain, gave him a wonderful boost to face the day. In due time, he appeared in the living room, showered and dressed, with a smile and a lovely compliment for me on my cooking.

"You outdid yourself again," he would say. "Next time around, why don't you write a cookbook? You could outshine any Julia, Marcella or The Galloping Gourmet". My heart swelled hearing these words. I was making him happy, for a little while.

One morning, when I went into the bedroom to make the beds, I stopped in my tracks. They were already made. The flowered shams were on top of one another instead of side by side and the little peach satin neck rolls were at a strange angle but all was neat and trim. I didn't say anything but I felt my throat tighten.

"Oh, my," I said. "Bob, will you come and look at this? The beds are made. Beautifully, I might add. I can't believe it. I think we have an elf that's come to live with us." He smiled and nodded and our make-believe elf became a character we turned to when the going got rough. In the beginning we didn't realize how important this illusionary elf would become in helping us release the awful tension in our days. We started inventing scenarios.

"Have you noticed how raggedy our little guy is these days?" Bob would ask me. What do you say we get out of here and take him shopping? There's a place that sells clothes for elves and I know he would love the latest in elf fashion."

We'd walk to Saks Fifth Avenue, our make believe-elf at our side wearing his favorite hat—a Parisian beret. In the men's department we would continue our latest scenario. "Hey, little friend," Bob would say. "Try on this straw hat—and here's a navy jacket and white shorts to go with it—perfect for when you go to parties at the seashore. You'll knock 'em dead." And then we'd go to the shoe department, where we'd act silly asking if Armani ever designed shoes with tuned-up toes. At times, I was fearful the giggle inside of me would end up as a sob.

And so we would take refuge in a fantasy world far away from the deadening despair threatening to envelope us. We were children again, running from the bogeyman, making up stories starring our tiny companion from make-believe land. We took him along when we went out to dinner. He was a clever raconteur, regaling us with tales of his escapades. "Tell us again," we begged him one night, "the story when you got tangled up in a king size bed sheet and the maid accidentally threw you down the laundry chute." And Bob and I in describing the plight of this tiny man would dissolve in hysterical laughter. One night, a lone lady at the next table leaned over and asked us who this fellow was. She wanted to meet him and hear more of his stories. When we told her he was a character we had made up, she immediately said, "How romantic! Write about him—you would charm the world!"

During the first two years of his illness, Bob managed to look and feel relatively well but as the months went by, he became more fatigued and needed longer naps. I noticed there were gaps in his memory now and each day brought more of a faraway look in his eyes—like he was beginning to see a different place —a place that was welcoming him—a place free of pain and fear. He was trying to be brave in front of me and I tried to match his moods as well as I could, but it was like a game of hopscotch in my head, hopping from one subject to the next. Like characters in a Greek tragedy, we both knew his time was getting shorter but he never wanted to talk about his death. This was so typical of Bob's private side. Perhaps I should have been more honest and forthright, but it was clear to me that he was going to face the challenge his way and he didn't want other people telling him he could find a miraculous cure with some doctor in Germany or how visualizing the good little white cells in his body would knock out the bad invaders. Bob was pragmatic and his mind demanded concrete facts and answers so he scoffed at Bernie Siegel's "laughter is the best medicine" or any ideas like it. But the little elf was always near; ready to lighten our hearts a little. All we needed to do was to say "elf" and the door to our world of "pretend' opened and we stepped inside to forget for a while.

In the fall of 1988, Bob came to me with an idea. He had summoned his courage and wanted to go to Europe, while he still could, and see again meaningful places he had been to as a soldier. He had never forgotten any of these places and I think he realized he needed to relive, for the purpose of closure, the horrors and high points of his WWII experiences. Perhaps he needed to feel once more the courage he once had. Did I want to do this with him? Of course I did!

"And let's take Brooks with us," he said.

It was a strange trip that started out badly, with missed connections that left us sitting in the Munich airport in the wee hours of the morning, waiting for our plane to Vienna. Just when we could have used our little elf and his bright spirit, he was nowhere around. Bob worried me. His face was gray and drawn and he seemed confused—kept asking me what time it was.

Tired and cross, we arrived hours later at the two-hundred-year-old Hotel Sacher, situated across from a lovely old park in the center of Vienna. What a beautiful city! It was hard to believe we were in the twentieth century. Here, time stood aside in favor of preserving all the grace and beauty that filled Viennese life in the 1800's—horse drawn carriages—the Hapsburgs and the fashionable culture when Vienna glittered like a star throughout Europe—when young Johann Strauss was shocking and delighting the elite with his daring waltzes. We felt Vienna's spirit the minute we walked into the Sacher's lavish lobby where bellboys, in their smart red and black military uniforms, were ready to help with our baggage and reservations.

It was still early in the day and our rooms were not ready so we were shown big cushy sofas. Gratefully we sank into their softness and the tension of the trip began dropping away. Soothing strains of violins and piano came like cool hands on my jet-lagged brow and I could have curled up right there and fallen fast asleep. Brooks was already dozing, her head on a down pillow. Bob's head was nodding. I was blinking hard trying to stay alert. We were a sad, travel-weary trio. I prayed this trip would prove to be worth all this discomfort and clarify some of his hazy memories of the war..

Hours later, freshened by a long nap and all the generous accoutrements of the well appointed bath, we all met in the bar before dinner. Half way through our second Sacher special cocktail, I leaned over to Bob and pointed to the empty bar stool and mouthed "elf." Instantly, we jumped into our fantasy world There he was—our imaginary friend—all decked out in his brand new Austrian boiled wool jacket and lederhosen. Perched rakishly on his little head was an Alpine hat covered with pins from all the posh ski resorts. Bob was in a good mood. Winking at me, he turned toward the empty stool said, "Where have you been? You were nowhere around when we left New York and we thought you didn't want to come on this trip."

For a moment, the little elf hung his head. Then his eyes twinkled and he fairly jumped up and down as he held out his hand with a gold medal in it. He broke into a big grin and told us he had just come from the big winter games for elves and had won the high jump! He was a champion! We clapped him on the back and ordered drinks all around. Time to celebrate! By this time, we were on our third Sacher special and when the bar tender served us, he had a very peculiar look on his face.

For two days, Brooks and I explored Vienna from the tiny coffee houses and very expensive boutiques to the Hapsburg crypts. Bob joined us one morning for a tour of the "Austrian Versailles" the Shoenbrun Palace, but he was sagging by lunchtime and headed for his bed and a long nap. I spent the afternoon trying to smooth Brooks' feathers. She was not enjoying any of this and tried to opt out of the trip and go home.

Early the next morning, Jurgen, our driver, met us in front of the hotel for the long drive to Salzburg. Three adults squeezed into the back of a medium-sized car is a recipe for sour moods and there was little bright and cheery conversation on the way. Brooks sulked and Bob slept.

Bathed in a golden glow from the late afternoon sun, Salzburg appeared, quaint and charming, not at all like Vienna's formal architecture. After inquiring at the post office, we found the road up to the castle-turned-hotel where we were going to stay. It was right out of a children's storybook. The elegant assistant manager, chic in every detail, made me feel like I had hay in my hair but was all smiles as she led us to our rooms. Each room was decorated in a different period and they were all extraordinary in every detail. She then introduced our chambermaid, whose freshly starched uniform fairly crackled with her every movement. She took us around the bedroom and bath, explaining everything and how it worked and that our beds were made with duvets. What were duvets? We found out. By the end of our stay, we were totally in love with our down comforters encased in fine linen sheets. And Brooks' good humor came back in a flash when she saw her turret room with windows overlooking the city of Salzburg. She could have stayed there a long time, she told me.

That evening, when we walked down the wide marble staircase, dinner was being announced in dulcet tones by the butler. I gave Bob's arm a couple of quick squeezes as we slowly entered the paneled dining room This whole ostentatious presentation was giving me the giggles and made me feel just like an extra in a period movie. Liveried footmen showed us to our places at the table. Then like statues they took up positions behind us watching every move we made. This made me self-conscious but I did manage to get through the dinner hour despite the footman behind me and the stilted conversation with the other dinner guests. On the other side of the table, Brooks was having a fine time but Bob and I, bored by the whole flossy evening, declined the invitation for after dinner coffee in the library. Instead, hand in hand and accompanied by the ghosts of centuries past, we climbed the ancient staircase to our beds and the blissful comfort of our new indulgence—our duvets.

We gathered for breakfast the next morning in the same gloomy baronial room, and although there was a blazing fire in the mammoth fireplace, it didn't radiate much cheer. I stood in front of the old leaded windowpanes, absently stirring my coffee, watching the rain that was now a steady downpour. My coffee did little to warm the chill inside of me. I felt as dismal as the scene outside. This will never do, I said to myself, and I went in search of Brooks and Bob to plan the day. Hours later, when the rain had slackened, Jurgen drove us to Mozart's birthplace. Again, Bob sagged, and sat on a bench in the hallway while Brooks and I followed the tour for a while. That evening, armed with a flashlight and a very large hotel umbrella, we sloshed our way next door to a highly recommended restaurant. I remember that night vividly; for that was the night our make-believe friend, our elf, was given his name.

The heavy oak door swung open to a cheerful room fragrant with delicious smells that woke up our taste buds. Bob was feeling especially fit after his long nap and eager to have a few laughs. He looked around nodding his head with satisfaction and rubbing his hands in delight. "Hey," he crowed. "This is great—couldn't be a better place to be on a cold wet night." The maitre'd led us to a cozy corner by the fire, the wine steward at his elbow. Bob in his limited German, said "A bottle of your best German Liebraumilch." I was a very happy traveler at this point, grateful to be warm and dry, instead of splashing through puddles. I sat back in the upholstered bench, warming myself by the fire, feeling my dissipating along with the smoke curling up the fieldstone chimney. The smiling waiter arrived with very elaborate menus in gold embossed leather covers and when I looked down on mine, there in the center was the word "Winkler's. Suddenly, I knew. "Hey, everyone," I announced gleefully. I know our little elf's name. Vinkler!

Bob's head came out of the menu.

"You've got it Punchy," Bob cried, his face full of happy wrinkles. Immediately, the tone of the evening changed. Now we had a reason for a party! He pulled up another chair for our little friend.

"Come on, hop up and join us," he said, and signaled the waiter for another bottle of wine so we could toast our little guy. Even our taciturn daughter Brooks stepped into our fantasy and I think for a while she loved our game of "let's pretend." The waiter, overhearing all the nonsense, raised his eyebrows at the glass in front of the empty chair but decided to mind his own business and went ahead and poured the wine.

The next morning Jurgen and Bob had a long conversation about a prisoner of war camp somewhere in southern Austria. It was here where Bob, as aide de camp to General MacKelvie, witnessed the liberation of allied officers who had been taken prisoner by the Germans. Even though the war had ended forty years before, Jurgen assured Bob he knew where this camp had been located. But despite his easy breezy no problem attitude, we were having no luck finding the place. We spent the morning crawling back and forth on a dusty country road, peering into the thick underbrush on each side. Yurgen was hunched over the wheel, looking for familiar signs in the landscape that would point him in the right direction. We just had to find this forgotten camp. Bob had come too far to go home empty handed.

All of sudden, Jurgen slammed on the brakes and then put the car into reverse. We had driven by a half-hidden road a dozen times but this time, Jurgen's memory cleared. We turned in and not far up the overgrown lane we found the clearing.

"This is it," he said. Slowly, we all got out of the car and stood looking at this little patch of land that held so much history for Bob. There were perhaps a dozen monuments from different countries still standing in this forgotten meadow. A chill ran over me. I stood looking at these testaments of love as sharp little whirls of air whooshed through the tall dried grass, ruffling the faded bouquets fastened to three-legged stands. A crow in a treetop called to warn of our presence. No one spoke. We were silenced by something larger than the moment. Here, in this weed-choked field, Bob walked back into 1945. This is what he had come to find. I watched his face crumble revealing the anguish, as well as the triumph, of those last hours in his army career when he was General MacKelvie's Aide de Camp.

"It was an unforgettable day," he finally said quietly. "I saw the hollow-eyed men assemble themselves to stand at attention before our contingent of Third Army brass—all seated next to each other at a table under a field tent". Bob paused, visibly shaken.　　　"There were two and three star generals, colonels, majors, and on down the line. I sat behind my commanding officer General MacKelvie. The former prisoners lined up— I guess there were thirty-two or three—a pathetic group." His voice broke. "They were wearing dirty and ragged uniforms and it was obvious they had not had fresh food or clean clothes for a long time. I wanted to bawl. The Germans in charge of this camp hadn't given a damn about them or their rank."

Bob continued. "One by one, their names were called. They came up to the table and stood tall and proud while receiving their commendation. I remember one guy especially—a Polish officer—he was different, somehow—had a royal bearing. As he moved forward in answer to his name, I could see the lice crawling all over him. I couldn't stop my tears. I've never forgotten it." Jurgen, Brooks and I walked quietly back to the car, leaving Bob alone with his memories.

The next day, we headed south to "Eagles Nest," Hitler's last bunker where he supposedly committed suicide in April 1945, along with Eva Braun, his mistress/wife. Overnight, the temperature had fallen and the skies forecast bad weather.

Brooks started to grumble." Mom, do we have to do this? I am feeling goose-bumpy. It's freezing in this car and I don't care a hoot about seeing Hitler's last stand."

I understood the soul-searching going on with Bob and I gave Brooks a look that said 'be quiet'. She hunched in the corner of the car and pulled her coat collar up.

Jurgen headed the car up the mountain road toward the fortification. It was getting colder by the minute and the rain was now mixing with sleet, slowing us to a crawl. What a perfect backdrop, I thought, for remembering the misery caused by one man's insanity. We rounded a curve to find ourselves in front of a barricade. The guard held up his hand and spoke to us in guttural German. Jurgen turned to us, translating and said, "We're not allowed beyond this point. The road is icy and too dangerous for cars."

There were remnants of bunkers still dug into the mountain, harsh reminders of the blackness that Hitler brought to Europe. In my heart, I was glad to leave all this and go on to Alt Aussee where the salt mine was located.

Bob clearly remembered the day Division Headquarters, stationed in Vocklabruck, received word that much of the priceless art stolen by the Nazis during the war was stored in salt mines in southern Austria. As we were in the area, General MacKelvie was given orders to open the Steinberg salt mine in Alt Aussee. Bob was at his side when there, in a damp, dark bowel of the mountain, they uncovered some of the world's priceless art. It must have been a thrilling moment—an unforgettable memory to share with their children and grandchildren in the years to come.

Bob had been on a quest that finally ended here at the salt mine. Satisfied with the trip and all that was accomplished, he was ready to go home.

While I would never be able to understand the horror of those days when Bob walked in hell and came out a different person, I was deeply grateful he was spared in the war. Those two years in Europe took a heavy toll, nevertheless. It was killing of a different kind where realism snuffed out innocence; where idealism turned into disillusion and joy became despair. Bob would forever be haunted by what he had been through. I prayed that the future in front of him would be easier, now that he remembered how courageous he had been during those fearful days.

Anne called the day after we landed. She had been so impatient for our return because she had "big news," she told us. Her voice was full of excitement.

"Mom! Guess what? I'm pregnant! We didn't tell you before you left because we weren't sure but it's true. I'm having a baby at the end of May. Isn't that great? Now Christie won't have to grow up all by herself."

"Oh, Anne, how wonderful!" I managed to say, my heart sinking with this news. The doctor's warnings were screaming in my head. "Please," he advised. "Don't get pregnant. It could cause the cancer to flare up."

But Anne loved to thumb her nose at bad scenarios. She was fearless and confident that she would not fall prey to statistics.

CHAPTER 19

A Bottle Of Pills

BOB was starting to leave me. I saw it happening in the long pauses when he spoke to me; in the cane he now used to steady him on his morning walk; in the excruciating time it took him to accomplish the simple task of dressing. Gone was the lively response—the eagerness to tackle the day. Gone was the vital spark that used to shine in his eyes. Now his eyes were clouded and far away, as if he were looking at something he couldn't quite understand. Steroids kept his flesh filled out, so he was spared the emaciated look of many cancer patients. But it was false flesh, far from healthy. No amount of diversion could bring him out of his depression. Added to this burden was the troubling news of Anne's pregnancy.

I wanted to scream at the universe—lift my head to the night skies in a mournful howl. My aching heart robbed me of sleep at night and in the morning despondency lay like a heavy quilt on my being. I guess my prayers for strength helped, but my resolve was dragging. Each day my concern for Bob grew and pushed my worry over Anne into the back of my mind. I could only do so much. How I longed for another trip to the make-believe land of our imaginary elf. But the fantasy that had given us so many hours of pleasure was gone forever. A few references to Vinkler were not answered, but instead brought forth Bob's sad smile that said it won't work anymore. It's too late.

Still, Bob would not talk to me about his fears, his despair or his hopelessness. He kept all of this in a very private part of himself. He loved his books and his one pleasure was reading but I knew many words were not registering. He had so little to do, as the days stretched long and empty in front of him, that a book in his hand must have given him him a sense of purpose. The one bright spot in our days was the cocktail hour, which now came earlier and earlier. There wasn't much conversation. We would hug and toast each other and then he would go back to reading.

One evening, as I made him another drink, I made a remark about it being his third or fourth and did he really want another. He startled me by shouting, "What the hell difference does it make? If I want sixteen drinks before bed I'm going to have them." I started to cry, which released some of the tension in him and he broke down, apologizing for shouting at me.

"We aren't doing very well, are we?" he asked pitifully.

"No," I answered in a tiny voice, full of defeat, "but I guess we're doing the best we can."

This was the closest we ever came to consoling one another.

One night, after I had made us both another drink, he was quiet for a long time. Then he turned to me with a request.

"I want you to do something for me and if you love me, you will do it," he started. He paused for a long time. Then he opened his hand and in it was a bottle of pills. "I have enough here to put me to sleep permanently. I want you to leave me alone all day—I'll decide the day—just leave me alone for twelve hours. By that time, we'll both be out of our misery.

This knocked me completely off base. What he was asking of me was unthinkable, against all standards by which I lived. I don't know how long I sat there before I shook my head. My hands were shaking, spilling my drink. In a trembling voice I answered him. "You are asking me to assist you in taking your life and I can't do it. I burst into tears and, choking and sobbing moaned, "I just can't do this."

"How dare you refuse me?" he ranted. "It's my decision, not yours or anybody else's. Who do you think you are, playing God this way?" He lashed out with bitter accusations. "Now I see your true colors," he shouted. "You're turning your back on me, thinking of only yourself and your precious beliefs".

Cringing before his anger, I remember wailing "No. No. " The horror of what he was contemplating sent panic creeping up my throat and started quicksilver thoughts darting through my brain; *he doesn't believe this is a sin; how could he do this without somebody finding out; where would I go for twelve hours; what could I tell the doctor, the ambulance driver, the doorman, my children, for God's sake! What would I say to them? Where did he get the pills?*

"Help me, God," I prayed. My head was pounding. I couldn't think straight. Finally when I could speak, I kneeled in front of him, putting my arms around his waist. "Bob," I said, trying to steady my quavering voice, "you can't ask this of anyone—you just can't. If this is what you want to do, then it is your decision and you alone can act on it. But you must know that I believe differently than you. I believe what you intend to do is wrong and not the plan that God has for you." I cupped his face now wet with tears in my hands and said, "Won't you try to understand that? It isn't that I don't love you—you know I do. But because I *do* love you, I can't stand by and see you do this. It isn't the answer."

He bent his head and let his tears flow freely through his hands. I kneeled in front of him, crying with him, feeling helpless and lost. After a long time, he whispered, "I should have known better than to think you would help."

It was a slap in the face. I had fallen way short of the person he needed and now he had no one to turn to. In his eyes I was branded a traitor.

It wasn't long after that his final stage began. One night around midnight, I woke to hear Bob moaning and groaning in the next bed.

"Please get me something for the pain—call the doctor, do something, please!" he begged. I did as he asked and the doctor told me what to administer. It didn't help. I gave him a second dose and then a third. It was not helping. Again, my shaking hands dialed the doctor's number. He picked up immediately. "Please," I pleaded. "You've got to come over here now." He said he would come immediately. Thank you, God, I breathed.

Inside of fifteen minutes, the doctor arrived and when he examined Bob, he showed me Bob's back, which was purple, a mass of broken blood vessels. "His extreme pain is caused by massive hemorrhaging, " the doctor explained, and we can control this only in the hospital. We must get him dressed and to the hospital. In the car, I held Bob's hands. It was cold that night—no snow as yet—but inside of me the storm of the century was raging.

The hospital, quiet and shut down for the night, had an eerie, unreal quality. We entered through a side door accessible only to staff. Our emergency now had an aura of a covert action, adding to the nightmarish evening. We took a back elevator to the eighth floor where the doctor had arranged for a private room. It was dark—no nurses anywhere. Bob shuffled in, shoulders slumped, his face pleading for someone to help him. The doctor and I helped him to the bed. It was stripped—the mattress bare of linens-giving the room a forlorn look.

The doctor helped Bob to the bed and left saying he would be back. Bob sat down wearily on the striped ticking, still in his Brooks Brother Harris tweed overcoat. He looked forlorn and frightened and my heart started whispering words of comfort but they were stuck behind a huge lump in my throat. All I could do was stroke his hands. The doctor returned. "Everything is in order so let's go," he said. Bob turned to me, his face lined with anguish. "Where are you going?" he cried in alarm. "You can't leave me. Stay with me, please."

The doctor started behaving like a robot with no words of consolation. "We must leave," he ordered. "We are breaking rules and if we are found here, I could lose my privileges. I have given orders to the head nurse, who will be here shortly, and we must get out of the hospital now. He turned to leave but I grabbed his coat sleeve.

"You have to stay—you have to help him," I sobbed. And then I started yelling. "What kind of a doctor are you, anyway. If you cared you would stay and see Bob put to bed properly." He grabbed my arm and pushed me toward the door. "Get a hold of yourself," he demanded. "And be quiet. Do you want to get us thrown out?"

"NO!" I won't leave," I cried. "Stop pushing me that way. I can't leave my sick husband, sitting on that bare bed in the dark with nobody to help him! Don't you have a heart?" I screamed. He grabbed my arm. I wrenched free and then he grabbed me again and half carried me to the door. My last look at Bob tore me in two. His shoulders were shaking and his head was bent in a posture of defeat. I could hear him crying, "You are betraying me—you are both abandoning me." Stumbling and sobbing, I let the doctor lead me out of the darkened room. All the way to the car those words burned deeply into my very soul. Yes, I think we both abandoned Bob when he needed us the most.

It was snowing. The doctor helped me into the rear seat of the waiting car, slammed the door and climbed in beside the driver. "Beekman Place," he told him. Through the window, I watched the darkness become polka-dotted with big white flakes. Watching the snow calmed me down and slowly my sobbing ceased. In its place came a fury as cold as those flakes falling on the windshield. I was beginning to hate this doctor with a deep passion. He had no right to treat Bob and me in such an insensitive way and I would see that my doctor, who had referred him, was told everything.

In the morning, I went back to the hospital and found Bob's room buzzing with activity. Nurses were flitting around and annoying him. No, he didn't want a bedpan but when they tried the bathroom, it was too painful. No, he didn't want to sit up in a chair. He just wanted to lie down, please! Our family doctor came in the midst of all this confusion and told them to leave.

When order was restored he explained to both of us that New York Hospital was a teaching hospital and although Bob had one of the best rooms, the staff and students would still visit him. The doctor gave me the person to call for round the clock care for Bob and I found three highly recommended terminal patient nurses who were available. He would have excellent care, my doctor assured me. I stayed with Bob until visiting hours were over and when I left, Bob was resting comfortably, even managing a smile. "Thanks for coming," he said.

I cried all the way home.

It took thirty days—thirty sorrowful days—until Bob was finally ready to say goodbye. We did all we could to make him comfortable but we could sense when he wanted his time alone. Not so one of his friends, though, who insisted on visiting him faithfully every afternoon. Talk was stilted and forced and when it ran out his friend would pick up the New York Times and rattle the pages endlessly until Bob yelled at him to get out—this wasn't the New York Public Library's reading room, he said.

What little patience Bob had was gone and his nerves, as well as ours, were stripped and raw. I remember him asking over and over what time it was, saying it was taking a hell of a long time to die.

When it was apparent that Bob couldn't last much longer, Anne and Budd flew in from the west and joined Brooks and me in the daily vigil. Always close at hand, they would often urge me to leave and take a walk or get a quiet lunch.

The Boston kids phoned every day, offering to come, but I begged them to stay home. I wanted to spare them the pain of again losing someone they loved. What we needed most of all were their thoughts and prayers for the end to come quietly and soon. But each day came and went with hardly a change and I went home for another sleepless night filled with tortured thoughts and tears, intermingled with fervent prayers for strength.

Day twenty-nine. I walked into the room and immediately noticed Bob's breathing was interspersed with low rhythmic moans. Danielle, my favorite nurse, was on duty and she was talking to him.

"That's all right, Mr. Betts. You go ahead and moan all you want to."

"Is he conscious?" I whispered.

"He hears us, but doesn't want to talk. The moaning is a result of a change in his condition, a preparing of the body for what lies ahead. We have given him maximum doses of morphine, plus other painkillers, so the moaning isn't from pain. It is a reaction we can't exactly put our fingers on, scientifically. He can't control it. We hear it in terminal patients all the time."

"God, I hope she's right," I said to myself. It was a mournful sound that I could only stand for short intervals so I walked every inch of the hallways in the hospital—sometimes with one of the kids—most of the time alone. Whenever I felt strong enough, I went back to see if there was any change, only to hear him still moaning. How many hours this went on I cannot say. It seemed interminable. The day inched toward darkness and visiting hours were over and the nurse kindly told us to leave. I recall that last night standing by the side of the bed, conscious of the sickly sweet smell of death –the same gagging smell I remembered when I was with my parents and my brother and sister in their final hours. You can never forget that smell. Brooks, Anne, and Budd stood by my side as we said goodbye to a wonderful man who had given us so much and who we loved from the bottom of our hearts. We knew before long he would be in another place.

Back home, I threw myself down on my bed, exhausted, and fell into a deep sleep. Toward dawn, something awakened me. I lay on my back, trying to clear my head, when suddenly; a movement near the ceiling caught my eyes. I watched a wispy emanation dipping and swirling, back and forth over my bed for a long time. In that period of half- consciousness, I idly wondered what it was, calmly accepting this extraordinary happening. Then someone was knocking on my door. It was Anne, in tears, telling me the hospital had called. Bob had died a short time ago. The time of his death coincided precisely with the phenomenon I had just witnessed. I knew that the emanation was Bob, who had come to bid me farewell.

I dressed quickly and Annie and I took a cab to the hospital. In the hall outside Bob's room, we found our family doctor along with Brooks and Budd. We clung together, crying, for a long time, desperate to push aside the sorrow and the emptiness.

The mechanics of making funeral arrangements gave a purpose to the long days and nights that followed. Bob had given us written instructions that we were not to have a big memorial service in New York. He wanted to be cremated and his remains shipped to Wyoming where, sometime after Jackson's winter snows had disappeared, he wanted a small service for the family and close friends in the chapel in Grand Teton National Park. The obituary in the New York Times was matter of fact—no picture— again honoring Bob's wishes. When the news of his death reached the public, the response was heartwarming. Phone calls and flowers, cards and letters expressing sympathy, arrived daily. It was a beautiful tribute to an extraordinary person.

For weeks after Bob's death I stumbled through the days in a dream state, managing somehow to help handle all of the necessary details. Despair hung on my shoulders like a sodden shawl, which was to be expected, I suppose, along with the shutting down of my daily life. Friends stopped calling after a while, and the family left to take up their own lives once again. My days were now gray blurs keeping pace with my aching heart, a pain no amount of aspirin could dull. Heartache? Can a heart actually ache like a backache or a headache? How naïve of me to believe this only happened in Shakespeare or in romantic novels. In the empty chasm following Bob's death, I learned all about this ache—so big it radiates through your body, causing you to throw yourself down on a bed and cry yourself into a state of exhaustion. But tears don't alleviate the ache or staunch the bleeding. I longed for some relief, but knew only time has the power to heal.

One bright spot saved me from complete collapse. Anne's second child was expected in May. When Jim and Anne invited me to come and be present at the birth of their second child, it did wonders for my gloom. I joyfully accepted the invitation. Anne had been just fine with this pregnancy and we all had our fingers crossed, praying that she would be spared any flare-up of her cancer.

Witnessing my daughter bring forth a child was a precious gift of sharing. I clasped my hands in joy, tears misting my eyes when I saw Anne holding Catherine in her arms. The look of wonder on her face was exactly how I remembered feeling. She told me later that the moment she and Catherine looked at each other, it was instant bonding.

I remember Anne's doctor carefully examining the afterbirth and declaring there were no signs of cancer—"no enemy infiltration," he said. We all let out a sigh of relief and gave deep thanks to our benevolent power; I accompanied the proud parents and baby home. I stayed a few days until the house was running smoothly, then packed up and left for my Wyoming house on the hill to plan for Bob's memorial service.

It had been a long three months since he died and everyone in the family felt the need for a final loving tribute to Bob. But before we could do this, winter had to loosen its hold on Jackson Hole so we decided to hold the memorial service in June. By that time, the weather would cooperate, Anne could travel, and the rest of the family would be free to join us. The whole family came except my sister whose frail health made traveling out of the question. What they say about weddings and funerals being like family reunions is so true. It was the first time my brother Buddy and his wife had met any of the Boston kids and there had been many years since they had seen Brooks, and Anne. It was a bittersweet time of high emotion

The chapel in Grand Teton National Park was the perfect place for the service. It was small and rustic, holding about fifty people, and built of lodge pole pine logs. Behind the pulpit was a big picture window framing a glorious view of the Grand Teton Mountain. I remember sitting numbly in the front pew listening to my children speak lovingly of their father. Through the chapel's window, my eyes focused on the mountains. I felt their strength and serenity tying this humble ceremony to a much larger world beyond

The reception afterward at the Strutting Grouse restaurant gave everyone a chance to relax and meet with each other. I suppose I must have appeared normal but I felt disembodied. What a strange misty void I inhabited. Maybe this was nature's way of taking the horrible cutting edge off the reality.

Later, the family gathered at our mountain house. A spot had been cleared in the woods and a lichen rock from Budd's ranch had been placed under a sheltering pine tree. It now had a bronze plaque set into the top. On it were these words Bob had chosen:

I will lift up my eyes to the hills from whence cometh my help.

The pine boughs sighed in the gentle wind. We came forth, one at a time, to pay homage, each one taking some of his ashes and scattering them to the wind. We placed the simple bronze urn deep in the waiting hole and one by one, we all threw a handful of dirt on top of the urn until it was completely covered. We stood and held hands. It was then I heard the *scree, scree* of the red tail hawk high overhead, soaring high above the hold of the planet. He was glorying in his freedom and suddenly, I felt comforted. This magnificent bird was giving me a message. As I watched him catch a thermal and glide effortlessly through the sparkling air I knew he was telling me that someday we all would be set free to soar to the heavens.

When everyone went back to their homes, the buzz of humanity for me stilled and the resulting silence in my little Wyoming cabin grew unbearable. It made me decide to go back to New York to start putting my life back together.

It was late in the afternoon three days later when I unlocked my apartment door and stepped inside. The room felt cold and unfriendly and I saw with dismay how the ficus tree by the living room window had withered, dropping yellow leaves all over the floor. Even quickly turning on the lights didn't dispel the funereal gloom. Memories of Bob's last days were everywhere and I knew I would quickly sink into depression if I stayed here. I had to get out.

Fortunately, Brooks had a small cottage on her property in Sag Harbor and she asked if I would like to stay there for a while. I grabbed at the chance. It was a charming little place so like the enchanted cottages from my childhood storybooks. It even had small casement windows and a white picket fence around it covered with climbing roses. Brooks gave me this welcoming space and with it came thirty days of quiet contemplation.

I walked the beach road everyday, drinking in the solitude and salt air, wishing I were a gull and could fly away from all my sorrow. I did some renovating for Brooks—bought an under-the-counter refrigerator and some new cupboards for the little kitchen. I hung lace trimmed café curtains— the kind you would see in an Irish country cottage—on the casement windows. Armed with fresh watercolors and paper, I attempted some watercolor painting; and I went on a diet, which required hours of vegetable preparation and cooking. I wrote letters and wrote in my journal. I read and read and read.

At the end of the month, I had dropped a dress size and welcomed a return of some purpose in my life. I wanted to take a trip through New England to visit old friends. I felt ready. So, regretfully, I packed up and said goodbye to Brooks and the little white cottage. I loved being there, but it was time to move on.

The Long Island Expressway was bumper-to-bumper. In-between stops and starts, there was plenty of time for woolgathering and I automatically braked and accelerated while allowing my thoughts to wander. Out of the blue, something jolted me into the present. In my peripheral vision I saw a large white truck in the left lane creeping up on me. As it came alongside,

I saw there was one word written in oversize letters on the side: WINKLER. Tears spurted out of my eyes. This had to be a message from Bob saying all was fine and not to grieve. Just one word—that's all it took but for a moment, I was happy. I never saw that word again—anywhere—but on that busy Expressway, I could feel Bob right beside me

This was the second time I'd felt him close by. The first time happened in Central Park not long after he died. A funny little man playing an old-fashioned hurdy-gurdy caught my attention. He had a monkey, dressed in a red hat and matching vest trimmed in gold braid, cruising the crowd for donations. As the wind carried the notes my way, I recognized the Mozart composition—the same piece that played in my antique music box where the music set two tiny figures dancing. I sat there, on the park bench, weeping quietly, as I remembered the Christmas Bob gave me the lovely gift. "I hope you like it," he had murmured rather shyly. "I wasn't sure when I bought it." It was clear to me. All of these loving signs were necessary for saying my final goodbyes—the ones where I would at last let Bob go and take up my own life. .

The trip through New England was a bit more stressful than I had anticipated, with too many parties and long days of antiquing, visits to historical places, straw-hat theaters. I loved my friends but I found I now tired easily and would have loved a quiet lakeside retreat instead of so much "doing".

I had saved a long weekend, before going home, to stay with George and Jean in Hancock, New Hampshire. This little town, dating back to the Revolutionary days of John Hancock, had much to soothe some of my rough edges, and as I stretched out on their patio, iced tea in hand, a small sigh of pleasure came from deep inside of me. I could feel the chord of life, which had been stretched to breaking point, begin to loosen and very faint hums begin.

Jean and I were busy preparing dinner one night, harmonizing one of our favorite show tunes, when the phone rang. Jean picked it up. I heard her say "She's right here" and handed me the phone with a worried look on her face.

"Mom," I heard Anne crying at the other end, "They found cancerous growths in both my breasts." Instantly, the little angels of hope for Anne flew before dark reality. "Oh, my God," I cried. "It just can't be. Say it isn't so. Say they made a mistake." But it was true. This was the phone call I had been dreading in my night's darkest hours.

Memory is fuzzy about my trip back to New York except remembering it was interminable and full of wrong turns. One turn landed me in the middle of the Bronx with no signs to anywhere. At that moment, I felt I was literally falling to pieces. But I straightened up and followed my nose until an approach to the Triborough Bridge told me where I was. I knew how to get home to Beekman Place.

When I turned the key in my front door, I walked into a room of cold, stale air. This time I spent no time feeling sorry for myself but, just as Bob would have done, I sprang into action. I called a neighbor of mine in Florida who had been cured of breast cancer, she said, by a wonderful doctor in Germany. She gave me all the information and I persuaded Anne and Jim to make the trip to see him. They came home unimpressed with the German cancer specialist but Anne dutifully followed his prescribed regime—dozens of his pills of special foul smelling formulae every day that made her throw up. After a few weeks, she threw them all in the trash. I shook my head when she told me this but said nothing. This was her decision and her courage was humbling. I had no part in it except to be there when she wanted me.

There was nothing in their lives now that gave them any pleasure except Christie and Catherine. The joy they gave Anne and Jim was a thousand times the sum of their lives here on earth. Without those toddlers, the days would have been unbearable.

It had been about six months after the trip when Jim called. "Emmie," he said with a trembling voice. "I hate to ask but you did say you would come when we needed you. Well, the time is here. We really need to have you here—Anne needs you, I need you and Christie and Catherine need you." His voice trailed off, pitifully.

I booked a hotel suite close to their house, which was brown outside and in with windows that were heavily draped—not much sunlight penetrated the gloom. It was such a depressing, sad household that I could only bear to stay there for short intervals. Each day I shopped and did errands and spent a couple of hours playing with the girls. Anne never came downstairs. Fortunately, I met a lovely Spanish lady who cleaned my apartment unit and told her about Anne and asked if she had any free time. She quit her cleaning job and went to work for Jim. She came every day and cleaned, did the laundry, cooked and cared for the little girls. Without her, the whole situation would have been totally chaotic.

Jim was a mess, half out of his mind with grief and unable to cope. He would take off for hours, trying to get himself together, I suppose, but his bitterness grew daily and it vented itself in ugly scenes. I remember one afternoon I arrived with some groceries and found total bedlam. The girls were crying and Jim was screaming. "I want this damn dog out of here," and he picked up the little cocker spaniel and threw it across the room. He started yelling at the girls. "Shut up, shut up, both of you," which terrified them and only made them scream louder.

I quietly put the groceries away and made an offer to put the girls to bed but Jim waved me away. I felt utterly helpless so I quietly slipped out the door and walked the four blocks back to my rented rooms and spent another sleepless night.

Each day when I sat in the living room, watching TV with the girls, my heart was upstairs in the room where Anne lay in her bed. I longed to be with her but her orders were no one was to come up unless invited. She wanted no visitors. But one day, Jim came to me and said Anne asked for me. I remember climbing the stairs with a heart beating so hard it threatened to jump right through my sweater. I went to her bed and she patted the side of it for me to sit. "Hi, honey," I croaked. I was so choked up I could hardly breathe. "You wanted to see me?" I asked?

"I want you to sing to me. Sing me that song "Tammy". I remember you used to sing "Tammy" when you were putting me to bed. Please. Sing "Tammy" to me. Her soft brown eyes were full of remembering. I cleared my throat and started. I had to start over more than once. Then, through a trembling throatiness that barely sounded like singing, I sang the song from her childhood. When I was finished, she said "I always loved that song, Mom. Thanks." I bent to kiss her but she turned her head. I told her I loved her and I went back to her little girls and Jim.

Then the day came when Anne said she was ready for the hospice. We all stood at the bottom of the stairs as she slowly came down, one step at a time, on the arms of Sylvia, her minister.

"I guess I'm an invalid now," she said softly. I made a move toward her but she shook her head. She didn't want any help from us—just Sylvia. Even at this final stage of her life, it was hard for Anne to accept a loving touch. She would always draw back from an embrace. It was a life-long rejection that hurt me, and one I could never understand.

Anne wanted to be surrounded by things she loved and the hospice encouraged us to bring anything she wanted. I can still see Jim and Budd carrying in the loveseat from their den as well as her favorite chair and coffee table. Brooks and I followed Anne's instructions and arranged it all like she was furnishing a new home. Perhaps she was.

One of us was always with her and the little girls were in and out all the time. Of course, they couldn't comprehend what was happening. The hours I spent sitting on her favorite loveseat were rich ones, taking me back through the years with this irrepressible free spirited daughter of mine who embraced life. I had to smile as I remembered how as a toddler, she seemed to be thrown out of nursery school daily for kicking or biting her classmates and even her teacher. And my heart swelled with pride when I remembered the times when she befriended someone in trouble or brought home a homeless kitten. Life with Anne was turned on high. It was never dull. The contrasts between her dark and light sides were extreme and when something tickled her funny bone her infectious laughter would shatter the air.

The day before she died, I sat on her bed and fed her chicken soup. I can still see her huge brown eyes, looking into mine, full of love. "Thanks, Mom," she whispered. "That was good."

I held her hand until it was over. In death she looked like an angel painting by Raphael, peaceful and touched by heaven. No more would Anne's laugh and unique take on life add spice to my days. No more would I hear that enthusiastic, "Hi, Mom!" on the phone. Now an even vaster landscape of empty days stretched ahead of me, ending in a colorless horizon. I was just beginning to climb out of the pit of despair after Bob died and now I felt I had slipped and fallen into an even deeper one.

The ache in my heart returned with a vengeance, taking away sleep and bringing despair that clutched me in a merciless grip. The tears never stopped. Losing Bob was, I thought, the worst kind of sorrow anyone could imagine, but now with my child gone I felt myself falling apart. But nature had shut me down to idle speed and allowed me to.function. I hardly remember Anne's funeral and the church packed with her friends. During Sylvia's loving tribute to Anne, I had to smile when the little girls, in purple velvet dresses, ran all over the church, stealing everyone's attention and it reminded me of when I was flower girl and stole the show from my sister at her wedding.

Back in New York, the sense of loss closed in on me like a chilling fog. My mind was fuzzy; my movements slow and unsteady. I suffered from vertigo and was fearful of walking to the corner store. The simplest daily chore loomed up as high as Mt. Everest, and, as a result, I accomplished little. Budd and Brooks urged me to seek help. The state I was in must have alarmed and angered Brooks greatly for she began to berate me for not keeping my checkbook balanced, for my loss of memory, for making foolish purchases, for my apathy. At the time, it hurt to be treated so harshly, but now I realize she was scared—frightened of what might happen to me. It was the lowest period in my sixty-seven years and it was a painful two years before I began to feel like myself again.

CHAPTER 20

Running On Empty

MY heart started beating a little bit faster as the plane began its approach to the Phoenix airport. I peered out the window. It had been twelve years since Bob and I had enjoyed a great weekend here with Anne- twelve years that had pulled me apart and rearranged my whole life. The plane dipped lower and Camelback Mountain came into view, along with the palm trees lining the drive to the Arizona Biltmore. As the plane taxied to the terminal, I thought how strange life is. Here I was retracing steps I had taken with Bob so long ago. With a shrug I collected my belongings, exited the plane and made my way to the baggage claim area. The shuttle driver introduced himself and helped me into the station wagon. We were off -to the retreat I had booked—Rancho Los Cabelleros.

Two hours later, as a haze of the late October day gently touched the mountains, the driver stopped the shuttle in front of a charming hacienda. The staff greeted me warmly and showed me to the Bradshaw room, a snug efficiency, which would be my home for a month and a half. I unpacked my clothes and art supplies, and prepared to settle down for a while in an entirely new world. I liked my little place. It was comfortable and pleasant, decorated in sunlit Arizona colors, with the right amount of Mexican influence here and there. The easy atmosphere soothed my harried spirit and I felt contentment creeping over me like a covering of down.

It was just a short walk to the dining room, my connection with humanity. Although my quarters included an efficiency kitchen, eating by myself was just too painful and I preferred the dining room with its buzz of people enjoying themselves. I hoped the time would come when I would no longer dread walking into a restaurant by myself and asking for a table for one. Now being alone made me feel vulnerable, and making friends with this feeling of separation would take time. So I took great comfort in cozying up to people whenever I could.

The days were long and lazy. The ranch had a station wagon shuttle to the small town of Wickenburg nearby. A couple of other gals and I found some interesting spots—a wonderful book store, a hardware store that delighted the creative do-it-yourselfer, including great watercolor paint and paper, and a boutique filled with stunning one-of-a-kind hand-made clothes. The owner was fun loving, slightly nutty, and soon became my soul sister. I couldn't help comparing her shop with Threadneedle House. It had the same caring atmosphere that welcomed us whether we bought anything or not. In six weeks, over many pots of coffee, we became close friends.

One beautiful morning, I hopped into my rental car and made the two-hour drive to Scottsdale. I was anxious to see some old friends from Chappaqua who were now confirmed desert lovers. It was a wonderful get-together and as I was leaving one of them called out,

"Hey, Emmie, why don't you move to Scottsdale? You would love it here and we would love to have you here." I laughed and answered, "Find me a house and I'll do it!"

The more I thought about it, the more living in the southwest appealed to me. My friends knew of a realtor in Scottsdale who just happened to know of the perfect house for me. I called and made an appointment. She knew what she was doing. I loved the house. The deal was cemented and in record time I found myself the surprised owner of a "fifties" ranch house on the Mountain Shadows golf course. It was badly in need of a complete update and my head was already busy designing the changes.

Through my years of moving from place to place, I trusted my intuition to tell me if I was on the right track and this time was no exception. When I told the kids I now had a house in Scottsdale, they were not at all happy with my decision. Budd's reaction was "Mom, you have got to stop building nests every two years. Get a hold of yourself. Isn't the Wyoming house enough?" Brooks was really worried about my mental state.

"What am I supposed to be doing?" I demanded. "I promised your father I would leave New York after he died and establish residency in tax-friendly Wyoming. He wanted to save you kids from having to pay huge inheritance taxes when "the bus hit me,"—a euphemism my accountant was fond of using. "So now you are unhappy with my house purchase here in Scottsdale. You know I can't stay up on the hill in Wyoming all winter. Please tell me where I have gone wrong?" They couldn't give me a good reason.

Richard, a fun-loving highly skilled builder, appeared on the scene and luckily he had time to give to my project. His enthusiasm for my ideas and his fertile imagination were in perfect sync with mine and together we transformed a dingy ranch house, circa 1950, into a charming French country cottage. Working on the house saved me from real trouble with depression— the kind that takes you so far under you can hardly find your way back. I knew how close I was to that dark world. I knew how frightened I was at times seeing reality dancing just beyond my grasp. I guess I didn't know how very ill I was but this house project made me get out of bed every morning, get dressed, and show up when the workman arrived and then pretend I was fine.

Slowly, the days completed their cycles. The weeks turned into months and at last, the house was finished. The transformation was stunning. With this came a satisfaction that boosted my morale and brought back my confidence. The first thing I did was to give a big open house party to show it off. What a thrill it was to hear all the oohs and aahs from my friends. But when I turned out the light that night, the longing I had deep inside to be back in New York crept into bed beside me.

In all the conversations I had with Brooks and Budd, I don't think they ever realized how homesick I was. I never told them. I know they were vastly relieved that their squirrelly mother now had a lovely country cottage in the sun-belt to run to in the winter and the little cabin on the Wyoming hillside for the summer months. It seemed the perfect combination.

For three years, I was satisfied in Scottsdale. Besides my beautiful house I was discovering the fascinating land around it. I had never been close to the desert and the more I paid attention to this ever changing landscape, the more it proved to be a wonderful balm to the hurt in my soul. I never dreamed the desert could be so spectacular. In my mind's eye, it was painfully dry land, dotted with cactus and sagebrush—a place where the wind's hot breath sent the tumbleweeds flying across the snake-laden sand.

But I learned there was much more to the desert. I learned it was a patient teacher and I learned patience in getting to know it. I soon learned to get out of bed early so I could stand under its clear sky and watch it get ready for the new day—watch the deep azure blueness lighten to lavender then fracture itself into streaks of pink and yellow. It always filled me with awe, feeling I was standing on the brink of something big, like watching creation itself.

I had loving friends who invited me to many benefit parties, dinners and luncheons—all part of the oil that makes social life hum in Scottsdale. Appointments dotted my calendar like so many dead flies. Busyness filled my days. In spite of all this, at the end of each evening soiree when I turned the key in the front door, the silent emptiness reached out and gathered me in. Also, the restlessness persisted. I decided to call my accountant.

"Ok, Jeffrey, just how much money am I saving the kids by living like a refugee out here in play land? I have to be honest with you. It is fine for vacations but it isn't New York. I want to come home. Can you make this work financially?"

He called the next day with a very positive solution and I was thrilled!

The house didn't sell quickly. The house hunters, it seemed, wanted southwestern décor with Navaho rugs and mission furniture—not country French. Weeks went by. Finally, my savvy real estate broker turned up friends of hers who always wanted to live in Mountain Shadows. She persuaded them to make the trip from California and they loved the house. A closing date was decided. Only one more month and I would be on my way home.

The night before the moving truck arrived I sat on the patio a long time watching an evening sky the color of newly blossomed lilacs throw warm shadows behind the stately saguaros. In the stillness of the early desert evening, my thoughts turned to the strange pattern of my life. What was I running to or running from back and forth across the country? What was causing this restlessness that would not leave me alone? Most of my friends were happy and content, or so I thought, to stay put and not go running from pillar to post, as I seemed to be doing. I looked to the heavens for an answer but saw only the first stars beginning to blink their message. Oh, well, I sighed, feeling a tinge of sadness about leaving. I did have these wonderful years here in Scottsdale. Locking the patio door behind me, I went into the house leaving my question hanging in the soft evening air and thinking how happy I was to be going back home

The Stanhope hotel in New York was a quiet and gracious retreat from the city's steady beat. Breakfast served in my room with the morning New York Times, messages carefully taken and given at the front desk, and a freshly made bed turned down at night with the offering of a chocolate rounded the ragged edges of my being. Of course, all of this luxury came with a price and as I signed one bill after another, I began to sense the financial urgency of finding my own place.

"Lois," I wailed to my friendly realtor, "we've been searching for two weeks! We have to find something. I'm getting damp palms making out all these checks to the Stanhope Hotel!" She laughed and suggested we go back and take another look at a pied-a-Terre at 1060 Park Avenue that had possibilities. It was very small but charming. The kitchen would not hold more than one person at a time and you could not open the oven door all the way because the sink blocked it. But the tiny living room had a fireplace! Gas fired, yes, but still a fireplace. To have a fireplace was one of my dearest desires so I bought the apartment.

My Lilliputian apartment was within seeing distance of where Brooks lived. To find an apartment so close was not planned and far from ideal and it caused a few shouting matches between us. I tried to stay out of her life as much as possible as she was working hard for her MFA at New York University and stressed to her limits. But now and then, when she felt up to it, we did get together for dinner.

One night I remember standing by Brooks' kitchen window, looking down on the steady stream of yellow cabs on Park Avenue. She was rinsing lettuce for a salad. We were talking about a friend from high school she was still in touch with here in the city which brought to mind her very serious heart throb in her senior year.

"Brooks, what ever happened to Bob Macduff? Does anyone know where he is? You're still close with that old group except Bob. It seems he just dropped off the edge of the earth."

She stared at me and then laughed.

"It's funny you should ask. I just had a long telephone call from him. He's in Los Angeles and wants to come east to see me." She couldn't hide the wonder and excitement I saw in her eyes.

This turned the pages back to the turbulent decade of the sixties, when Brooks and Bob were in high school.

Brooks and Bob. Even their names flowed smoothly together. When this shy, quiet boy with the ponytail came into Brooks' life, she blossomed. But after graduation, they went to different colleges miles apart and after a while, they drifted apart.

Now, twenty-four years later, Brooks and Bob were about to bridge the divide. Brooks went to the airport to meet Bob. When they arrived at my apartment they were both lit up like Christmas trees, stumbling over words and giggling like kids. It was obvious they were still crazy about each other. Brooks called often from her tiny house in Sag Harbor to say what a wonderful time they were having and hinted that if Bob asked her to marry him, she would. By the end of the week Bob popped the question and of course she said yes. They didn't want a church wedding but instead planned a ceremony at Budd's ranch.

On a windy hilltop overlooking the vast Wyoming landscape I watched the long ago high school sweethearts come together as man and wife. Brooks was radiant in a beaded native Indian dress and Bob wore a western hat, which he wore throughout the whole ceremony along with his buffalo plaid jacket. The families stood in a ring around them, wiping away joyful tears as the local judge's right-hand girl, pronounced them man and wife. We all let out a whoop and true to Western tradition, sailed our hats high in the air. Life seldom gives you a second chance and I watched this fairytale come true with a singing heart.

For a while, my life was going along pretty well but I needed another project. So, I decided to put an addition on the Jackson Hole house. My family thought me whacko but I reminded them it was much better for me to do this than to spend my time on a psychiatrist's couch. Only I knew the therapeutic benefits I would get from this creative endeavor. So, again, they watched their impulsive Mom launch another project.

I flew to Wyoming and threw myself into this with everything I had. It took hours of planning and decision making—waiting for the weather to cooperate—and then the frustration of waiting for workmen to show up to do their jobs. It was a nail biting time watching the bank account shrivel but when I stood in front of the completed restoration; I knew it was worth every penny.

The little mountain cabin had grown into a gracious summer retreat. As far as spending any winter months there, I had given that up after one try. Once, I had convinced Bob to spend Christmas in our original cabin. We flew to Denver with Chris and John and were ready to board the plane to Jackson when the cancelled sign appeared on the monitor. The airport in Jackson was closed because of blizzard conditions. We all groaned. But instead a giving up the whole idea, we rented a car and after a hair-raising trip on roads covered with black ice, we finally found ourselves snug in our mountain cabin with plenty of food and logs for the fireplace. Everything was picture perfect until the clouds rolled in bringing the worst kind of blizzard. It was so fierce that we had to evacuate and spend Christmas in an almost deserted hotel in Jackson. Bob never let me forget it. "You and your little girl fantasies," he said shaking his head. "Are you ever going to give them up?"

I was feeling very guilty and sorry I had persuaded him to do this. But as we were having a very dry and tasteless turkey dinner in the hotel dining room, the snow stopped. The blizzard was over. "Bob," I said plaintively, "Why don't we walk to St. John's for the midnight service." To my delight, he agreed.

There, in that tiny chapel, a small group of people gathered around the chancel holding hands and singing carols. At midnight, we wished everyone a merry Christmas and walked back to the hotel under a sky full of stars. The frigid night was silent—not a sound except our crunchy footsteps on the snowy sidewalk. It was forty-two degrees below zero but inside of me was a flame of love burning as bright as the Christmas star.

When winter in New York gradually surrendered to the sun and warm temperatures of spring, I often found myself taking the Hampton jitney to Sag Harbor to spend a lazy weekend with Brooks and Bob in their charming house in the woods. A short five minutes away was the great Atlantic. It drew me like a magnet.

I loved the wild wind coming off the water. I loved walking the beach with them, throwing sticks for their dog Gabby, laughing at her biting the waves as they rolled in. The clean salty air and the roar of the ocean always brought back that carefree feeling of my summer in Ocean City and for a couple of hours, I was a kid again, when Buddy and I would roam the beach like little earth children. When he married and left for California, he took a part of me with him and I missed him terribly.

Ten minutes away from Sag Harbor lay the village of Southampton, New York —the summer playground of the rich and famous—a place where people who desire to rub shoulders with those of the manor born, flock to be seen by whoever happens to be looking. Although the trip from the city sometimes took three hours of bumper to bumper traffic, it was worth the discomfort for there was nothing about the Hamptons that didn't please the senses—clean ocean breezes, twenty-seven miles of empty beaches, open farmlands and charming villages that evoked a Long Island of long ago. I yearned to have a taste of this famous place and my curiosity led me straight to a realtor's office.

When Lianne, the realtor, and I pulled up in front of an attractive white-shingled Cape Cod house surrounded by blooming azaleas and hydrangeas,

I gleefully told her she didn't have to show me anything else. This was perfect and I'd take it for a month.

It was the month of April—a fickle month –warm and sunny days interspersed with damp chilly ones. When the sun shone, Brooks and I loved walking the beach, Gabby running happily along with us. Then, when the skies turned gray and everyone huddled inside, I turned on the sound system in my little Cape Cod house and built a cheery fire, relishing the snap and crackle from the apple wood logs. But, no matter what the weather served up, inspiration came easily in this friendly house and I found my paintbrush fairly flying across the watercolor paper leaving trails of just the right colors.

The end of the month came much too soon. I hated to leave Southampton and hoped I could return to this little house someday. For thirty lovely days, it had gently nurtured every part of me and I silently thanked the generous lady who let me share a part of her life.

Back in the bustling city, I started thinking again about purchasing a computer. I knew it would be a big change for me but the lure of the exploding field of high technology was hard to refuse. Here I was well into my seventies, going down the microchip path, fearful but intensely curious about this awesome bit of machinery and a little scared of how it could take over my life. Nevertheless, I ordered an IBM computer and when it was installed, I sat in front of it not knowing whether to laugh or cry. But little by little, I discovered how easy it was to type out my thoughts as fast as they came to mind and then edit and move them around just as fast. I found this whole new world fascinating. I was hooked.

June came and it was time to go west to Wyoming once more. I packed up my writing, my cowboy clothes, and boarded the plane, looking forward to long, sun-filled days and gentle evenings with my western friends. Summer was the season to celebrate and there would be benefits and parties almost every weekend. Too soon colder temperatures with a few snow showers would visit the valley and then the north would send its chilling breath to shrivel the wild flowers and send the geese to warmer climes. So, "let's play while we may—winter's on its way"—we all said.

The Wyoming summer was beginning to wind down when I got a telephone call from Brooks.

Hi, Mom," she said. "Bob and I found you a house to rent in Sag Harbor. Are you interested? We went over to see it and we think you will love it. It is an old nineteen-twenties type house and has a view of the bay and is furnished. They're willing to take a six month lease."

I was thrilled. "Oh, Brooks, this sounds perfect and if you and Bob like it, that's good enough for me. Go ahead and sign me up."

In a couple of weeks, I was back on the Hampton Jitney once more—this time to meet Brooks and Bob and see the rented house. Three hours later, I stepped down from the bus and into their car and we were on our way.

We finally turned into a very pretty, tree-lined side street. Another turn and there we were in front of the house.

This was it? I was a bit crestfallen. It was not what I expected at all. This wasn't the white house with black shutters and a striped awning I had been envisioning. This house was gray and somber looking and immediately reminded me of that dull toady house I lived in on Porter Street so long ago. My high hopes were slipping. We went up the steps and put the key in the front door. No go. Another attempt on the side door but that door wouldn't budge either. Finally, we pried open the front door and when I stepped inside the hall; the air that hit me was stale and unfriendly.

Something was not right but I obediently followed Brooks and Bob through the downstairs. To the right of the front hall was a very dark living room. I looked around. A shiver went through me. There was a fireplace but the owner said I was not to use it. This was a big disappointment because one thing I was looking forward to was a cheerful fire on cold, blustery days. Behind the living room a couple of tiny rooms led into a very large kitchen with a big table that could seat twelve. At the far end of the kitchen there was a bank of windows overlooking a small backyard with a very narrow view of the bay. Upstairs there were four bedrooms—great space for the family coming from Wyoming. This was a big plus as I visualized a happy crowd in that kitchen on Thanksgiving. I prayed I would begin to feel better about all this but I still couldn't say anything.

"Well, how do you like it, Mom? Bob and I thought it was just darling and wanted to move into it ourselves." I smiled weakly, not knowing what to say. My silence did not sit well with Brooks and Bob and I saw them rolling their eyes at one another.

I sat down on the window seat feeling like a lost puppy.

"Why aren't you saying anything, Mom? We looked all over the area and this was the best we could find and if you don't like it, too bad."

She pulled on her coat impatiently and turned to leave. "Don't ask us to do anymore house hunting for you," she said crossly. "This is your place for the winter and you might as well settle in and love it 'cause there's no way you can break the lease."

I finally found my voice. "It's fine, Brooks. I'm just a little befuddled with it all so please forgive me. I really appreciate all you and Bob did."

They finally left in a huff. I sat by the window for a long time, feeling guilty and sorry for myself. I had to face up to the fact that I was downright foolish to sign on to something sight unseen. Back and forth my thoughts flew like a nest of starlings in my head. Houses have always spoken to me, sending either a positive or negative message and this house was sending me a message as chilly as a fog off the bay. I would have loved to chuck the whole thing. But it was too late.

I lugged my suitcase up the stairs and unpacked in the cold bedroom that oozed dampness from every corner. When at last I climbed into the lumpy bed it was with a heavy heart. My vision of a lovely retreat by the bay had crumbled just like my sand castles in Ocean City so many years ago.

Making friends with a strange quirky house is not easy. The hot water spigot in the kitchen would only work if the cold water one was off. The sink sprayer leaked and sprayed me instead of the dishes. . The stove's oven was unreliable, and the first time I used it, the gas finally ignited with a mini explosion that scared the daylights out of me. Opening the side door was a daily tussle, and the front door would lock only if I threw my whole weight against it. The TV had such a bizarre hook- up I finally had to ask for help at the local TV store. The bed in the master bedroom was a disaster—not a soft spot anywhere in the thin mattress—so, from then on, I slept in the guest bed, which wasn't much of an improvement. On winter mornings, it was hours before the heat took the damp chill from the rooms. It reminded me of the bitter mornings in Prospect Park years ago when it was so hard to leave the warmth of my bed and face up to the icy room— how the crackling and hissing of the burning wood in the fireplace downstairs was such a wonderful wake-up song. But there was no chance of that here.

When you rent someone else's house and are observant, you can tell what kind of people lived there—whether they were fun loving or sober— kind and generous or stingy and mean. When I rented the Southampton cottage the previous spring, I found the warmth of kindness everywhere. I hoped that I would have left the same warm mark in the many houses I lived in. But there were no friendly feelings in this house even though the owner was an acclaimed writer and about to have one of his books made into a Broadway musical. From living in his house I knew a lot about him and I was happy we never met.

The weekends were not the happy ones I had anticipated. Some weeks, I made excuses to myself not to make the trip. The house was just too depressing. I never realized how the constant beat of New York gave me comfort—pushing away my loneliness. But the minute I opened the door of my Sag Harbor house, those dark days I had been battling all came rushing back. I had only myself to blame. I started counting the days until the lease was up.

We did have a great time over Thanksgiving when Budd and his family came east from Wyoming. I was happy having the whole family together. For almost a week, we filled that dreary, worn-thin place with the sounds of love and laughter and for a while my disappointment with the house was forgotten.

But too soon they left and I could feel the house withdrawing into its mean existence.

It was the first day of 1999—a brand new year with the gift of clear air and bright sunshine. I was staying with Brooks and Bob. It was early morning and the house was quiet. Even sweet Gabby, the dog was still in her bed when I silently crept into the kitchen and though she opened an eye and looked up at me, she didn't stir. As I busied myself with the morning coffee routine, I gazed out of the window letting my being meld with the dense wooded land.

How fortunate Brooks and Bob were to be tucked away in this peaceful corner—away from the noise of the summer pleasure seekers. Here their companions were the unseen creatures who lived among the trees and the undergrowth that sheltered the property. As I stood there musing, a special feeling began coursing through me. It was a feeling I hadn't experienced since I lived in my house of sunshine when I was a toddler—a feeling light and fluffy, full of sparkles and joy—singing like the hum of a tuning fork. I remember looking up at the sky at the beautiful clouds edged in pink. And I noticed the lily of the valley—how startled I was at the whiteness of the little bells against the glistening, dew-studded green leaves. It was as though I had just been placed here on earth and was looking around me for the first time. I remember looking at my mother and noticing for the first time how her laugh transformed her face. This was a time of great awakening for me when I was first reaching out from the tight little cosmos sheltering me. It was the first step in a very exciting journey and now, here again, after so many years, was that same wispy glimpse into a state of grace that defies description. I was totally bewildered by this all-encompassing feeling washing over me—so strange and beautiful.

This morning Brooks and I were going to drive to the ocean for a special ceremony. I had written down my hopes and aspirations for the New Year—thoughts that deserved the finest parchment but all I could find was a sheet from a yellow legal pad. I wrapped it around a stone and secured it with a rubber band—not very fancy, but it would have to do.

After breakfast we drove to the beach. A short walk from the parking lot and we were on top of the dune. The sight that met us was stunning. The sea must have known we were coming for she had dressed carefully. She wore an exquisite silken shimmer in iridescent hues of the palest mother-of-pearl colors—peach and gold, chartreuse, mauve and blue—all woven together like a splendid sari, stretching from shore to horizon, where the sky was embroidered in a slightly deeper blue border. We stood, dazzled by the beauty. I was aware of the air's caressing softness, the gentle shush of the waves. Time was holding its breath, waiting for our little ritual. In all my hundreds of days by the sea, I had never seen anything lovelier than what was before us, touching our very souls. With a prayer in my heart, I threw the stone as far as I could into the water. As the stone sank from sight, Brooks' delighted voice shook my reverie.

"Did you see what happened?" she cried joyfully. "Did you see the light around your stone when it hit the wave?"   It was the blessing.

The next afternoon back in the City, I found it disturbing to walk into 935 Park Avenue. It was my building and my apartment, but things felt slightly askew. It was hard to orient myself when part of me was still on the beach in Sag Harbor, dumbstruck and touched by something I couldn't name. The experience had gone to the very depths of my being and I couldn't shake it. Was it real or was it a trick of the subconscious?

I did not have the answer but I threw myself into my work, grateful that I had something concrete to do. Much to my relief, the writing took over my thoughts and my energy.

The months slipped by and again, it was time for the annual pilgrimage to Wyoming. I had to admit I was uneasy about the house on the hill. It no longer seemed a vital part of my life and something told me this was the time to look for the next step in my life.

CHAPTER 21

Mine Eyes To The Hills

IT had been a rainy, summer day in Jackson Hole. I did the town thing; post office; market; a little shopping for this and that. When I turned my trusty S10 Blazer north, my whole attitude changed. I shivered. Sadness, a most unwelcome passenger, had sprinkled its frostiness all over me. Why did I feel this way about going back to my house on the hill? Reluctantly, I had to admit that I could never recapture those carefree years and no good was ever going to come from sitting around in the lonely house. I knew I had to find another place to live.

But I wanted desperately to hold on to something real in the valley. I think I was afraid that once I sold our Kelly house, I would be tempted to leave Wyoming and end thirty-five years of joyous vacation living. It saddened me to think of giving up my friends and the art organizations I had helped build. I also was thinking practically. What I needed was a place here in Jackson Hole that would be cared for while I was absent. Being so far away most of the time, I no longer felt I could rely on just an occasional check by neighbors. This uncertainty pushed me to Teton Pines, a new golf course community at the base of the Teton Mountains. .

When I walked into the Pines Real Estate office, Dave, my friend, and one of the fathers of this development, was just ending a telephone conversation. He looked up with surprise. "Hi, Emmie," he said, extending his hand "What brings you over on our side of the valley so early this morning? —Coffee?" he asked.

I sat in the chair across the desk from him and savored the hot liquid. "I know you are wondering why I am here. It's not hard to figure out. Curiosity brought me. I'd love to take a look at some of your cluster homes or building sites. I think it's time for me to get off the hill."

We drove to a building site by a tranquil pond. The water softened by rushes and willows shimmered in the morning sun and the open view to the valley seemed to enfold me. "Yes," I sighed. "This is lovely. Let's go back to your office and talk."

I left him smiling with a deposit check in his hands.

The car and I floated back to Kelly in a bubble of happiness. Later, on the deck of our little mountain cabin, I celebrated my decision with a drink in hand. "Bob," I whispered, "please forgive me for leaving our house here on the hill, but you know as well as I it's time to leave the shadows behind."

I could feel Bob standing next to me, saying, "It's all right."

In the space of a couple of hours, a new house and a new life lay before me. How many times had I done this? How many times still lay ahead?

Dave suggested one builder and I signed on.

After months of long distance haggling over hundreds of details and the mounting costs, the Teton Pines house was ready. Moving day arrived. As I watched the men empty my mountain cabin piece by piece, I was not prepared for the emotional storm this would trigger inside of me. Leaving this house that Bob and I had built with love and dreams was one of the hardest things I ever had to do. Finally, the last box had been stowed, the door shut, and the truck was on its way to the Pines.

Slowly, I walked through the empty rooms and stood on the deck, gazing at the mountains, feeling their magic. I let my mind travel back over the past. Every corner of this little house held a fond memory—every bit of floor or kitchen counter, windowpane and chimney stone told hundreds of tales about the friends and family that had shared these spaces over twenty years. I could take my memories with me but I couldn't take the heart of the house. It would always stay within these walls. I looked around for the last time and quietly closed the door. As I drove away I was stricken with guilt. I had turned my back on something I had loved. All of a sudden, I was sobbing, tears running down my face so fast I could hardly see to drive. "Please, dear God," I prayed, "send someone who will love this house and take care of it the way we did."

The house went on the market. In the beginning, there was a lot of activity but no offers. Weeks and then months went by. Nothing. Then one afternoon in late summer Dave called.

"Guess what, Emmie? I have a good offer for your house!"

A surge of delight went through me. "Whatever it is, I'll take it. The house needs people in it. It has been empty long enough.

Now that the Kelly house belonged to someone else, I relaxed and began to enjoy my Teton Pines house. The first two summers were quiet ones, where I took my morning coffee out on the deck with only the company of the blue heron, quietly waiting for his breakfast to glide by in my pond. In the evening, I would patiently wait for the owl's first tentative hoot from the pine tree. I loved the hush that evening brought, when all the birds had found their perches for the night and nature slowly pulled her curtain down..

Then in 1999 the building boom took hold in Teton Pines with a vengeance. It came on with little warning and filled the air with shouting construction workers—the staccato of staple guns—of hammers and whining saws splitting the air with their harsh sounds before eight in the morning. All day, a constant stream of workers' pick-ups and huge trucks filled with everything from top soil to trees to imported decorative rock, lumbered by my house, turning the quiet road into a busy thoroughfare.

To my dismay, foundations were dug for three new houses within a stone's throw from mine, much too close to each other. I shrugged my shoulders and tried to accept the inevitable. But after these houses were built and occupied, the serenity I had enjoyed was shattered. The racket caused by kids, their friends, doors banging, shouting back and forth and the never-ending parade of cars on my side road was making me see red! Had I been more cautious and studied the plans and ultimate goal of Teton Pines I probably would have reconsidered. But I didn't. As usual, I had acted on impulse.

The end of summer came and, once again, my bags were packed, boxes shipped off to New York, and I was ready to go home. It was a repeat of so many years -back and forth between Jackson and New York—bracketed between June and Labor Day. I knew I needed change but I was beginning to feel like a nomad, wondering where I really belonged.

On one of those gray-blue February days when the city was least appealing, I picked up the phone to hear a friend from Jackson on the line. Her voice was high with excitement. Would I be interested in a condo in the quiet, wooded development where she lived? It sounded like the answer to my problem in The Pines.

In less than a week I was winging across country to Jackson, hoping that the weather would be relatively calm with no blizzards. My friend met me at the airport and drove me to a spacious three-bedroom townhouse in a quiet secluded area. Nice, I said to myself. But when I walked in I thought I was in California. I was astounded. The owner had tried to turn this modest country condo into a sophisticated Hollywood dwelling with crystal chandeliers, black lacquered floors and oversized furniture upholstered in white ultra suede. The kitchen was black with gold floor tiles and the guestroom walls and ceiling were painted bright red in contrast to the brilliant green wall-to-wall carpet. The hideous décor was almost laughable and would drive away most buyers but I was confident I could restore the condo. I swallowed hard and told the realtor I would take it. My friends were ecstatic!

Going back on the New York bound plane gave me time to evaluate what I was doing. To an outsider, and my family, I was irrational—plunging into another sale, another move and yet another renovation. How many times had I done this? I counted up the number of places I had called home. It was hard to believe there were nine, including three summer rentals. And then Bob and I had moved ten times in the forty-three years we were married. This was bordering on insanity. I may never know why fate propelled me into such a wandering life

The Aspens condo satisfied my itch for just two years before a delightful one floor apartment with a wide open exposure came on the market in the same building complex. The lively stream running by called to me like mythical sea nymphs. Telling myself I was simplifying my life, I put my townhouse on the market, and purchased the smaller one.

It was my first summer in my "tree house" by the water. I was enjoying a quiet time on the porch when the ringing phone broke the stillness of the hot August afternoon. A neighbor called to catch up. During the conversation, she asked if I knew that my former Kelly house had been torn down. I was dumbfounded. Why would anyone do this to a charming little western hideaway? Why? I put down the phone, bewildered, feeling intruded upon.

I contacted the architect for more information. He told me an amazing story. Apparently, just when the owners were going to demolish it and have it carted away to the land fill, one of the construction workers offered to take down the house piece by piece and take it over the mountains to his property in Idaho. For months, this young man and his wife, along with three children, cousins and grandparents came from Idaho every weekend. With beaver-like determination, they carefully disassembled the house, loading everything piece by piece in their pickups and trucked it over the mountains to Idaho. It was a monumental task but, finally, it was gone, all except the lichen rock chimney that was left standing—a lonely monument to the past. This story touched my heart. I had to find this young man.

It was frustrating. No one seemed to know who he was. Finally, after months of inquiries, I had his name and phone number. My fingers trembled as I dialed the number in Driggs, Idaho. The soft voice of a woman answered. I asked for Reed and she politely told me she would put him on.

"Hello, this is Reed," he said.

I told him my story starting at the beginning—how we came upon the site in the pouring rain—how it filled us with awe and thanksgiving to have found it. I then told him about the trials in building it—how we had to dig five hundred feet into the mountain's skin before we hit water for the well—how for twenty years we filled the little house with the love and laughter of our family and many friends. As I was speaking, my throat was tightening and I felt the sting of tears behind my eyes. I couldn't forget what I had done.

Reed spoke. "I have a wife and three children and we hope for more. Your house was like a gift from heaven. We could never afford anything this nice and we can't thank you enough."

I ended by saying, "Well, I want you to know that twenty years of love comes with every piece of wood, every window, every door, every fixture. His answer touched my heart. "Well, we plan to put back all that love, for sure."

I hung up the phone and sat deep in thought. My prayer had been answered and the house would go on sheltering the lives of the people who loved it. Selling the house had caused a deep emotional wrench in me and now it was lifting like morning mist over the Tetons. Here was the affirmation of a belief I have held since childhood. Even though life as we know it is no more, that energy will transform itself into a different form and go on.

Reed Dayton and his family gave me a wonderful gift.

Over coffee one afternoon in Wyoming, one of my friends pressed a book into my hands. It was a book about angels.

"You've got to read this," she said earnestly. "It tells you angels are always around us and we can write to them with our problems. You'll be amazed."

The minute I got home, I started reading the angel book and from the first page, I knew this information was meant for me. I had always been aware of a presence around me—an unexplained cool breeze—a strange fragrance —a sort of humming in the air. I felt there was something or someone unknown smoothing my path —traffic lights turning green for me—cars exiting the exact parking space I needed—getting the last seat in the front row of a Broadway hit. And I shudder when I remember the day in New York when a gentle force pushed me back on the sidewalk just before a car came careening around the corner.

The book was fascinating. It had easy instructions for starting a dialogue with my angel. All I had to do was write a letter to my guardian angel at night and then in the morning, sit quietly with pen in hand, start writing and the answer would come. This was a new and unusual concept, hard for most people to accept, but my heart said "Do It." Now perhaps I would find out who she or he was. I found a beautiful journal in my desk, named it my angel journal, and sat down and wrote my first letter to my angel. I was filled with curiosity.

Eagerly the next day I took my pen and the angel book and sat by the kitchen window in my house in The Pines, watching the sun backlighting the hills with the golden glow of early morning. The urge to write came quickly. My pen wrote "Dear Emilie." How odd. Hardly anyone calls me Emilie but, as that is my given name, it was altogether proper for my angel to use it. I kept on writing. It flowed easily and it wasn't long before I noticed the words did not sound like me at all. Sometimes a word would be repeated three times. According to the book, this was a sure sign that an angel was talking to me.

I kept writing faithfully to my angel all summer and each morning there would be gentle reminders to take my walks or spend the day in the studio working. "Get to your painting now, now, now," would be the counsel —" don't fret— things are working out perfectly—be patient—all is well—be creative—stay open to our nearness and we will enrich your life."

September came and with it time to return to New York. Much as I loved 935 Park Ave. I felt a pressing need for space for my art and writing so Lois and I began the hunt again for new quarters. It was an exhausting time, traipsing back and forth in the Upper East Side of Manhattan, and the process was beginning to unravel me. In my impatience, I almost signed the bottom line on two apartments but was stopped in both cases by a very curious happening. One apartment Lois showed me was lovely in every detail. I told her I would take it. On the way home I said to myself, "It's a beautiful apartment but where is the space for my writing and my art work?" I took my problem to bed with me.

In the middle of the night, I awoke and sat bolt upright. Something had awakened me with loud protestations! "No, No, No" a voice inside of me was shouting loud and clear. There was no mistaking the message and I felt a great weight lifting from me. In the morning, I made the call. "Lois, I hate like anything to tell you this, but I can't take the apartment. I love everything about it except it doesn't have that extra room for my art studio". She was dismayed, but understood.

Two days went by. The phone rang and there was Lois with another place that I just had to look at. I fell in love with it and told her yes. Again, I was awakened by the same warning and had to back off. I was beginning to wonder about my sanity.

Then I remembered the angel book described angels engaged in all kinds of special work—some tended the sick and aged—others helped children in trouble and still others were, believe it or not, in real estate. Yes! Why not ask for their help? That night I wrote to my angel asking her to contact them. The next morning, as I wrote, the words flowed across the page, telling me they would help me but they needed more specific information. Could I draw a floor plan in my angel book, showing as much detail as possible and giving a preferred location? You bet I could! I set to work that night and drew a floor plan in my angel book of what I wanted filling in all the details.. As I drew, I pictured myself in all the rooms.

Soon after, I was invited to a cocktail party. I didn't know it then, but what happened at the party quietly rearranged my future.

It was a November evening. The last glimmer of the day had disappeared and streetlights were pooling their glow at all the corners. My friend's apartment was located on the corner of Fifth Avenue and Ninety-Fourth Street in Carnegie Hill, an area new to me but very low key and family oriented..

As the taxi drove up Park Avenue, the buildings were coming to life. One by one, apartment windows were lit from within sending their radiance into the gathering darkness. This nostalgic time of day always spelled home to me—home, where it was warm and the smells of dinner cooking greeted you with a friendly welcome. Inside these apartments, families were gathering after their day, happy to see each other and looking forward to the evening together. I was thankful to be going where there were people. At times, I found living alone was too much of one's company.

The doorman greeted me and showed me where to hang my coat. The host was by the front door and after a hello and an introduction to another guest I wandered into the living room to find a familiar face. I didn't get very far when, suddenly, I saw through the huge oversize windows, a breathtaking view of the Upper West Side of New York City, sparkling like jewels laid out on black velvet, thousands of lights blazing and blinking from thousands of apartments. It was spectacular!

I'm not sure how long I stood there. Someone eventually came up behind me and said, "Pretty, isn't it?" I took a deep breath and said softly, "I could take a lot of this."

That weekend Lois called again. She sounded excited. "An apartment just came on the market on the corner of Ninety-third and Fifth Avenue. It's on the fourteenth floor of an historic 1926 land-marked building—a top building in one of the best neighborhoods. Do you want to see it?"

My heart took a giant leap. Ninety-Fourth and Fifth? That was just a block away from my friend's apartment! "Oh, yes," I answered.

Lois was waiting in the lobby of 935 Park at precisely 9:00 the next morning and we began walking the twelve blocks up to Ninety-Third Street. Anticipation put wings on my feet and we arrived at 1115 Fifth Avenue ten minutes early. While we were waiting for the seller's real estate agent, we talked about the unusual turn of events that brought about this day. The party had a lot to do with it. Had I not seen that view from my friend's living room and breathed a silent wish for something like it, we would not be sitting here in the lobby of a very similar building. I shook my head in wonder.

The agent finally arrived and we took the elevator to the fourteenth floor and entered a long, spacious entrance hall. At the end of the hall, we stepped into the living room and dining area with four large windows overlooking the reservoir and the West Side of Manhattan. I was speechless. The view was identical to the one in my friend's apartment but on a much higher floor. This apartment was like a penthouse, far beyond my fondest hopes, with views to the south and the east as well as the west. The rooms were large and gracious and, wonder of wonders, were laid out almost identically to the drawing I had made in my angel book. A shiver of delight fluttered across my shoulders. This close resemblance was no coincidence.

We wandered from room to room in a daze, hardly believing this very special place. Lois raved on. She had never seen anything like it. I counted the windows. Twelve, and through them all, I could see miles and miles of sky and cityscape. The living/dining area led into a large library which would make a perfect studio. It had a fireplace, too, and I visualized a cheery blaze warming me while the snow fell outside. I knew this was it. My angel and her real estate friends had done their work well. They had guided me to Eleven Fifteen Fifth Avenue—my house of sunshine in the new century.

And so I began five years of New York City living at its best —five years that satisfied the desire I felt when I was a budding teenager and thrilled to the sight of the towering skyline of Manhattan. I couldn't wait until I was old enough to be on my own and escape the boring environment in Easton that was stifling me. I longed to be a part of the teeming life of this unique city with its many-sided culture. That time had arrived.

I became a member of the Metropolitan Museum—treated myself to season tickets to the ballet—engaged a personal shopper at Saks. My art blossomed. Through the many artists I worked with in my studio, I became active in the art community, sold some paintings and hung my work in a gallery in Soho.   Gradually, I was enfolded into the support group of Yaddo, a prestigious art organization, and hosted several fundraisers that opened my eyes to the surprising politics of the art world.

For a while I had fun being a part of the diplomatic scene, attending black tie affairs at the Foreign Policy Association. Several jury stints in the impressive downtown courthouse gave me a new look at our judicial system, and volunteering with the city's sadly understaffed housing department, was a lesson in how New York City operated behind the scenes. And when Bette Midler was organizing her green team, I signed up and wore my ball cap with pride. Life was full and interesting.

Day after day, I responded to the beat of New York and my apartment was rarely quiet as friends and family were always coming and going. Budd especially loved to make the trip from Wyoming. There was a part of him from his days working at Esty that needed to belly up to the bar again at some of his Third Avenue haunts. Once he brought Emi and Lindsay and Robert and we had a great weekend playing tourist. There wasn't much we missed—from the Statue of Liberty to the Empire State Building. I was the tireless New Yorker delighted to share all the wonders of this great city.

.

During this time, my brother Buddy's wife passed away in Las Vegas. He flew to New York and together we drove to Easton, Pa. for the burial service. While he stayed with me, we welcomed the chance to do the reconnecting we both sorely needed. And wedid a lot of reconnecting that we both sorely needed-and we had a chance for some fun. One morning we took a cab downtown and he was thrilled to view the opening of the stock Exchange. Then back uptown, where we sat on a bench in Central Park, eating a vendor's hot dog, watching the people—line skaters, bikers, grandparents and young parents pushing strollers, joggers, and dogs everywhere. And then after dinner at Tavern on the Green, we took in a performance of the famous Rockettes in Radio City Music Hall. It topped off a perfect day. But the best part of his stay with me was his visit to his old battleship, The New Jersey, now a tourist attraction in Camden, New Jersey. When Buddy made it known he was part of the original crew, the operating Captain and crew bent the rules and allowed us free range of the ship.

Buddy took me to the flag deck and nearly broke down as he relived some of his experiences as signalman first class in the Navy. For the first time since the war, I began to understand the hell he went through being attacked by the Japanese and their Kamikaze pilots.

It had taken us two wars, three divorces, five new kids and now five deaths for us to find once again the closeness we had as children. After almost sixty years, I felt the circle beginning to close.

CHAPTER 22

An Inspired Move

HOW can I explain my latest folly—if it is that? I loved my sunny aerie high above the street. I could look down on the most exciting city in the world and feel its heartbeat—a city that copes peacefully with its eight million people, tending to their daily needs, offering them a place where they can be who they are without fear of recrimination. And I had a front seat for the weather's full repertoire, from brilliant sunshine to dark-as-night thunderstorms that sent me scurrying to the other side of the apartment…gray misty days and nights when the fog was as thick as pudding…silent snow, soft as eiderdown…or ice storms slashing at the windows in staccato bursts. I felt that I was in the right place at the right time. The restlessness that had plagued me for so long was quiet. Dared I think that perhaps now the rainbow ended here?

On a sunny Tuesday morning in September, I took my coffee into the den and turned on the news. Channel 7 came on with a picture of a plane crashing into a building. Oh, no, not a promotion for yet another one of Bruce Willis' action movies, I said to myself. I switched to CBS and there it was—the same picture. An adrenaline charge hit me like a blast from an oven and I thought I was going to fall over. Staring at the horror unfolding on the screen, I groped behind me and finally found a chair. I could hardly breathe as I witnessed the second plane crashing into the second World Trade Center tower. I began to shake from head to toe. I wasn't looking at an accident. And then, when I learned that the Pentagon had been hit with a third plane, waves of fear threatened to unravel my fragile self control.

As I sat crying and shaking in front of the television, my house guests at the time came bursting into the den, their faces white and stricken. They had been watching TV in their room. Karen grabbed my arm. I saw that her pupils were dilated and she was sobbing hysterically. "Oh, my God," she cried, "What are we going to do? What's going to come next?"

"I don't know," I cried, "but we must get word to our families," and I rushed to the phone to call Brooks I got her on the first ring and was able to tell her I was OK just minutes before the entire New York City phone system, overloaded with thousands of calls, cut us off. As none of us had cell phones at that time, our only link to the world outside was the TV. For hours the three of us sat on the edge of the sofa, clinging to each other, murmuring things like "it will be alright—we will rise above this," not really believing it but trying to reassure each other. We were survivors in a turbulent sea, clutching the TV like a piece of driftwood.

It must have been late afternoon—I really can't remember the time—when I finally made a move. "I think we should make our appearance outside," I said, "at least alert the doormen that we are OK. And we should think about dinner and maybe get some food into the apartment." We had calmed down—we were no longer hysterical—just numb.

After we managed to comb our hair and apply some blusher to brighten our faces, so that we didn't resemble figures in Madame Tossaud's wax museum, we ventured out to Madison Avenue in search of water and food. The owner of the Korean market across Madison Avenue greeted me kindly but shook his head at his sadly depleted shelves. We did buy the last case of water and some canned goods and then went looking for an open restaurant. Many had run out of food by this time. No food delivery trucks were able to come into Manhattan as the bridges and tunnels—the city's life lines—had been closed down all day for security reasons.

There was a strange surrealistic atmosphere surrounding us as we walked slowly along Madison Avenue, where the normal din of grinding buses, honking horns, shouting workmen and chattering of dozens of school kids was now muffled. On this late afternoon of September eleventh, 2001, the vibrant song that New York sang so proudly was barely audible.

We were all suffering from trauma and desperate for any connection with our remembered world of just yesterday. So we bought ice cream cones from the sad-faced Italian vender, an everyday afternoon fixture at the corner of Madison and Ninety-second Street. We sat on a bench, and carefully licked the ice cream in our cones round and round in an orderly fashion while the F16 fighter jets endlessly circled the sky above us.

The career moms and dads, their faces strained with worry, went by us on their way home holding their children securely by the hand. There were very few nannies that afternoon.

I cannot say how long we continued to sit there like zombies but no one felt like talking. To be silent with our own thoughts was all we could manage. I found myself on strange turf, dealing with an enormous sense of loss. Having lived in a city as powerful as New York, I thought nothing could make me lose faith in its untouchable magic, but now I was feeling like a crystal goblet, wobbling but still in one piece, after the magician whisked the tablecloth from under me.

There was very little sleep for any of us that night. In the morning, we tuned in to Mayor Giuliani's news conference. "Get out of your houses," he said. "Go to the parks with your families and meet with your neighbors." And so, as weary as we were, we walked to the Great Lawn in Central Park and mingled with thousands of people who needed to share their grief with each other and realize they were not alone in this tragic time. While it looked like any Sunday afternoon in the park, we all knew it was a Wednesday—a sad and abnormal one. The laughter and squeals of little children filled the air with happy sounds but even this couldn't cover up the sickening smell reaching us from the burning towers downtown.

Tuesday turned into Wednesday, to Thursday and by Friday, a stunned city began to stir. Upper East Side ladies once again strolled Madison Avenue with their little dogs.   the familiar grinding sound of buses and garbage trucks was heard once again. Traffic began to flow in and out of the city as the bridges and tunnels, now heavily guarded, were reopened. We no longer felt marooned on the island of Manhattan. My friends were finally able to go back home to Pennsylvania, taking with them memories they will never forget of New York City on September 11, 2001.

As I made my daily rounds in the neighborhood, I was saddened to see shrines on the sidewalks, lovingly arranged with flowers and candles and pictures of a lost loved one. I would come home shaken, my eyes brimming with tears and I didn't care who saw me crying.

There was to be a candlelight vigil all over the country. . I wanted to be with Brooks and Bob for this somber ceremony, so I hired a car and went to their home in the suburbs. I can remember the three of us standing outside on their patio. We each held a white taper and at the prescribed moment, lit it and said a silent prayer. We could barely speak but together we gave thanks to the brave policemen and firemen who had given their lives to help others. And with compassion we remembered those who never made it back home on that fateful day.

By the time October came, there had been dozens of warnings about new attacks. Nothing happened, but the fear stayed with us. Christmas came and went quietly. The New Year was full of tentative hope. Big crowds were expected in Times Square and New York's finest were everywhere. Again, nothing catastrophic or destructive happened and our daily lives once more moved on with a semblance of normalcy.

I began pondering whether or not I should stay in my fourteenth floor ivory tower, where it felt as though nothing could touch me, or flee to the countryside as so many others were doing. I decided to stay—for the moment.

When May 2002 came, and I was almost fully recovered from the harrowing events of September 11, I decided to take a train trip across Canada, through the magnificent Canadian Rocky Mountains and down to La Connor, a picturesque town on Skagit Bay, Washington. It was a soothing antidote for the stress in my life.

Every morning, I stood on my balcony of the LaConnor Inn and let my spirits soar with the gulls over the peaceful blue water. The unscheduled sunny days spiced with clear, crisp sea breezes cleared my mind and I began to realize my perfect life in New York City had lost its appeal.

Living in a small town near water had always been one of my fondest fantasies but in all my moves I had never managed to do this. Here, the taste of life in LaConnor started a pulsating desire in me to make my fantasy a reality.

When I returned to Jackson in June, I sprang into action. I called two realtors—one in Greenwich, Connecticut, on Long Island Sound, and the other in New York City. Brooks offered to accompany the Greenwich realtor on her search for a waterfront house while I stayed in Jackson close to the phone for my New York agent. Needless to say, my quick decision to sell my beautiful home in New York City had me wondering if I had gone completely haywire. But I was driven by that all too familiar chorus inside of me that kept saying it was time for a change. Time to move on.

Within three days of inaugurating my plan, I was winging my way back east to look at two houses on the water in Greenwich. Neither one appealed to me. However, Brooks urged me to stay another day—this time to look at waterfront properties in Rowayton, Connecticut, an old oystering village that is only an hour from New York City.

Rowayton, a haven for New York City commuters, was a charming town that retained much of its original flavor. It was a place where narrow winding streets and jumbles of clapboard houses standing in orderly disarray seemed to lean towards one another like clusters of daffodils. The only main street in the town led up a curvy hill where, at the top overlooking Long Island Sound, there was an attractive sprinkling of condos lining the blue waters. Ooh, I said to myself, "This is a beautiful spot." When the realtor stopped in front of condo number six, and we opened the door into the sunny interior, I fell completely in love- again.

Many windows wrapped the front and sides of this cozy space, allowing a stunning view. Every room held wonderful surprises like a fireplace in the bedroom as well as one in the living room, and a generous deck off the kitchen. The sale included a boat, a dingy, and a deep water mooring. "I'll take it," I said, shooing away a little cloud of uncertainty. Right now, I was feeling like I held four aces in my hand.

I had to admit to myself that my constant moving was telling me something I had yet to decipher. From the first days of living in Rowayton, the tight armor I had worn around me since 9/11 began to fall away and in its place came contentment. To walk into the tiny post office in Rowayton and say hello to the friendly red-headed postal clerk and then read all the notices and personal ads on the community bulletin board took me back to a side of living that I had almost forgotten - like the town of Jackson when it was still undiscovered or the tiny town of Kelly with its miniscule post office. In New York City I had been fortunate to have somewhat of a small town atmosphere. Ninety-third Street and Madison Avenue is a neighborhood where the people who lived there knew me by name. The Maitre d's in the restaurants would save my favorite table and the polite Korean dry cleaner always greeted me with a smile.

But the sophistication of Manhattan's upper eastside, with its proper dress and weekly manicures, was in direct contrast to the easy atmosphere I found in Rowayton. Here, there was always time to savor the moment. The morning ritual consist of picking up a newspaper and a container of coffee at the Rowayton Market—then crossing the main street to the local hardware store for a visit with Lou, the owner, whose customers wouldn't think of going to Home Dept. Once again I found myself poking around in an old-fashioned hardware store and eavesdropping on the native's gossip. This delightful diversion became a must on my daily rounds. One day, while I was fishing through Lou's clearance bin, a shrill voice rose above the store's normal hum.

"Four million? Apiece? For that kind of money you can have a 5000 square foot house and three acres of wooded land—maybe even a pool? Four million? Huh." I turned to look at a diminutive lady whose family had probably settled in this old seaside village centuries ago.

"These developers," she went on, outraged, "robber barons, I call them, come in, tear down an old house full of charm and sturdy beams, and put up something God awful and charge the heck out of the buyer—shows you the crazy things people with money will do to get a place by the water."

Having said her piece, she pulled her watch cap down over her wispy hair, picked up her package and hastened off, huffing all the way. This interesting scene was my first bit of gossip about the town's business side. No doubt about it. The real estate hounds had found this sleepy town and the last vestiges of quaint living would not last long.

While my head was stuffed with ideas for my new condo in Rowayton, my other real estate lady in New York had bids for my apartment at 1115 Fifth Avenue. In less than a week's time, I had switched from city mouse to country mouse but that switch also meant that the many roots I had put down in Wyoming over thirty years needed my care—especially those roots that couldn't be transplanted to Connecticut. I immediately flew west, put my Jackson condo on the market and made arrangements to ship my furniture to Connecticut.

Before leaving Jackson for good, my one concern was Bob and Anne's gravesite. When I sold the mountain cabin in Kelly, I had purchased a plot in the cemetery in Jackson where I moved Bob and Anne's burial urns. It was a hillside plot in full view of the Grand Teton and many times I thought that the Biblical quote Bob had chosen for his headstone—"I will lift up my eyes to the hills" was so apropos.

But when I last saw the plot it was filled with debris and the weeds had taken over. It needed a good spring cleaning. I called a friend who was kind enough to help me. We set out one sunny morning armed with rakes and shovels, fertilizer and new plants. Hours later, I was satisfied it was deserving of Bob and Anne. The next day, I went back to water the new plants we had put in. I climbed the steps to the spigot and when I walked back down, there on the bottom step was my funny little bell—a talisman that was part of my twenty years in Chappaqua. I didn't remember taking it to Wyoming. How did it get there? With wonder, I picked it up and held it in my hand, remembering all the times I rang it to call the kids in from the back yard for dinner. Far from elegant, the bell did have a certain

charisma and certainly the lives of a cat. It had been packed and unpacked
a dozen times since leaving Chappaqua in 1979, showing up in the most
unexpected places—like the bottom of a tool box or among my art supplies.
It was now a sentimental keepsake—no longer in use. At that moment, I
felt a cool breeze—almost like a hand gently ruffling my hair. I shivered
slightly. This wasn't the first time something of mine had disappeared only
to show up in a totally different place from where I thought it might be.
When the worn family dinner bell reappeared here at Bob and Anne's
gravesite, I experienced something far beyond my understanding. But I
did know it was all about love and caring.

Finally, when the keys to my Jackson condo were turned over to the
new owner, the phone disconnected and my accounts closed, I felt that the
physical break to Jackson was complete. Yet I knew the heartfelt attachments
I had with treasured friends and the memories I had made over many years
would stay with me forever.

As the plane lifted over the verdant valley of Jackson Hole, I did not
look back to the Tetons but set my sights to my new home. My thoughts
turned to Bob and I wondered how he felt about my ever-constant
journeying. Would he understand why I had to leave Wyoming?

In a few months, fall came to Connecticut with a blaze of color I had
not seen for years and I welcomed back the wonders of the New England
trees with a joyful and thankful heart. After flying back and forth to
Wyoming, and the clamor of New York, I found the whooshing of the oaks
in high winds as melodic as the string section of the New York
Philharmonic—their swaying back and forth as beautiful as the ballet "Swan
Lake." And when the night owls were calling to one another, it was the
best of lullabies. I loved watching the coming and going of the daily tides
in Long Island Sound, and depending on whether the tide was in or out, I
was always rewarded with a never ending theater of water birds, from gulls
to stately white swans. Being here by the water answered a deep need in
me but every now and then, my heart gave me a tiny stab. I was still
weeping for New York City, and in a way, I felt that I had deserted her just
when she needed my support.

I had been in my waterfront condo for less than a year when Betsy, my
realtor and now good friend, asked if I wanted to spend some time driving
through the area. She knew how curious I was about all the new
construction. We picked up Brooks and Bob, who were also curious and
had asked to come with us.

It was a lovely, sunny, spring day and we were all in an adventuresome mood. In and out of the streets we went, noting many new houses, men in hard hats tearing down old houses, dumpsters and cement trucks pouring foundations and streets blocked and ripped up for new sewer lines. It was a relief to put the noise and activity behind us and continue to neighboring Wilson Point, a residential area that dated back to the 1920's.

We drove down winding roads under a canopy of century old trees, and passed by stately stone homes looking like castles and others like Spanish haciendas or villas from southern Europe. Many homes reminded me of College Hill in Easton when I was growing up. The more we drove, the more my body tensed with a strange expectancy. Oh, how lovely this is, I kept murmuring. The car barely moved along the empty byways, free of the normal buzz of traffic. It was as if here in Wilson Point, time had been turned down a notch. It must have been a couple of miles before we rounded a bend in the road and came upon a fairytale cottage just like the pictures I used to love in my children's books. I gasped with pleasure. "Oh, Betsy," I pleaded. "Could we stop here please? I want to get out and look."

She turned into the driveway. "I have the key," she said smiling. "I wanted you to see this house. It would be perfect for you." Was she crazy? Was I now totally mad? Another house?

Eager to see more of this lovely property, we all jumped out of the car. I remember standing there in the driveway, transfixed, my mouth open, unable to say anything as I gazed at the gabled roof and many windows and the little greenhouse in the back with attached shed and chimney A greenhouse! Instantly, I knew this enchanted cottage was meant for me.

I walked through the front door and a sense of belonging came over me. Beamed ceilings, classic cottage walls of white plaster, and the sun spilling across the gleaming cherry wood floors transported me back to my childhood when I once lived in another enchanted cottage—my house of sunshine. All my life, I had carried with me a vision that someday I would find another enchanted cottage that would still my longing for a sense of home. Today, eighty years and twenty-nine houses later, my vision had led me to the house at twenty-three Valley Road.

I bought the new house of sunshine and again I feel the same lightness of being I had as a child. Once again I can taste the thrill of discovery and find the joy in creativity. In a way, the long years between these two houses seem but a moment apart. To me, this house has never stopped living. Imprinted on the walls is an invisible record of many families—a record of births and weddings and deaths and more births. I feel the heart of 23

Valley Road, beating for eighty years, now beating in tandem with my own, as if it had been waiting for me. I see my name on the deed and many other names as the house passed from one owner to the next. And now the house is mine to pass on.

Not long ago a friend called to tell me that the River Road cottage in Easton, my first house of sunshine, was up for sale. Memories flooded my head. I could almost hear my German nursemaids singing—hear the river rushing by—see the white swans gliding majestically across the pond. I had to go back to see the place that had been in my heart all my life—the place I had been seeking to find again. My friend put me in touch with the owner who said she would be delighted to see me.

A few days later, I drove to Easton through almost forgotten territory— the winding two-lane road dimly remembered—an age-old cement plant, a little general store with a gas pump outside. All still there but dreamlike. When the house I hadn't seen in seventy years came into view, my breath quickened and I could feel my temples throbbing. I eased the car down the driveway and parked by the front steps. At first glance, the house was as I had remembered it, but where were the flowerbeds filled with scarlet sage? What had happened to the green and white striped awning over the porch? And the swan pond? The big oak trees? They were all gone.

I knocked on the weathered wooden door. A smiling gray-haired lady opened it. "Please come in," she said, and led me past piles of wood and a carpenter's bench that stood in the middle of the living room.

"Sorry about the mess," she said, "but we're slowly getting back to normal after the last flood." We sat down at the kitchen table, where she had coffee waiting. She told me how the house had been flooded three times in the last two years. I tried imagining myself wading through thigh-high water, rescuing sentimental items. It was a dismal picture.

"But what interests me," she said, "is that you lived here as a child. How strange it must be to see your birthplace after so many years."

"Yes, it is very strange. So much of what I remember isn't here- the beautiful old oak trees-what happened to them? She sighed and led me out the back door. I couldn't believe the devastation. There were gaping holes in the river bank and an inaccessible slash of mud and rocks where once a lush lawn had led gradually to a sandy beach. All the trees had toppled leaving naked roots reaching to the sky. Brown lifeless bushes hung precariously onto what was left of solid ground. In a shaky voice, she said "It was as if a big claw came and ripped the bank to shreds." The shady back yard of my childhood, where I spent hours on the tire swing, had been swept away. I felt a pang of loss like a mourner leaving the gravesite.. There was no reason to stay at River Road any longer. I thanked the kind lady and headed back home.

As I drove, questions flew around me. What made me come back today? What was I trying to find? My idyllic life had disappeared when the stock market crashed and took away everything we owned. So, was I trying to replace what was lost? Had I been searching in all the houses I had lived in for some piece of the happiness of those fairytale days of long ago? Did I go back today hoping to find the last piece of the puzzle—the answer to my life-long searching—a reason for the constant need to move?

Three hours later, I eased the car between the stone pillars of the driveway at 23 Valley Road. When I turned the key to my front door, I knew why I took the journey back to Easton. It was to finally put to rest all my unnamed longing. For so many years, I had been mourning the loss of my house of sunshine. All my life I had been trying to find, in the many places I had lived, the happiness I remembered as a child. But I had made a big mistake. My happiness didn't depend on the things I could see and touch—big windows and fireplaces—big back yards and cozy kitchens—cashmere sweaters. It was born out of the precious gifts of love, home and family that I learned early in my first house of sunshine. But during the bleak Depression years these treasures were tarnished and had been buried under days of deprivation. In my search for the good life, I thought if I had more creature comforts, they would bring me the happiness I remembered. So year after year, I was like an idling motor, always waiting to dash off to another place.

I put my pocketbook on the hall table and hung up my coat. When I opened the windows to the garden, the delicate perfume of lilacs in bloom filled the room. My heart began to sing such a song of joy and thanksgiving that I picked up my journal—the one that says on the cover "Angels can fly because they take themselves lightly"—turned to a blank page and wrote, "No more will I be looking down the road to find something new and different than what I have. Everything I need or desire is right here."

Maybe my enchanted cottage by the water will still my restlessness. Maybe this time I will find all I have been looking for.

But, then again, I believe I have said this very same thing before.

About the Author

In eighty-five years, Emilie Betts has lived in seven states and in twenty-nine different dwellings. She has been a private secretary, a defense factory worker during WWII, wife of an advertising executive, mom to three and later five more children, a soprano soloist, writer, and publicity chairman for the New York Area Girl Scout Council.

She also worked in the publicity department of the New York City Housing Bureau. In 1964, after earning a degree from the New York School of Interior Design, she and three other suburban housewives opened a fabric shop in Chappaqua, New York.

In 1929, the stock market crash left her family homeless, forcing them into a nomadic life. But these years provided rich experiences that became the theme of *Shadows in My House of Sunshine.*

Today, she lives in a 1920s English cottage in Norwalk, Connecticut—much like the home of her childhood—and is at work writing another book.